Relations in Indian Philosophy

Sri Garib Dass Oriental Series No. 147

Relations in Indian Philosophy

Edited by

Prof. V. N. Jha

Director

Centre of Advanced Study in Sanskrit,

University of Poona

SRI SATGURU PUBLICATIONS

A DIVISION OF :

INDIAN BOOKS CENTRE

DELHI-INDIA

Published by:
SRI SATGURU PUBLICATIONS
Indological & Oriental Publishers,
A Division of
INDIAN BOOKS CENTRE
40/5, Shakti Nagar,
Delhi-110007
INDIA

ISBN—81-7030-329-X

First Edition : Delhi - 1992

Printed at:
D.K. Fine Art Press, Delhi.

PRINTED IN INDIA

Preface

The present volume contains 17 articles presented and discussed at the National Seminar on Relations in Indian Philosophy which was held on 25th to 27th March, 1991 at the Centre of Advanced Study in Sanskrit, University of Poona.

It gives me pleasure to present these articles in the hands of scholars of Indology, Logic and Philosophy. Briefly speaking, focus has been put in these papers on the following aspects.

1. Nature of a relation.
2. The role played by a relation in generating a cognition.
3. The role played by a relation in creating a precise language of philosophical and logical communication.
4. The Philosophical implication of a relation.

Any Philosophical analysis requires clear idea about these aspects of a relation. The studies included here cover a very wide range of philosophical and logical literature in Sanskrit. Although the main source of information has been the literature on Prācīna Nyāya and Navya-Nyāya, some articles also have taken into account the position of relation and the problems of relation in other systems of Indian Philosophy. As can be seen, there are views on relations being Ontological facts and also there are views which deny the Ontological reality of a relation. The discussions in this volume incorporate both the ranges.

The Navya-Nyāya system of Indian Logic started paying more attention to the problem of relation because it was the necessity of the time. There was a great need for evolving a precise language of communication for logical and philosophical discussions. The Indian logicians realised that this cannot be achieved without introducing the idea of delimitations through property and relations and this is why they had to pay more attention to the discussion on relations. I wish that the readers will read this volume with the perspective presented above.

I thank the Indian Books Centre, New Delhi for undertaking the publication of this volume. I am sure, the scholars in the field will highly appreciate this venture.

V.N. Jha
Director
Centre of Advanced Study in Sanskrit
University of Poona,
Pune - 411007

Contents

1

Saṁyogasambandha in Nyāyavaiśeṣika

Nirmala Kulkarni

I.0.0. *Saṁyoga* or contact is a relation accepted by the Nyāyavaiśeṣika (NV) system of Indian philosophy. Present paper takes a brief account of this relation in the light of the discussions presented in the texts of this system. For the convenience of description, I have divided the discussion into the following parts:

1. Necessity of accepting *Saṁyoga* relation
2. Definitions of *Saṁyoga*
3. Nature and role of *Saṁyoga*
4. Objections on *Saṁyoga* relation and their refutation.
5. Conclusion.

I.I.0. **Necessity of accepting *Saṁyoga* relation**

NV system upholds doctrines of realism. According to this system, certain object is true, unless it proves to be an object of erroneous cognition. Valid cognition of such an object which can be verbalised is always a विशिष्ट ज्ञान, i.e. a qualified knowledge. विशिष्ट ज्ञान is a cognition which includes विशेषण, a qualifier, विशेष्य a qualificand and a सम्बन्ध, a relation, between these two. Without a relation qualified knowledge cannot arise. Therefore, a relation in general must be accepted.

Now, the relations between two things are not of similar type. There are various relations by which two things are related. e.g. when we know a black pot i.e. नीलघट, we know that it is नीलत्वविशिष्टघट i.e. a pot qualified by blue colour. Here, नीलत्व and घट are related to each other. In the case of दण्डी पुरूषः the form of the cognition is दण्डविशिष्टः पुरूषः, a person qualified by a stick, and the person and stick are related to each other. Can we say that the relation between नीलत्व and घट is similar to the relation between पुरूष and दण्ड? No, because the relation between नीलत्व and घट is a permanent relation; we cannot separate these two from each other. However, the relation between दण्ड and पुरूष is not permanent, because दण्ड can be removed from पुरूष at any time.

Thus, to explain our behaviour NV system has introduced many relations. *Saṁyoga* is one of these. In our routine behaviour we find hundreds of things connected with each other e.g. when we stand or sit, we have contact with the earth, when we eat there is a contact between our mouth and our hand. On table, a few things lay and certainly there is contact between the things and the table. We also use a verbal expression, 'these two things are connected with each other' i.e. इमौ संयुक्तौ. To explain our experience of 'connectedness' 'conjecture' NV system has coined a term called संयोग, which is the central theme of this paper.

Thus, to explain such behaviour we must accept a relation in general and संयोग in particular.

I.II.0. Definitions of *Saṁyoga*

I. "अप्राप्तयोः प्राप्तिः संयोगः"

Saṁyoga is that relation by which two substances come together, which are not so before. This definition is found in *Praśastapādabhāṣya* (*Prapābhā*), in *Upaskāra* (U) and in the *Nyāyasiddhāntamuktāvāli* (*Nyā Si Muk*).

II. संयुक्तव्यवहारहेतुः

A cause of the verbal behaviour in which connectedness is expressed.

Prapābhā, Tarkasaṅgraha (*Tar Saṅ*) define *Saṁyoga* in this fashion. *Kiraṇāvalī* on *Muktāvali* explains—

'इमौ संयुक्तौ इति यो व्यवहारः तस्य असाधारणहेतुत्वं संयोगत्वम्।

It is a particular cause of the verbal behaviour, in the expression 'These two things are connected. In this definition the term असाधारणहेतुत्वं is added to avoid काल and दिक् which are general causes of anything. From the above quoted definitions of *Saṁyoga* one can observe—

(1) *Saṁyoga* is possible between two things which are two separate द्रव्यs. By the adjective अप्राप्त, संयोग is differentiated from समवाय. Udayana in *Kiraṇavalī* explains—

प्राप्तिः संश्लेषः। स च समवायोऽपीत्यत उक्तम् अप्राप्तयोरिति। प्राप्तिः means a relation. समवाय is also a relation. Therefore, the adjective अप्राप्तयोः 'which are not related' is used.

(2) From the same definition non-eternality of संयोग is suggested. Because when the substances are separate संयोग does not exist there. Thus, since it exists for a limited time it is अनित्य, i.e. non-eternal.

(3) The second definition संयुक्तप्रत्ययनिमित्तम् suggests the necessity of accepting संयोग relation in explaining the verbal behaviour इमौ संयुक्तौ.

I.III.0. Nature and Role of संयोग

(1) *Saṁyoga* is accepted as a relation. A relation is defined as द्विष्ठः सम्बन्धः i.e. a relation is that which resides in two objects. For example, when we say हस्तपुस्तकसंयोग, संयोग resides in hand as well as in the book.

(2) *Saṁyoga* is defined as सर्वद्रव्यवृत्तिः i.e. which can reside in all substances. Being a *guṇa*, it can reside in all substances.

(3) *Saṁyoga* is described as अव्याप्यवृत्तिः i.e. that which does not pervade entire locus, when we say दण्डी पुरूषः, दण्ड or stick has contact only with the palm of the hand and not with the entire hand or body. Thus, संयोग does not pervade the entire locus.

(4) संयोग is many a times described as वृत्तिनियामक-सम्बन्ध, whenever it shows आधाराधेयभाव, it is occurrence-exacting, e.g. when there is contact between a table and book, it shows that book is on the table, i.e. book is आधेय and table is आधार. In such a case संयोग can be called as वृत्तिनियामक-सम्बन्ध i.e. occurrence-exacting relation. However, when we join our hands vertically, this position does not prompt an understanding of आधाराधेयभाव. Here we can not label it as वृत्तिनियामक.

(5) *Saṁyoga* is described as अनित्य i.e. non-eternal. The definition अप्राप्तिपूर्विका प्राप्तिः shows its non-eternal character. In this context two questions are raised.

(A) Could there be नित्य संयोग in between two विभुs i.e. all-pervading substances? *Saṁyoga* is possible only in substances. आत्मा, काल, दिक् and आकाश are substances. Thus, there is no harm in having contact between these two and since these are eternal substances, the contact with these must be treated as eternal.

The answer is no, because

(i) For *Saṁyoga*, action or क्रिया is required at least in one substance. All pervading substances do not have क्रिया and therefore, since there is no cause there can be no contact between them.

Upaskāra says in this context—

विभुनोस्तु न संयोगः, कारणाभावात्। कर्म तावत्तत्र नास्ति।

(2) नित्य संयोग is never possible, because संयोग is defined as अप्राप्तिपूर्विका प्राप्तिः। This definition contradicts नित्य संयोग.

(3) Moreover, युतसिद्धि i.e. existing separately prompts contact i.e. contact is possible only in युतसिद्ध substances युतसिद्धि is defined as

(i) द्वयोरन्यतरस्य वा पृथग्गतिमत्त्वं युतसिद्धिः।

It is that state in which, either out of the two substances possesses movement. This definition is applied only in the case of eternal substances.

(ii) पृथक् आश्रयाश्रयित्वम्।

It is the state of residing in different loci. This definition is applied in the case of non-eternal substances.

Thus, विभु substances can not be युतसिद्ध, since these do not possess पृथग्गतिमत्त्वं and therefore can not have contact relation.

(B) Now, the second question is raised in the case of contact between परमाणु and आकाश. What is the status of such contact? Can we label it as नित्य? Because both of the substances are नित्य परमाणुs possess action, and so पृथग्गतिमत्त्वं is seen in परमाणुs. Thus, since these substances are युतसिद्ध, they must be having contact. This contact must be नित्य because both are eternal substances.

The answer is, there is a contact no doubt. But it is not नित्य. Because परमाणुs do not possess गति or movement all the time. Whenever there is क्रिया in परमाणुs these can have contact with the ether. Since this contact exists in segmental time it is अनित्य.

6. *Saṁyoga* is further divided into three sub-kinds.

(i) अन्यतरकर्मज is caused by the action in one substance. *Prapābhā* explains क्रियावता निष्क्रियस्य तथा स्थाणोः श्येनेन, विभूनां च मूर्तैः। When out of the two substances one possesses action which causes the contact, such contact is called अन्यतरकर्मज. The contact between विभु substances and मूर्त substances is अन्यतरकर्मज. It is caused by the action in मूर्त substances. मूर्त substances having limited size possess action. This action is the cause of the contact.

(ii) उभयकर्मज - उभयदिक्क्रिययोः संनिपातः। मेषयोः मल्लयोः वा। A contact caused by action in both substances from two different directions. Two goats or two wrestlers have contact with each other, because of the action in both.

(iii) संयोगजसंयोग A contact caused by contact. *Prapābhā* defines it as follows:

उत्पन्नमात्रस्य चिरोत्पन्नस्य वा निष्क्रियस्य कारणसंयोगिभिः अकारणैः कारणाकारणसंयोगपूर्वकः कार्याकार्यगतः संयोगः। तन्तुवीरणसंयोगात् द्वितन्तुकवीरणसंयोगः।

It is a contact of a product (just produced or produced before long time) with substances which are not its cause, however these are connected with its cause and this contact is in between a product and non-product which proceeds a contact between a cause and non-cause, e.g. तन्तु is a cause of पट. (द्वितन्तुक) It has a contact with वीरण, a kind of grass. Because of the contact between तन्तु and वीरण, another contact is produced in between पट and वीरण. This contact is called संयोगजसंयोग .

7. ***Samyoga* is described as द्रव्यगुणकर्महेतुः। It is a cause of द्रव्य, गुण and कर्मः**

(A) घट is a द्रव्य, it is formed because of the contact between two पृथिवी परमाणु^s when two कपाल^s come in contact with each other घट is produced. Thus, संयोग is a असमवायिकारण of घट.

(B) *Samyoga* also produces गुण, ज्ञान is a गुण which is produced in आत्मा. It is produced in आत्मा when आत्मा and मनस् have contact with each other.

(C) *Saṁyoga* produces कर्म in द्रव्य when there is contact between वायु and तृण, कर्म is produced.

I.IV.O. Objections

With this background now, let us see some objections on *Saṁyoga* which are refuted by Naiyayikas.

(1) *Saṁyoga* does not exist, because it is a relation.

Unless we accept relation, we cannot express valid cognition. Our behaviour depends upon valid cognition. Thus, we cannot explain our behaviour if we do not accept relation. Moreover, we do not have any proof to establish valid cognition as erroneous and therefore, the argument that *Saṁyoga* does not exist is not valid.

(2) What is a *Saṁyoga*? Is it the state of having no gap in two things (नैरन्तर्यम)? Or is it absence of gap in two things? If so, it is a अभाव पदार्थ and cannot be included in *guṇa*. Moreover, if 'having no gap' can be a relation 'having gap' will also be a relation.

This objection of Buddhists is refuted by Śridhara. He says संयोग is not नैरन्तर्य or अवधि-अभाव, rather it is a cause of the experience that these two things have no gap. Being a cause i.e. an existing entity, it must be included in भावपदार्थ. To quote himself verbatim—

नैरन्तर्यनिबन्धनोऽ यं प्रत्यय इति चेत्? कि द्रव्ययोः परस्वरसंश्लेषो नैरन्तर्यभ् अन्तराभावो वा? आद्ये कल्पे न किञ्चिदतिरिक्तमुक्तं स्यात्, द्रव्ययोः परस्परोपसंश्लेष एव हि नः संयोगः। द्वितीयो कल्पे सान्तरयोरन्तराभावे संयोगादन्यः को हेतुरिति वाच्यम्।

(3) We can use the term रूपश्लेष for संयोग, and it also does not exist. Because रूपश्लेष with what? With another परमाणु. If so, it does not exist, because by total amalgamation two things become one and the definition द्विष्ठः संयोगः cannot be applied.

Prabhācandra on *sambandhaparīkṣā* says—

नापि रूपश्लेषलक्षणोऽसौ, सम्बन्धिनोरभावे सम्बन्धायोगात्, द्विष्ठत्वात् तस्य।

This could be refuted as follows:

(i) संयोग as रूपश्लेष is possible only in परमाणुऽ. Because संयोग in substances having महत्परिमाण can be perceived by eyes. In case of परमाणुसंयोग we have to infer it. Because as घट is a product of कपालसंयोग. Similarly कपालऽ are products of परमाणुसंयोग .

We can also point out another case of रूपश्लेष. In मसीक्षोदसंयोग or दुग्ध-आप-संयोग we find रूपश्लेष i.e. total amalgamation. In मसीक्षोदसंयोग ink and ink powder are together with the relation of contact. Similarly if we add water in milk, the form of milk does not change. So there is रूपश्लेष. However, we cannot deny संयोग since by विभाग produced because of पाक or any other क्रिया we can also separate water from milk.

(ii) If we accept रूपश्लेष is it with the part? Or with the whole? If it is with part, whether such a part is identical with the whole or not? You cannot say yes, because no part will be left separately and thus रूपश्लेष i.e. संयोग cannot be established as a relation.

The answer is अवयविन् exists in the अवयवऽ So, though the contact will be with the part, still we can say that it is connected with अवयवी.

Conclusion

Saṁyoga is the most important relation according to the NV system, since it is intensely involved in our day-to-day experience. It is refuted by Buddhists and Sāṁkhyas. However, Naiyayikas and Vaiśeṣikas have tried their best to establish संयोग as per the necessity of the system. Vaiśeṣikas no doubt have included it in *guṇa*. Prācina Naiyayikas do not enlist it under any category, since their classification is dialectics oriented. However, while discussing perceptual cognition संयोग is discussed as सन्निकर्ष. Later on NV system has followed categorisation of Vaiśeṣikas and therefore, *Saṁyoga* has retained his place in *guṇa.* In the later period though Raghunatha Śiromaṇi in his *Padarthatattvamnipaṇa* has reduced the number of categories which are excessive according to him, could not discard संयोग because of its immense need. Moreover he has broaden the corpus of संयोग by adding परत्वापरत्व to it. Thus, through the development of Nyāya philosophy place of *Saṁyoga* is undisturbed.

Bibliography

1. Ed. Tripathi, Bhagirath Prasad, "*Praśastapāda bhaṣyam* with Kandati", Ganganath Jha Granthamala, I, Varanasi, 1971.

2. Ed. Mishra, Narayan, "*Vaiśeṣikasūtropaskāra* of Saṇkaramiśra", Kashi Sanskrit Series 195, The Chowkhamba Sanskrit Series Office, Varanasi, 1969.

3. Ed. Jha, V.N. "सम्बन्धपरीक्षा *The Philosophy of Relations*". Bibliotheca Indo-Buddhika, No.66, Sri Satguru Publications, Delhi, 1990.

4. Ed. Athalye Bodas, "*Tarkasangraha*", B.O.R.I., 1980.

5. Shastri Narayana Chandra and Swetavaikuṇtha Sastri "Nyāyasiddhāntamuktāvali" with Kiraṇavali, Kashi Sanskrit Series 212, Chaukhamba Sanskrit Sansthan, 1983.

6. Ed. Jetly, J.S. '*Praśastapādabhāṣyam with Kiranāvali*', Gaekwad's Oriental Series, No. 154, Oriental Institute, Baroda, 1971.

2

Samavāya

B.K. Dalai

1. The Problem

The problem of relation is one of the most baffling problem of Philosophy and rightly claims the most fundamental position in all metaphysical discussion. It is indeed a very difficult task, or so it is thought, to attempt in giving a meaningful analysis to the concept of relation. The observation in this context made by Perry is worth quoting here. He observes:

"But to answer the question 'what is relation'? is a difficult affair; for, to define relation is impossible". Either it may be taken as an ultimate logical category or one should face the dialectical difficulties as shown by Bradley[1]. Following his steps Alexander holds a similar view: "Relation according to Alexander is 'the vaguest word in the philosophical vocabulary'. It is used as a symbol indicating a connection and is generally left undefined"[2].

But the Indians' mind has gone far away in expounding the nature of the relation and presenting a criterion to define what relation is[3]. The *Naiyāyikas* define relation as a special determinant of a qualified knowledge[4]. Jagadiśa defines relation as the contentness (*Viṣayatā*) other than the qualificandness (Viś*eṣyatā*) and the qualifierness of a qualified cognition[5].

The relation is broadly divided into two groups. (i) *Vṛttiniyāmaka*, (ii) *Vṛtty aniyāmaka*[6]. The first group consists of three types of relations namely, *viśeṣaṇatā* (the qualifierness,) *saṁyoga* (the conjunction) and the *samavāya* (*inherence*). These three types along with *tādātmya* (identity) are called relations in the primary sense of the term[7]. But in the secondary sense, as has been rightly pointed out by Prof. Ingalls, the relations are many[8].

Amongst these, the relation of Inherence is of great importance and is the most controversial one; controversial in the sense that there are at least three main streams of thought from three prominent schools combatting with each other. On one side stand the extreme realists amongst whom the *Naiyāyika* is the chief and holds purely an objective view of the relation in general and the relation of Inherence in particular. To them the relation of *Inherence is a Real Entity* intervening between two terms as a tertium quid[9].

On the other side we have the idealists, the Buddhists followed by the *Vedāntins* who hold a subjective view of the relation of Inherence. To them any relation is a conceptual fiction fabricated by our mind having no objective reality[10].

Still there is a third group which stands in the middle keeping the realists in one side and the idealists in the other, maintaining a relative view of the relation of Inherence. According to them Inherence is neither absolutely subjective as hold the *Buddhists* nor absolutely objective as hold the *Naiyāyikas* but both. They dub this relation as identity-cum-difference or identity in deference[11].

2. With the introduction of controversy atleast three significant questions, are in order, to be answered.

1. What is the nature of *Samavāya*
2. Why the *Naiyāyikas* postulate a relation like *Samavāya*
3. How and why the idealists like *Buddhists* and *Vedāntins*; the realists like *Bhāṭṭas* and *Jains* do not accept *Samavāya*.

It is proposed here to attend these questions with some amount of justification.

3. Nature of Inherence

According to the *Naiyāyikas* the relation of Inherence is a real entity (*vāstava*). It acts as a relation as a tertium quid between two terms or relata which are inseparables. A *Naiyāyika* believes that every bit of human experience has its object which is existent in the eternal world. In other words, the object of a true cognition has to be accepted as an eternal objective reality.

Thus, in a cognition say 'this rose is red', we have three separate entities namely, (i) the rose, (ii) the redness, and (iii) the relation connecting the two, i.e., the rose and the redness. And all these three are objective realities. This third entity is precisely what the Inherence is.

This relation of Inherence is supposed to exist between five pairs.

1. The whole and the part.
2. The quality and the qualified.
3. The motion and the moved.
4. The generic character and the individual manifestation.
5. The particulars and the eternal substances[12].

It is said to be a necessary relation in the sense that the relata never exist without being related to the other. We have pointed out earlier that the relation of Inherence exists between such entities as whole and part, quality or motion and substance, the universal and the individual.

The Inherence has been established in many ways; but at any case of dispute it can be established by inference. Any qualified cognition can be analysed as having three primary objects as its content namely, 'the qualifier', 'the qualificand' and the relation between the two. In case of the cognition like quality, motion etc., this relation cannot be that of conjunction[13]. Thus, this relation will be Inherence.

The Inherence is not conjunction, because conjunction takes place exclusively between two substances as between a *kuṇḍala* and the *puruṣa* but Inherence does so between (i) two substances as in the case of part and whole, (ii) between substance and non-substance, as in the case of quality etc., and substances; (iii) and between two non-substances as in case of universals and the qualities etc. The clear distinction of the two has logically been established in PDS of *Praśastapāda.* The grounds may be summed up here:

1. Conjunction occurs between objects those have separate existence prior to the conjunction whereas Inherence subsists between objects those have no separate existence at any time.

2. Conjunction is brought about by the function of either one or both of the members related, whereas in case of Inherence we do not find any such cause and the only for the relationship lies in the productive potency of the cause bringing the substance into existence.

The conjunction of two hands say 'A' and 'B' is possible by the action of either of the hands or by both the hands i.e., by the movement of the hand 'A' or 'B' or both 'A' and 'B'. But any such cause is not seen in case of Inherence.

3. Conjunction ceases as soon as there is a disjunction of the members related whereas Inherence is indestructible. The conjunction of the component conjoined loses its continuity by the disjunction of the members related; but Inherence is an ever lasting and eternal entity.

4. Conjunction occurs between two substances that have independent existence; for instance the various fingers of the hands come into mutual contact whereas, Inherence subsists only in such substances as stand to each other in the relation of the container and the contained.

The aforesaid discussion presents a clearcut picture as to why conjunction must be treated as distinct from Inherence. In this context the observation of K.C. Varadacari is worth mentioning. He observes: "There is an essential difference between the two types of contact and we cannot say that *samavāya* and *saṁyoga* are identical. If *saṁyoga* can connect, then *samavāya* also can, but the differential between the two lies in the fact that in *saṁyoga* one can disconnect oneself from the object just like a copulary link between two carriages but one cannot disconnect the *dravya* from *guṇa* in a mechanical way. It is a metaphysical distinction not a mechanical disjunction that is possible between the *dravya* and *guṇa* or *guṇa* and *sāmānya*"[14].

It is already said that 'whole' exists in its parts', quality in their 'substance' by the relation of Inherence. It amounts to say that Inherence should exist in both the relata; for, it relates the two. But the *Naiyāyika* accepts only the container to be *samavāyin* that is containing something in it by *samavāya* relation while the contained entity called *samaveta*' (contained in some by *samavāya* relation). In this regard Praśastapāda says:

The property of being *samavāyin* belongs to all the first five categories", namely substance, quality, movement universal and particularity[15]. Commenting on this Śridhara points out that the property of being *samavāyin* only means subsistence by *samavāya* relation[16]. But the real difficulty arises here is, what is the relation for *samavāya* to exist in an object? If it is accepted that it exists by some other relation it would lead to an unending regress ad infinitum[17]. The *Naiyāyikas*, therefore, hold that inherence does not require any other relation for its substances. It subsists by itself. Regarding this Praśastapāda holds: In the case of being with regard to substances, qualities, and actions we have seen that it has no connection with any other being and in the same manner Inherence, being inseparable from its substrate and of the very nature of 'subsisting relation' could have no other relation[18].

While commenting on this Śṛidhara says that inherence being independent does not subsist by any other relation as conjunction does. It means that conjunction being a quality does exist in the object by Inherence; but Inherence itself is not a quality or property of any other object and hence no relation is necessary. For, the propriety of the question as to by which relation that relates two entities, is related to the relation is also doubted[19]. In this connection Udyotakara, to the question—why Inherence is regarded as independent—answers: "It is because it has no other *samavāya* relation for its subsistence. Whatever subsists elsewhere must subsist by some relation" and there we conclude "Inherence which has no relation for its subsistence does not subsist any where[20]. In his typical way he argues: "*samavāya* does not subsist anywhere because it can be designated by the term *pañca-padārtha vṛtti*. What ever can be designated by that term does not subsist anywhere as for instance an atom[21]. The term *pañca-padārtha vṛtti* can be interpreted in two ways. In case of atoms it means 'in which there is the substence of five categories[22]; for, all the five categories reside in an atom. But in case of *samavāya* it is interpreted to mean something different, that is the relation of five categories. This view has been criticized by Vācaspatimiśra like this:

"In that way it can be argued that because a 'cow' and 'speech' are both designated by the word *go*, speech should also possess horns like the cow"[23].

Being confronted with the question that if *samavāya* does not subsist anywhere why there is a notion of the Inherence of cloth in the thread, Udyotakara answers:

"That notion of subsistence of *samavāya* is an illusion"[24]. Fortunately Udyotakara is the only person to hold that Inherence does not subsist anywhere.

On the other hand all other philosophers maintain that *samavāya* does not exist in its substratum by another relation. They never say that it does not exist at all. To Prasastapāda, *samavāya* is subsistent (*āśrita*) in some object[25]. In clarification, Śridhara, however, maintains that subsistence means 'being cognized as dependent'[26]. This is in fact a clear contradiction on his part, for he maintains Inherence as independent.

According to *Naiyāyika samavāya* can be the object of perception[27]. However, there is difference of opinion among the philosophers of *Nyāya-Vaiśeṣika* school as to whether *samavāya* could become the object of perception. Even amongst the philosophers who favour the theory that Inherence can be the object of perception are not unanimous even in holding that Inherence is always the object of perception. Some philosophers think that it is always perceptible while others point out that it is not always so. It is perceptible only when the relata are perceptible and even it may exist when one of the relata is not perceptible. But in that case the Inherence is not perceptible.

On the otherhand the Vaiśeṣika holds that *samavāya* cannot be known by perception[28].

According to *Naiyāyika* there is a regular contact of the sense-organ with the *samavāya* and hence it can be known by perception. One can have the perceptual knowledge of *samavāya* in the form *rūpasamavāya ghaṭaḥ*. Here the *ghaṭa* comes in contact with eye, where inhers the *rūpa*. In this case *samavāya* also exists in the *ghaṭa* by *svarūpa saṁbandha* and becomes a qualifier of the jar which has direct contact with the organ, eye. Now, the *viṣayatā* which exists in the form of qualifierness is in *samavāya*. That is why in the perception of *samavāya* the qualifierness determined by the object having its contact with the sense-organ is the cause[29]. The reason behind the difference of opinion among the scholars of the two sister schools may possible be like this. The philosophers of the *Vaiśeṣika* school think that it would be difficult on their part to explain the subsistence of *samavāya* in an object. Further, it was difficult for them to establish a sense-organ contact with the *samavāya* which leads them to hold Inherence to be inferable. Praśastapāda himself has said that *samavāya* is itself in the nature of subsistence and has no other relation of subsistence. In the same context he says, *samavāya* is inferable, because it has no relation of subsistence[30].

This Inherence is one in number[31] and is conceived as eternal. By 'eternality' what is meant here is uncausedness (*akāraṇatva*) and therefore it is indestructible. It is obvious that the idea of eternality is intended to be aimed at avoiding the fault of infinite regress; for, whatever is produced must need a productive agent and that too would need a further productive agent, and so on. Praśastapāda in his PDS has established that *samavāya* is uncaused and repudiates the view that it is other-caused or self-caused[32].

Very interesting question is raised against the notion of Inherence as one. If the relation of Inherence is one and the same, then the Inherence of touch and the Inherence of colour being identical, the air also should be endowed with colour, because the Inherence of colour is also there[33]. Praśastapāda who normally avoids controversy in his PDS has introduced an objector who argues: If *samavāya* is one then *samavāya* of *dravyatva* and that of *guṇatva* being the same, the *dravyatva* will reside in the qualities also, and *guṇatva* in the substance also[34]. To this he replies; "although *dravyatva* and *guṇatva* have the same *samavāya* there is the difference of potentiality of manifestation (*vyañjya vyañjaka-śakti*) on account of which there will be a restriction in the relation of the container and the contained[35]. To this adds Śridhara; "the potentiality of manifesting *dravyatva* resides only in *dravya* and therefore the universal *dravyatva* will reside by *samavāya* relation only in substance and nowhere else[36].

Viśvanātha in his NSM meets the objection with the answer that although the *samavāya* of colour is present, yet there is no colour in the air[37].

It has been answered further that the relation of colour is not Inherence but the locusness described by Inherence qualified by the association of colour by virtue of its being the describer of Inherence[38].

The modern neologicians chief among whom is Raghunāth-Śiromaṇi are of the view that Inherence is not one but many. To them the cognition in the form of 'the Inherence of smell is in the earth and not in the water' clearly proves that Inherence is not one but many in number[39].

4. Need of Accepting *Samavāya*

The *Naiyāyikas* accept the relation of Inherence as a real entity intervening between two inseparables, as an independent padārtha; it is further postulated as one and eternal. But the question is: Why do the *Naiyāyikas*, accept such a peculiar relation like Inherence? Would it not be possible for them to dispense with Inherence? What would be the difficulty if they do so? The following are the answers to such questions:

The idea of dispensing Inherence may involve three possibilities. 1. There is no necessaity of postulating any relation at all and nothing is related from the ultimate point of view (*paramārthya dṛṣṭyā*), as do the *Buddhists* and the *Vedāntins*[40].

2. The relation is to be accepted but not the relation of Inherence but in some other forms and can be replaced by *tādātmya* i.e., *bheda ghaṭita abheda* as do *Bhāṭṭas* and the *Jainas*.

3. The relation of Inherence is to be accepted but not all its characteristics like eternality and oneness as do the *Prābhākaras*[41].

But none of these alternatives would serve the purpose. Precisely the very acceptance or the theory of Inherence is at the root of the entire philosophical speculations and framework of the realists. It is indeed the bricks, so to say, on which the high mansion of *Nāyāya-Vaiśeṣika* takes its stand. Effect is different from its cause, whole is different from its parts, quality and action are different from their substrata, substances, universal is different from their individuals and still they are identical in the sense that they occupy the same space. These are valid cognitions whose validity cannot be doubted or contradicted. When thus is the case, how to explain such situations? How to justify the distinction between cause and effect, whole and part, quality and the qualified?

Thus, in order to give a proper solution to these problems and to avoid the difficulties, the *Naiyāyikas* accept the relation of Inherence. This involves the metaphysical aspects of the problem of Inherence.

From the epistemological point of view also Inherence is to be accepted, for a qualified cognition cannot be explained properly if the relation of Inherence is not accepted. To explain: Any qualified cognition having the structure of a qualifier-qualificand type has three essential factors as its object namely, (1) a qualifier, (2) a qualificand and (3) a relation between the two; i.e., the qualifier and the qualificand.

Thus, in order to explain a qualified cognition properly we do require the relation. It has been proved by the help of inferences by good many *Naiyāyikas*, how a qualified cognition having the structure of qualifier- qualificand type needs a relation. And this relation in case of qualified cognition of quality, motion and universal etc., would be nothing but Inherence[42].

5. Refutation of Inherence by Various Systems of Indian Philosophy

Among the opponents of the theory of the relation in general and the relation of Inherence in particular the *Buddhists* come first in the list the chief among whom is again the great *Buddhist* genius Dharmakīrti. He has attached so much so importance to the problem of relation that besides his referential and passing treatment of the problem here and there in his monumental work the Pramaṇavārttika, he composed twenty-five moemonic verses along with his own commentary which goes by the title *Saṁbandhaparīkṣā*, in order to refute all kinds of relations[43].

Dharmakīrti maintains purely a subjective view of relations. His attitude towards the notion of the relation is that all entities are momentary, simple moments enjoying isolated existence unrelated and fleeting[44]. Thus, according to Dharmakīrti a relation is a conceptual fiction fabricated by our mind having no objective reality at all[45].

The knowledge of relation is unreal for, it cannot be ascertained either by perception or by inference. And there is no third means of proof[46].

In the work of Śāntaraksita entitled Tattva Saṁgraha we meet with a fiar exposition of the position of *Buddhists*. He first starts to refute the theory that Inherence is eternal; for, he thinks that if he can crack this theory it would not be very difficult for him to refute the notion of Inherence as a distinct reality and to convert the *Naiyāyikas* to the *Buddhists* view of the world as a flux of momentary flash of energy. His argument may be put forth like this.

If there is only one and eternal Inherence, as the *Naiyāyika* holds, then there is no reason why when we see a pot we should not say there is a cloth or why when we see an elephant we should not think that we are looking at a cow[47]?

It should not be argued that even though one relation is destroyed the other still persists connected to its locus; for, it would amount to a very serious dilemma. He clarifies:

When one relatum 'A' which inheres, say, in 'B' by relation 'C' is destroyed what is that which continues to exist? Is it the Inherence which connect 'A' to 'B' or something else? If it is that Inherence then we have the absurdity of relation without relata,—a relation, which is designed to connect 'A' to 'B' which persists when there is no 'A'. On the other hand if it be something other than that Inherence which continues to exist then it is clearly not a single entity but a collection of bits of relations[48].

Coming to the *Vedāntins,* Śaṅkara[49] and his followers[50] are in agreement with the view of the *Buddhists* in denying the relation of Inherence as an independent objective reality. But what is most significant in case of Śaṅkara is that he had developed a very systematic and acute dialectical analysis on the problem of relation of Inherence. In a similar way he refutes the acceptance of Inherence. Instead they accept identity as the relation to explain the case where Inherence is postulated. Thus, according to Śaṅkara the notion of relation of Inherence is false[51].

Amongst the *Mimāṁsakas* Prabhākara and his followers are at one with the *Naiyāyikas* in accepting the relation of Inherence with certain reservations; for, they do not share the concept of Inherence in toto. They object to the acceptance of Inherence as eternal[52].

On the other hand the *Bhaṭṭas* unlike the *Prābhākaras* and *Naiyāyikas*, do not accept Inherence as a relation and also distinct category. While discussing on the relations of universals and its individuals Kumarila points out a number of difficulties in the theory of Inherence if it is accepted as a distinct *padārtha*, distinct from its relata[53]. To him this relation is *tādāmya* by which he means identity in difference (*bheda-ghaṭita-abheda*). The objection which Kumarila has pointed out follows the same line as that of the Buddhists or even *Vedantins*[54].

The *Jainas* are at one with the *Naiyāyikas* in maintaining relation as an objective reality. However, there are two important and significant points on which they differ from the *Naiyāyikas*. They are: 1. To postulate relations as existing independently of its relata as a distinct reality. 2. The acceptance of *samavāya saṁbandha*.

Regarding the first point the *Jains attitude* is that relation is something which is integral to the terms and not some absolute independent reality. It does not mean that it is subjective or mental as do the *Buddhists* and *Vedāntins*. To a *Jaina* philosopher the relation is indeed an objective fact serving as a link between the relata.

Regarding the second point, the *Jainas* do not accept the relation of Inherence. The arguments developed by the Jaina philosophers do not constitute and contribute anything new. The arguments are almost similar to that of the *Buddhists* and the *Vedantins*[55].

6. Observations

Logic apart what is more important for our purpose is: Why all these philosophers of different school are restless to refute the relation of Inherence? What do they achieve 'metaphysically' in denying Inherence. What precisely the difficulty would be on their part if they accept the relation of Inherence. Here follows some speculations which may clarify the aforesaid queries.

On the philosophical framework of Buddhist philosophy they have no other go than refuting any relation what so ever. Or else the entire construction of their philosophical framework would collapse and lose its base. They hold all realities to be momentary, simple moments, enjoying isolated existence and thus how can they think of any relation? Unless they accept the permanent existence of entity it will be impossible for them to accept any relation.

Coming to *Vedāntin*, Śaṅkara, he has a world of imagination, unreal, super imposition. He opposes the plurality of universe and that is why he has criticised the notion of Inherence. As observes S. Datta, "The theory of *samavāya* relation plays an important part in his *Nyāya-Vaiśeṣika* pluralism; if one wishes to criticise this pluralistic philosophy one just need criticise the theory of *Samavāya*"[56].

In case of Prabhākara he accepts Inherence but the eternality of it is not acceptable to him. He thinks that when Inherence is between two eternal entity it is eternal, but when it is between transient entity it is transient. Prabhākara thinks that if he accepts Inherence as eternal always, then it would be difficult on his part to explain how the relation can continue to exist when the relata or one of the relata is destroyed which is not the fact. Again it will not be possible for him to give a right answer to the objections posed by Śāntaraksita as to where the relation will exist when one of the relata or both the relata are destroyed. And if it is accepted that even if one of the relata is destroyed the relation can exist would amount to going against the fundamental notion of any relational situation that it is *dviṣṭha* (*dviṣṭhatvāt saṁbandhasya*), is the mind of the Prabhākara. Thus, in order to do away with all these difficulties he accepts it as permanent in case of permanent entities and then the question of the destruction of Inherence and a locus for it would not arise. In case of transient entity when the relata or one of the relata is destroyed, the Inherence would be destroyed. In fact the aforesaid difficulties can be explained even accepting Inherence as permanent, which has been already pointed out.

Prabhākara fails to see the underlying reason behind the acceptance of Inherence as one and eternal. If it is not accepted as eternal, the absurdities of finding a reasonable ground for its destruction would be difficult to explain. And again accepting Inherence as transient there will be no distinction between Inherence and conjunction. It is further cumbersome to have dual character of Inherence, which is *gaurava*.

Bhāṭṭas, on the other hand, oppose the idea of accepting the relation of Inherence. They want to replace the relation of Inherence by Identity-cum-difference. The underlying reason behind such commitment, most probably, is some thing like this. Bhātta being a realist cannot deny the ontological existence of relation in toto.

So in order to retain his fundamental claim as a realist he has to accept the relation. Nevertheless he wants to avoid the difficulties in the latter's conception of Inherence like regress ad infinitum & c. & c.; advanced by the Idealists. He, therefore, denies absolute difference between the sets of objects and accepts a natural relation (*tādātmya*). He intends to avoid the assertion of both absolute identity of the *Buddhists*' and *Vedāntins*' as well as absolute difference of *Prabhakaras*' and *Naiyāyikas*'. For, he fears, that the former would annihilate the plurality of particulars and would land him in a unpleasant mase of identity to the pleasure of the *advaitins*' and the latter results into a non-relational structure of the universe.

Notes and References

1. S. Datta, The Problem of Relation in Contemporary Philosophy, p. 8.
2. Ibid., p. 103.
3. This statement in no way implies that the Western Philosophers have not defined the relation at all. In fact there are a number of Philosophers who have taken great pain in analysing the nature of relation. Vide., James: A Pluralistic Universe, p. 282, Essays in Radical Empiricism, p. 42, Russell: The Problem of Philosophy, p. 152.
4. *Viśiṣṭapratītiniyāmakaviśeṣasyaivasaṁbandhatvāt* - *Vyādhikarana Dīdhiti Prakāśa* Chow. edn., p. 135.

   Viśiṣṭadhīniyāmasyaiva tathātvāt - *Siddhānta lakṣaṇa Jāgadīśi,* Chow. edn., p. 252.
5. *Viśeṣya-viśeṣaṇatvānya-viśiṣṭa-dhī viṣayatvaṁ eva saṁbandhatvam iti bhāvaḥ* - ibid., p. 256.
6. *Aviśiṣṭa vyāvṛtta viśiṣṭa dhī niyāmakaḥ saṁbandhaḥ—Tattva cintamaṇi*, p. 652, Kāmākhyānāth Tarkavāgiśa edn.

   Yathāsvā guṇakriyājātiviśiṣṭabuddhau viṣayībhūta samavāyo vṛttiniyāmakaḥ, ibid., p. 651.
7. *Tac ca tādātmya-viśeṣaṇatā-saṁyoga-samavāyeṣveva mukhyam*— Commentary on Pandita Anantakumar *Nyāya Tarkatirtha* on *Jñāna* lakṣaṇavicāra-rahasya, p. 3.
8. *Materials for the study of Navya-Nyāya Logic* —Article 47, p. 74.
9. *Siddhānta Lakṣaṇa Jāgadīśi*, p. 256, Chow, edn.

   cf. "Suppose for instance" observes Russell, "that I am in my room. I exist, my room exists, but does 'in' exist? Obviously the word has a meaning; it denotes a relation which holds between me and my room. This relation as something although we cannot say that it exists in the same sense in which 'I' and my 'room' exist. S. Datta. op. cit., p. 40.
10. *Sambandhaḥ kalpanākṛtaḥ*; *Pramāṇa vārtika*, III. 237.

    Vikalpite kalpanānirmite saṁbandhe..., Tattvārthaślokavārtika, pp. 148ff.
11. Bhāṭṭas and Jains comes under this group vide *Ślokavārtika*, VSS. 146-150 on sū. 4.

    cf. De Witt Parker: "Since everything exist both of an account of itself and of other thing there would be a part of the thing which would remain the same before the entrance into the new relationship and another part which would be different", The Theory of relations, pp. 250-251.

12. *Avayavāvayavinor jātivyaktyor guṇaguṇinoḥ kriyākriyāvator nityadravyaviśeṣayoś ca yaḥ saṁbandhaḥ sa samavāyaḥ, Nyāyasiddhānta Muktāvali* [= NSM] p. 3 with *Dinakarī* and *Rāmarudri*, NS. press edn.,

13. *Dravyayor eva saṁyoga iti niyamād iti*, *Dinakarī*, p. 87.

14. K.C. Varadācāri, "*Samavāya—A critique*", (presented to Dr. T.M. P. Mahādevan contributed by fifty one scholars, Eastern & Western, p. 178.

15. *Dravyādīnāṁ pañcānāṁ samavāyitvaṁ*; PadārthaDharma Saṁgraha, [= PDS], edt. D. Jha, p. 42.

16. *Samavāyitvaṁ samavāya lakṣaṇā vṛttiḥ*, Kandalī on PDS, p. 42.

17. cf. *Tataś ca tasya tasyānyonyaḥ saṁbandhaḥ kalpayitavyaḥ iti* anavasthā, Brahmasūstra Śāṅkarabhāsya, 2.2.13.

18. *Samavāyasya nānyā vṛttir asti, Tasmāt svātmavṛttiḥ,* PDS., p. 784

cf. a relation indeed has a kind of double personality; itself being a simple it has the characteristic of bringing other simples in to complex, S. Datta, op. cit., p. 118.

cf. The Hobhouse thinks that the so called infinite regress which Bradley points out is the result of a confusion. Bradley forgets that 'Relation implies analysis of a whole; it does not as such involve the analysis of its own terms'. So there cannot arise the question of relating a relation with its terms because... hence the question, how they are related is absurd, Ibid., p. 65.

cf. Thus relation r^1, r^2, r^3......, etc., are simply the specimens of the relation. R. to suppose such relation as the difference between the terms and itself is just a repetition. Cook Wilson, statement and inference, Vol. II, p. 694.

cf. Cook Wilson also thinks that Bradleys infinite regress is fallacious... ibid.

19. cf... the question of relating a relation with the term is meaningless and unreal. The idea of relation cannot be applied to the term and its relation., ibid.

20. *Anāśritaḥ samavāyaḥ*..., Nyāyavārtika, Benaras edn., p. 154.

21. *Pañca padārtha vṛtti sabdaviṣayatvāt paramāṇuvat*, ibid., p. 159.

22. Here it is a *tatpuruṣa* compound—*pañcānāṁ padārthānāṁ vṛttiḥ*.

23. *Mā bhūd go-śabda-sāmyena vāg-ādīnāṁ api viśāṇitvam*; Nyāya Vārtika Tātparya, p. 159.

24. *Mithyā pratyaya evas a iti* ; ibid.

25. *Āsrītatvaṁ cānyatra nitya dravyebhyaḥ* ; PDS. p. 785.

26. *Āśrītatvaṁ ca paratantratayopalabdhiḥ* ; NKL, p. 784.

27. *Samavāyasya pratyakṣa - varṇanaṁ Nyāya matena* ; Tarkāmṛta, p. 8.

28. *Vaiśeṣikamatetu samavāyo na pratyakṣaḥ* ; NSM. on verse 61.

Tasmād iha buddhy anumeyaḥ samavayaḥ ; PDS, p. 785.

29. *Evaṁ rūpasamavāyavān ghaṭa ity atra samavāya pratyakṣasthale cakṣusambandha-ghaṭe viśeṣaṇaṁ samavāya svarūpa saṁbandhena vartate-viśeṣaṇatā rūpa viṣayatā samavāyaniṣtaḥ atah samavāya pratyakṣe indriyasaṁbandha viṣeṣa na tu sannikarṣaḥ kārṇam*, *NSM*, p. 204.

30. *Ata eva atīndriyaḥ sattādīnāṁ iva pratyakṣeṣu vṛty abhāvāt, tasmād iha buddyanumeyaḥ samavāya iti*, PDS, p. 785.

31. *Sarvatraika samavāya iti gamyate* ; ibid, p. 697.

Naca saṁyogavat nānātvam ; ibid., p. 696.

Lāghavād ekasamavāya siddhiḥ, NSM, p. 88.

32. *Na hy asya kiñcit kāraṇaṁ pramāṇatā upalabhyate*, PDS, p. 697.

33. *Na ca samavāyaikatve vāyau rūpavattā buddhiprasaṅgaḥ* , NSM., p. 88.

34. *Dravya-guṇa-karmaṇāṁ dravyatva-guṇatva-karmatvādi viśeṣaṇaiḥ saha saṁbandhaikatvāt padārtha saṅkara prasaṅgaḥ* , PDS., p. 778.

35. *Tathā dravyatvādīnāṁ api samavāyaikatve'pi vyaṅgyavyañjaka śakti bhedād ādhārādheya niyama* ; ibid., p. 781.

36. *Dravyatvābhivyañjikā śaktir dravyāṇām eva, tena dravyasya eva dravyatvaṁ samaveiti, nānyatra* , NKL., p. 782.

37. *Tatra rūpa samavāya satvepi rūpābhāvāt*, NSM, p. 88.

38. *Rūpanirūpitatvaviśiṣṭasamavāyanirūpitādhikaraṇatayaiva rūpasaṁbandhatvāt*, Dinakarī, p. 89.

39. *'Pṛthivyām rūpasya samavāyo na jale' ityādi pratīteḥ samavāyasya nānātvam iti tu navyāḥ*, ibid.

'Jale snehasya samavāyo na gandhasya', ityadi pratīter eva samavāyasya nānātvam. Rāmabhadra Sārvabhauma commentary on Padārtha Tattvanirūpaṇam, Varanasi edn., p. 126.

40. Vide., infra., Fn. 46, and 48.

41. *Samavāyam Na vayam kāśyāpiyā iva nityam upemaḥ*, Prakaraṇa Pañcikā, p. 92.

42. *Guṇa kriyādi viśiṣṭa buddhir viśeṣaṇa-viśeṣya saṁbandha-viṣayā, viśiṣta buddhitvāt daṇḍīti buddhivat-Etena saṁyogādi bādhāt samavāya siddhiḥ*, NSM., p. 87.

43. The position of the *Buddhists* on relation has been fairly presented by Dr. V.N. Jha. Vide V.N. Jha, Philosophy of Relations.

44. *Tān miśrayati kalpanā,* SambandhaParīkṣā, Verse. 5; Prameya Kamala Mārtaṇḍa., p. 506.

45. *Saṁbandhaḥ kalpanākṛtaḥ saṁbandhacintā*, Pramāṇa Vārtika, III. 237.

cf. with the notion of Humes: "that all our distinct perceptions are distinct existences, and that the mind never perceives any real connection.

46. *Uktaprakārebhyaḥ pramāṇāntarasya pareṇanābhyu pagamat,* Prameya Kamala Mārtaṇḍa, p. 511.

47. Taṇ na saṁbandhinoḥ saṁbandha buddhir vāstavī, ibid., p. 506.

dvayor ekābhisaṁbandhāt saṁbandho yadi tad dvayoḥ, kaḥ saṁbandho 'navasthā ca na saṁbandhamatis tathā., ibid.

cf. Hence Perry thinks that it is a misconception of the idealist to say that independent entities would never come in a relation to one another. S. Datta, op. cit., p. 54.

48. G. Jha, Eng. Tra. of Tattva Samgraha, pp. 461-465.

49. Brahma Sūtra Saṅkar Bhāsya on 2.2.17.

50. Khaṇḍana Khaṇḍa Khādya, Chow. edn., pp. 1096-1099.

51. *Kalpanāyāś ca svāyattatvāt prabhūtatvasaṁbhavāc ca. Na cā vaiśeṣikaiḥ kalpitebhyaḥ saḍbhyaḥ padārthebhyo'nye'dhikāḥ śataṁ sahasraṁ vā na kalpayitavyā iti nivārako hetur asti;* Brahma Sūstra Śāṅkarabhāsya on 2.2.17.

52. *Samavāyañ ca na vayaṁ Kāśyapīya iva nityam upemaḥ* Prakarana Pañcikā, p. 92.

Samvāyo nityayor ākāśa mahatvayor nityaḥ, anityayor avayavāvayinor anityaḥ, Nyāya Siddhi of Nārāyana Bhaṭṭa, p. 92.

Tathaiva samavāyasyāpy adravyatvena saṁyogābhāvāt samavāyāntara śrayeṇa anavasthā prasaṅgāt Viśeṣaṇe viśeṣyabhāva eva sannikarṣa., ibid., p. 15.

53. Vide B.K. Dalai, Bhatta's Refutation of Inherence: A Critique, Deccan College Bulletin, 1988.

54. *Rūpādināṁ tu saṁyukta dravya tādātmyam eva naḥ pratīti kāraṇaṁ tasmān na sambandhāntare spṛhā;* Mānameyodaya, Theosophical Publishing House, p. 13,

55. *Samavāyasya samavāyāntareṇa vṛttyabhyupagame tu tatrāpyapara samavāya kalpane'navasthā nātidustarā*—Sarvadarsana Saṁgraha, Calcutta, edn., P. 252.

56. S. Datta, op. cit., p. 83.

3

The History of *Svarūpasambandha*

Baliram Shukla

Whatever object we pick up in this world if it exists, it does exist as related to something (*sambaddha*). Thus, when pot exists, it exists being related to its potness either as the qualifier or as the universal and that relation is known as inherence. We know all the entities in this universe distinctly on the basis of relation. The concept of relation plays a significant role in the Navya-Nyāya system and therefore, very often it is said as the relational logic. Showing the importance of relation the Naiyāyikas have been sometimes called as *sambandhin* 'who is related to someone by some relation' humorously.[1] .

A qualified cognition (*viśiṣṭajñāna*) has to have at least three contents (*viṣayas*): *viśeṣya* 'qualificand', *viśeṣaṇa* 'qualifier' and *saṁsarga* 'relation'. Among them *saṁsarga* alone becomes the regulating factor of a qualified cognition. Gaṅgeśa defines relation as the regulating factor of a qualified cognition that is different from the non-qualified one.[2] Rucidatta Miśra gives a clarification to this definition and says that not being a cause of non-qualified cognition that which causes a qualified cognition is treated as a *sambandha*. Jagadīśa criticizes Gaṅgeśa's definition only because that it is beset with the fault of *ātmāśraya* 'dependence on self'. Thus, *vyāpti* 'invariable concomitance' is a *niyama*. It has been defined as *pratiyogy asamānādhikaraṇaṁ yatsamānā-*

dhikaraṇātyantābhāvapratiyogitāvacchedakāvacchinnaṁ yan na bhavati tena samaṁ tasya sāmānādhikaraṇyam. [3] The term *pratiyogitā* as a relation enters in the definition of *vyāpti*. Here, our purpose is to know what the relation (*vyāpti*) is ? To know this relation we require another relation like *pratiyogitā* which is involved in the definition of *vyāpti* and hence, it is a fault of *ātmāśraya*. Avoiding this defect, Jagadīśa, therefore, gives a new definition of relation. That is: *viśeṣya-viśeṣaṇatvānyaviśiṣṭadhī-viṣayatvam* (*sambandhatvam*) 'it is the contentness of a qualified cognition, which is different from the qualifierness and the qualificandness.[4]

Relation is broadly divided into two types: (1) *sākṣāt* 'direct' and (ii) *paramparā* 'indirect'. The former refers to *saṁyoga, samavāya* and *svarūpa* and the latter, to *saṁyukta-samavāya, samavetasamavāya* etc. The present paper aims at discussing the history of *svarūpasambandha* 'self-linking relation'.

The Naiyāyikas define *svarūpasambandha*: a category (x) coming under its class with the help of some property (x-ness) when possesses a *saṁsargatā*, is called as *svarūpasambandha* .[5] As for instance, *pratiyogitā* 'counterpositiveness' (in *ghaṭābhāva*) relation that exists in its *pratiyogī* 'counter-positive 'pot' coming under the category of substance (*dravya*), and with the help of some property *pratiyogitā* when possesses *saṁsargatā*, we call it as a relation. In this type of relation we find that the relation (*Pratiyogita*) shows no difference from its relata (*pratiyogī*).[6] The Navya Naiyāyikas have accepted a huge number of relations under this category. Some of those relations can be cited as for instance in the following: *ādhāratā* 'the substratumness', *ādheyatā* 'superstratumness', *viṣayatā* 'contentness', *viṣayitā* 'containerness', *viśeṣyatā*' 'qualificandness', *viśeṣaṇatā* 'qualifierness' and so on.

In old Nyāya system *viśeṣaṇa-viśeṣyabhāva* 'the qualifier-and-qualificand relation was accounted for as one of the six *sannikarṣat* 'relations', by which the absence and the inherence were perceived. Again this *viśeṣaṇa-viśeṣyabhāva* was used only in terms of *viśeṣaṇatā*. But it is *Bhāsarvajña* who perhaps for the first time introduced this relation in the sense of both *viśeṣaṇatā* and *viśeṣyatā* and those two relations were found used as one intended. For example, (i) *ghaṭābhāvavad bhūtalam* 'the ground is with the absence of pot' and (ii) *bhūtale ghaṭābhāvaḥ* 'there is no pot on the ground'. In the first case, *ghaṭābhāva* is a qualifier, whereas in the second, it is a qualificand.[7] However, the relation *viśeṣaṇatā* in early period was taken into account only in the sense of *svarūpasambandha* . But in later development of this system, it became one of the varieties of *svarūpasambandah* like *pratiyogitā*, *anuyogitā* etc.

The *viśeṣaṇa-viśeṣyabhāva* as a *svarūpasambandha* which we explained before, is different from that of the cases like *daṇḍī puruṣaḥ* 'man is with a stuff' and *nīlotpalam* 'blue lotus' etc. Because the *viśeṣaṇaviśeṣyabhāva* between *daṇḍa* (qualifier) and *puruṣa* 'qualificand' depends on some other relation like *saṁyoga* for its accomplishment, but the case of *viśeṣaṇa-viśeṣyabhāva* as *svarūpasambandha* is altogether different, since it is explained by itself without seeking the help of any other relation.

The Navya-Naiyāyikas' account of *viśeṣaṇatā* shows its three varieties: (i) *abhāvīyaviśeṣaṇatā* 'the qualifierness related to absence', (2) *daiśikaviśeṣaṇatā* 'the qualifierness related to place' and (3) *kālikaviśeṣaṇatā* 'qualifierness related to space'. Jagadīśa includes the first variety in second on the ground that when we speak of 'the ground is with the absence of pot', the absence is seen in some particular place, i.e., ground and in that case, *abhāvīyaviśeṣaṇatā* should not be taken as its distinct variety, and accordingly he divides *viśeṣaṇatā* relation into two: (i) *daiśika-viśeṣaṇatā* and (ii) *kālikaviśeṣaṇatā*.

Ghaṭābhāvavad bhūtalam , in this cognition we have seen earlier that *viśeṣaṇatā* existing in *ghaṭābhāva* is treated as relation. But, Viśvanātha thinks it in different way and says that the particular ground (i.e., *viśeṣya*) in which the absence of pot exists in that particular time, is to be accounted for as the relation of the absence (of pot).[8] Relation has been described as the property that remains in a base-relatum (*anuyoginiṣṭhadharmaḥ sambandhaḥ*). Here, since the ground is a base relatum and since *viśeṣyatā* remains in *viśeṣya,* i.e., the ground, *viśeṣyatā* will refer to the relation, i.e., the self-linking relation.

Some of the Navya–Naiyāyikas are of the opinion that the *prakāratā, viśeṣyatā* etc. cannot be considered as the variety of self-linking relation. The reason is that by the possessive suffix like *vat* or *mat* no one does have such cognitions as *vahnimat jñānam* 'the knowledge is with fire' or *vahnimān abhāvaḥ* 'the absence is with fire', since it is inconsistent of human behaviour. If this is true, we cannot also maintain *prakāratā* or *viśeṣyatā* which remains in fire and knowledge or absence respectively as the self-linking relations.[9]

The self-linking relation is differentiated from the inherence on the ground that it is not different from its relata, though very often it is apprehended as an eternal relation like the inherence.[10]

From the above discussions we may draw the following conclusions:

1. In Old-Nyāya system *viśeṣaṇatā* is accounted for as *svarūpa sambandha*, but the later development of this system made its scope limited and it was used only in the sense of one of the varieties of *svarūpasambandha* like *viṣayītā, prakāratā* etc.
2. On the basis of the nature of objects, the Naiyāyikas have accepted a huge number of this relation.
3. Some Naiyāyikas have rejected the existence of this relation on the ground of their inconsistency in human behaviour. But this argument seems to be not sound in all the cases of *svarūpasambandha* .

References

1. *Bhāvād abhāvādy āpi nātiriktaḥ sambandhiḥ svīkriyate padārthaḥ, Nyāyadarisanabindu* of Paṇdit Kalipada Tarkacharya, Saṁskrita Visvavidyalana Varanasi, 2021 samvat, p. 11.

2. *Sambandhaś cāviśiṣṭavyāvṛttaviśiṣṭadhīniyāmakaḥ, Tattvacintāmaṇi,* ed. by N. S. Ramanuja Tatacharya, Kendriya Sanskrit Vidyapeetha, Tirupati, Vol. Ist, *Pratyakṣakhaṇḍa*, 1973, p. 663.

3. *Ibid.*, Vol. II, *Anumānakhaṇḍa*, Pt. I, 1982, p. 89.

4. Jāgadīśī, ed. by Somanathopadhyaya, Chowkhamba Amarabharati Prakashan, Varanasi, Part-I, 2nd edition, 1983, p. 256.

5. *Klṛptapadārthaḥ san kiñciddharmoprāgeṇa saṁsargatāvatvam,* Avacchedakatvaniruktivyākhyā of Śivadatta Miśra, Chowkhamba *Prakashan,* Varanasi.

6. *Ibid.*

7. *Nyāyabhūṣaṇa*, ed. by Svami Yogindrananda, Ṣaḍdarśana Prakāśana Pratiṣṭhānam, Varanasi, 1968, p. 168.

8. *Ittham ca tat-tat-kālīnaṁ tat-tat-bhūtalādikaṁ tat-tad-abhāvānāṁ sambandhaḥ, Nyāyasiddhāntamuktāvalī* on the verse No. 11.

9. *Siddhāntalakṣaṇajāgadiśī-vyākhyā* by Śivadattamiśra, Chowkhamba Prakashan, Varanasi, p. 252

10. As for instance, *Īśvarajñānam*. Here *jñāna* is *viṣayin* and *Īśvara* is *viṣaya*. Since *jñāna* and *Iśvara* are *nitya,* the relations *viśayitā* and *viṣaytā* existing in them are also to be regarded as *nitya*. And, hence *viṣayatā, viṣayitā* etc. as the self-linking relations are also *nitya*.

4

On Relation of Identity

(*Tādātmya-Sambandha*)

R.I. Ingalalli

1. The aim of this paper is to interpret the traditional concept of *tādātmya-sambandha* (identity relation) in Indian Philosophy[1] in terms of contemporary conceptual framework of the theory of identity as formulated in logic and epistemology. The word '*tādātmya*' has been rendered as absolute identity[1]/or essential identity.[2] However, in contemporary logic and epistemology attempts have been made to articulate the structural differences between absolute identity and relative identity (essential identity). The general theory of identity covers both absolute identity and relative identity, i.e., to say that absolute identity and relative identity are the species of identity. Parallel to this distinction in Indian tradition the concept of *tādātmya* has been used differently. In Navya-Nyāya system Gaṅgeśa and Mathurānātha treat *tādātmya* as *abheda*,[3] which normally captures the sense of absolute identity having the form 'a = a'.

1.1 *Tādātmya* (identity) as a relation (*sambandha*) plays a significant role in Indian thought in the formation of the conceptual frameworks of different systems. I would like to consider the concept of *tādātmya* in Navya-Nyāya and also in other systems of Indian philosophy. Even though etymologically the word '*tādātmya*' implies that a thing is identical with itself (*tasyātmā-svarūpam-tadātmā*),[4] there is a necessity for a theory of identity to provide a proper explanation of sameness or change in the world with reference to uses of such cognate expressions as 'same', 'identical', 'similar', 'like' and 'different' in order to understand the nature of the world. The world exhibits two features of permanence and change. If some one truly asserts of something that is changing then there is something which remains constant during the changes which occur in it. Most of the great theories of antiquity fall on one side or the other of saying that there is something which is unchanging reality or nothing in reality remains constant; if anything is real then it cannot change and whatever appears to be changing is illusory or unreal. There are also compromising theories to justify the common sense outlook of identity in difference (*bhedābheda*). The issues arise from differing conceptions of identity (*tādātmya*). On the metaphysical or ontological side identity as meaning permanence amid change and identity as unity amid diversity give rise to the problem of change and the problem of universals respectively. However, in the present context I am concerned with the logico-epistemological analysis of *tādātmya* as identity.

1.2 Modern authors have given different interpretations of Navya-Nyāya concept of *tādātmya*. Authors like Profs. Ingalls and Guha[5] interpret *tādātmya* as essential identity by way of using the sign '='. Accordingly 'x=y' means 'x is essentially identical with y'. Of course, this kind of interpretation is consistent with the Nyāya theory of identity which generally accommodates absolute identity and relative identity. However, on Ingalls' view *tādātmya* in Navya-Nyāya captures the sense of essential identity only and it does not imply the sense of absolute identity as conceived by Leibniz. He thinks that Navya-Nyāya possesses no term, the meaning of which is exactly synonymous with identity as usually defined in modern western logic. Nyāya makes use of expressions referring to baorder sort of identity; for example 'a blue pot is essentially identical with a pot' (a blue pot = a pot).[6] This example reminds us Buddhists notion of *tādātmya* in which the analytic statement 'a *śiṁṣapā* is a tree' ['Aśoka (tree) = a tree] represents a class membership relation. Accordingly a blue pot is a member of the set of all pots and an Aśoka tree is a member of the class of trees. However, there are textual evidences to support the view that absolute identity is also a basic concept in Navya-Nyāya system. There are several contexts in the tradition of Navya-Nyāya where *tādātmya-sambandha* has been treated as the relation of absolute identity.[7] Both the etymology of the word '*tādātmya*' (*as tasya ātmā tadātmā*) and the definition of *tādātmya* as the relation of thing to itself by virtue of non-difference (*abhedastādātmyam*), suggest that Naiyāyikas are aware of the importance of the absolute identity as basic notion of human discourse.

1.3 Normally *tādātmya* as absolute identity is a relation between individuals. Accordingly 'x is identical with y' means 'x is the same individual as y'. In modern logic equality, equivalence and identity are distinguished. Normally, equality is a relation between classes. Two classes x and y are said to be equivalent if and only if every member of x is also a member of y and conversely, symbolically [(x=y) = (a) (a=x) = (a = y)]. However, some authors like Quine and Stall apply definition of equality to individuals as well as classes. Equivalence may be sharply distinguished from identity, by virtue of truth functional characteristic of the former only, i.e., to say that equivalence as a truth function connects statements or formulas. For example, the sentence 'Aruna is Varuna's father" is equivalent to "Varuna is Aruna's son". In this regard authors like Ingalls think that in Nyāya system there is no word exactly corresponding to "equivalence", because Naiyāyikas do not distinguish terms from propositions. But as a matter of fact, Naiyāyikas have made the distinction between a word or term as '*pada*' and proposition or sentence as vākya. '*Vākyaṁ padasamūha*'—a sentence is a configuration of words' implies the distinction between words and sentences. Further necessary and sufficient conditions of a meaningful sentence need not be the conditions of a word. Of course, the expression '*sama-nīyatā-bhāva*' captures the sense of the expression "is equivalent to". In the relation of *sama-nīyatā-bhāvatva* x pervades y and x is pervaded by y.

2. For clearer understanding of the notion of identity (*tādātmya*) as absolute identity it is necesary to consider some of the definitions (of *tādātmya*).

2.1 In the generally accepted definition, d_1: *abhedastādātmyaṃ* (identity is non-difference), the defining property of identity is non-difference. This definition seems to be synonymous and authors like Prof. Guha think that even though "*tādātmya*" and "*abheda*" are used synonymously in Navya-Nyāya the term *abheda* would not give adequate characterisation of *tādātmya*. However *abheda* is a necessary condition of *tādātmya*. Another definition (d_2): "*tādātmyaṁ* svavṛtty *asādhāraṇadharmaḥ*" (Identity is the uncommon property existing in the self), implies the positive defining property of *tādātmya* in terms of specific or uncommon property (*asādhāraṇa-dharma*) existing in one and only object.[8] Since *tādātmya* is non-occurrence exacting relation (*vṛtty aniyāmakasambandha*), *asādhāraṇadharma* (uncommon property) cannot functions a a residing property, for it is the very nature of a thing itself. An uncommon property is to be distinguished from a common property like jarness (*ghaṭatva*), clothness (*paṭatva*) etc. which exist in many objects. And uncommon property (*asādhāraṇyam*) is understood as *ekaa-mātravṛttitvam* (occurrences in one and only one object). Accordingly '*tad-vyaktitva*' (that individual manifestationness) would be different from the common property like jarness etc. and individual manifestation occurs in *pratiyogi* or *anuyogi* (in case of mutual absence) but not in both. According to d_2 an uncommon property as unique property implies essence of an object, consequently d_2 may be taken to be a definition of essential identity. Nyāya-kośa refers to a type of definition (d_3) similar to d_2. According to it (d_3): '*tadvṛtti-dharmaviśeṣaḥ*'*tādātmyam* (identity is that relation which is characterised by self property). For example, pot and pot-ness are related by virtue of *tādātmya* (identity relation). Similarly, *yathā nīlo ghaṭaḥ ityādau ghate tannīlatvarūpaṁ tādātmyam* —the property blue-ness is related to blue pot by virtue of *tādātmyam*. But such illustrations also fit in the explication of *samavāya-sambandha* (relation of inherence). Authors like Ingalls and Matilal treat the relation between a blue pot and a pot as that of essential identity; (accordingly, 'a blue pot=pot') i.e., to say that a blue pot is essentially identical with a pot. However, in the above example blue pot (*nīlo ghaṭaḥ*) and *nīlatva* (blue-ness) are considered to be related, consequently blue pot is essentially identical with its colour.

2.2 Some modern writers in their enthusiasm to interpret *tādātmya* as essential identity have come across a certain paradox in the form of 'a blue pot=a pot'. Prof. Matilal acknowledges Prof. Ingalls' discovery of the paradox. Potter thinks that such a paradox of essential identity implies a conceptual flow in the Nyāya framework. I wish to examine the views of these thinkers in the sequel.

On Ingalls (1951:69-70) view it is generally accepted in Navya-Nyāya that "a blue pot=a pot". In this proposition the relation '=' subsists between the qualificands expressed on either side of it. The referent of the expression 'pot' is the type or framework that subsists in all knowledges of pots. 'According to Nyāya if one does not accept above identity, one must admit that a blue pot is not a pot.' However, the acceptance of the identity leads to certain difficulties. For instance, it would be an obvious fallacy if a blue pot is always substituted for a pot. On this point Potter agrees with Ingalls. In the given identity statement the known entities pot and blue pot are not absolutely identical; consequently 'blue pot' is in applicable to many entities or pots. Ingalls says: "Navya-Naiyāyikas are forced to keep constant guard against contradictions arising from (above statement)... It is because of this theorem that we have in Navya-Nyāya what at first looks impossible: 'x is essentially identical with y' used both where we should say 'x contains (or implies) y' and where we should say 'x is contained in (is implied by) y."

Resolution of the paradox

In this context I wish to argue that above interpretation does not reflect the spirit of the Navya-Nyāya theory of identity. As I have already pointed out (p: 2-3), both absolute identity and essential identity fit in the Nyāya theory of identity, i.e., to say that Naiyāyikas use '*tādātmya*' sometime in the sense of absolute identity and also as essential identity. Above interpretation of essential identity confuses absolute identity with essential identity. According to absolute identity in terms of non-difference (*abheda*), "a blue pot" is necessarily identical with itself; consequently 'the blue pot = the blue pot' or 'This pot = the blue pot'. In this formulation the qualificands are completely identical and there is a satisfaction of the principle' of identity that x and y are identical if and only if every attribute of x is an attribute of y and conversely. However, in case of 'a blue pot = a pot' there is no satisfaction of the principle of absolute identity, but it satisfies the principle of relative identity (or essential identity that a blue pot is necessarily a pot or a blue pot is a member of the class of pots. Accordingly essential identity captures the sense of set membership relation between individuals and their class. If *tādātmya* as essential identity is understood as set-membership relation then the following do not hold good: (i) that it would be an obvious fallacy that in a given identity statement 'a blue pot' is always substituted for 'a pot' and (ii) it is impossible that x (a blue pot) implies y (a pot) and conversely. Since (i) and (ii) are false, there is no contradiction in Nyāya theory of essential identity. The falsity of (ii) becomes obvious if the textual position '*na hi bhavati nīlo ghaṭo ghaṭānya* iti (a blue pot cannot be other than a pot), is properly understood. Accordingly a blue pot implies a pot but a pot does not imply a blue pot. That is to say that that x is a blue pot if x has blueness and potness and y is a pot if y has potness. Thus, potness is common to x (a blue pot) and y (a pot). Therefore, x is essentially identical with y.

2.3 It is to be noted that the notion of *tādātmya* as absolute identity has been used by Naiyāyikas to define an absential notion like mutual absence (*anyonyābhāva*): *anyonyābhāvatvaṁ tādātmya-sambandhā vacchinna-pratiyogitakābhāvatvam* and it has been noticed by the authors like Ingalls (1951:68) and Potter; Oddly enough the characterisation of mutual absence is taken for the definition of *tādātmya*. In case of an absential cognition "pot is not cloth", there is a denial of an identity between pot and cloth. Accordingly 'pot is pot' and 'cloth is cloth'. Symbolically, -(x=y) if true then x=x; y=y and (x=y) otherwise (x=y). In other words, if -(x=y) is false then x=y is true. Suppose there is a denial of relation of essential identity (=) instead of absolute identity (=) between x and y. In that case the formula '-(x=y), implies that x is not the same as y. But the usual example '*ghaṭo paṭo na*' (potcloth) does not fit in the schema of essential identity. Because *anyonyābhāva* implies difference (*bheda*) and the denial of *bheda* is *abheda* or non-difference. *Tādātmya* as absolute identity is a basic form of relation for every object, event and relation etc. are capable of being individuated on the basis of absolute identity.

2.4 From the above analysis of the definitions d_1, d_2 and d_3 it is clear that *tādātmya-sambandha* captures the sense of absolute identity in western logical theory. However, it is necessary to reformulate the definition of *tādātmya* in terms of d_1, d_2 and d_3 for comprehensive understanding. The necessity of reformulation arises in order to synthesise d_1, d_2 and d_3 in order that they function as necessary and sufficient conditions for the relation of identity (*tadatmya-sambandha*). Accordingly x is identical with itself if and only if (i) x is non-different (*abheda*) with itself, (ii) x has uncommon or specific property occurring in x only. (sva-*vṛtty asādhāraṇa-dharmaḥ- eka mātra-vṛttitvam*), (iii) x is characterised by self-property (*tadvṛttidharma- viśeṣaḥ*).

In this formulation, (i) appears as a negative condition compared to (ii) and (iii) as positive conditions of identity.

However, in case of relative or essential identity the defining properties are as follows:

x is essentially identical with y if and only if

(i) x is (not completely) different from y, (ii) x and y possess certain common properties *samānādhikaraṇyam*), (iii) x is not characterised by self-property (*tadvṛttidharma-viśeṣaḥ*).

3. *Tādātmya-sambandha* as relation of absolute identity having the schema (x) (x=x) provides a basic principle of reason in human discourse. And the principle of identity holds good for all possible worlds, i.e., to say that in every logically possible world no contradiction is involved in it. The law of identity is necessary for the articulations about things relations, properties etc. Aristotle recognised the importance of the concept of identity in the formulation of fundamental logical principles of thought which are involved in every reflective inquiry. Principle of identity as, if anything is A then it is A does not deny the possibility of change and also does not affirm that if something is green then it will always remain green. However, the law of identity does imply that if anything whatsoever in some definite context has some determinate character then it must have that character only.

3.1 For comprehensive understanding of the notion of *tādātmya* it is necessary to consider function of *tādātmya* in other systems like

Advaita-vedānta, Viśiṣṭādvaita and Mīmāṁsā systems. In Advaita-vedānta '*tādātmya*' functions as *samavāya-sambandha* of Nyāya system, for it holds good between substance and its attribute, universal and particular. Consequently the relation implies inseparable relation between two relata.[9] In the Advaita theory of propositions the concept of *tādātmya* is implicit. Statements like 'this is that Devadatta' and 'you are that' (*tattvaṁ asi*) are considered to be identity statements. The referring expressions of the first identity statements have the same referrent but different modes of presentations as sense (*pravṛtti-nimitta*). That is to say that the referrent of the words 'this' and 'that Devadatta' is the same person.[10] However, the identity statement is informative, hence, it is an instance of essential identity. It is to be noted that the judgment does not imply absolute identity because of incompatible attributes possessed by the same individual at different times at different places. And the only way according to which the judgment is to be interpreted as valid is to understand the identity of the substantive Devadatta by eliminating the contingent (or changing) or accidental attributes of Devadatta. Similarly, the great sentence (*mahāvākya*) 'thou art that' (*tat tvam asi*) is to be understood where 'thou' means an individual consciousness while 'that' means universal consciousness and the identity is due to deducting the two incompatible determinants 'individual' and 'universal' from both sides so that consciousness as the common denominator is the same. But it may be asked whether the relationship between thou, i.e., an individual soul, and that, i.e., cosmic soul is one of identity-in-difference? Prof. Hiriyanna (1973: 369-70) gives an interesting analysis. It may appear that the relation in question is one of identity-in-difference but such a conception will not do because it is against the spirit of Advaitic conception of non-dualistic reality. Hiriyanna illustrates the point by stating that let M and N be two entities between which the relation of identity exists. It may be said that neither M and N are identical nor they are different. It may mean that M is both N and non-N and that N similarly is both M and non-M and in that case, there is the violation of the law of non-contradiction. 'If M and N do not constitute an identity in difference directly, it may be thought that they do so mediately through features or elements in them and some of which are identical and others are different. Thus, we may say that M and N possess one or more common features which may be represented by *a* and, at the same time, exhibit differences represented by x and y respectively. According to this explanation, what is identical is quite distinct, from what is different; yet the entities, viz., M and N, by virtue of such features, it may be said, are identical with and at the same time, different from each other. Prof. Hiriyanna thinks that such an explanation merely shifts the difficulty to another set of things, because if M and N are characterised by ax and ay respectively, there is no satisfactory explanation regarding the relation between a thing and its characteristics. The relation between M and ax cannot be one of identity because in that case, the distinction between a and x would vanish, nor can a and x be different from M. So ultimately identity-in-difference is the only relation between these.

3.2 However, it is desirable to have some clear idea about identity-in-difference (*bhedābheda*) as advocated by Kumārilabhaṭṭa. According to Kumārila, every *dravya* is eternal even though its forms or attributes may change. For example, the clay that we see before manufacturing into a jar, at another time into a saucer; it may be red or brown, but in all these transformations the same material persists. Accordingly *dravya* endures and its modes appear and disappear; consequently things are not self-identical entities excluding all difference. This view implies *pariṇāma-vāda,* according to which the relation between the material cause and effect is one of identity-in-difference (*bhedābheda*). It is also interesting to find out whether Rāmānuja like Kumārila advocates *bhedābheda* view, for Rāmānuja does not admit identity of any kind whatsoever between the entities supposed to be distinct and the unity affirmed seems to be of complex whole. Rāmānuja's view may be illustrated by taking a common example like a 'blue lotus'. Blueness as a quality is distinct from its substance lotus. The complexity of a lotus being blue includes within itself the quality of blueness spoken of as unity. Rāmānuja in contradistinction with Advaitins recognizes a real distinction between the substance of lotus and the quality of blueness. In the proposition 'The lotus is blue', the quality of blueness necessarily points to some substance to which it belongs.

The identity that is expressed by the proposition is of the complex nature, because the two terms 'blue' and 'lotus' have distinct meaning but refer to the same substance (*prakavyadvaita*).

Thus, in the alleged identity statement *viśeṣaṇas* or qualities are also included. According to Rāmānuja, the identity of the soul and Brahman is different from Advaitic identity of soul and Brahman. According to Rāmānuja, all things are modes (*prakāra*) or forms of God. Rāmānuja's interpretation of Upaniṣadic maxim '*Tattvam asi*' implies that the term '*tvam*' which commonly stands for the jīva really points to God as the inner self (*antaryāmin*) of *jīva* and its physical body is like a mode; and the term '*tat*' refers to the same God as the cause of the universe. Thus, the identity meant by '*Tattvam asi*' is of two complexes namely—God as the indweller of the *jīva* and God as the cause of source of the universe. Consequently though the world and the individual souls are real and distinct, the Absolute or God in which they are included is one. However, Advaitins view that the relation between *saguṇa*-brahman and its constitutive elements are unique or as *tādātmya* which are not to be characterised as identity-in-difference. *Saguṇa*-brahman includes not merely reality but also appearance. The element of reality in it is the ultimate of Advaita or non-duality. According to Advaitic interpretation, the *mahāvākya* like '*Tattva masi*' implies the identity pointing to non-dual state of reality. Datta's (1972:324) analysis of the identity statement 'A is identical with B', in the context of Advaitic treatment implies that if am and bm are the properties of A and B respectively, it is not the case that am is identical with bm because a and b are different determinants; and after the sublation of 'a' and 'b' the identity in respect of 'm' alone is asserted. Consequently such identity statements are called as *akhaṇḍārthakavākyās*; such sentences are about the existence of a single content. But in case of ordinary judgements one content is applied to another content or two different elements are related to each other. In case of every judgement having the form 's is p,' p i.e., predicate is referred to subjects' and normally such propositions are called categorical propositions. But there are also other types of propositions which are relational propositions having the form SrP and an identity statement is relational statement. Datta thinks that Advaita conception of identity implies non-categorical but *akhaṇḍārthaka* type of statement in which a thing is uniquely related to itself.

It is interesting to note that the law of identity is also implied by the law of non-contradiction (*abādha*) as formulated by Śaṅkara.

The law of non-contradiction as formulated by Śaṅkara[11] is as follows: Contradictory predicates cannot inhere in the same subject (*na hy ekasmin dharmiṇi yugapat (sad asatvādi) viruddha-dharma-samāveṣaḥ sambhavati*). Since this law constitutes one of the fundamental laws of thought, Śaṅkara appeals to this law in setting the controversies of rival schools. And the characteristic of being non-contradiction is also a feature of reality.

From the above discussion it is possible to deduce the following consequences. The concept of *tādātmya* functions as absolute identity and essential identity. Essential identity presupposes absolute identity which is a fundamental notion for articulation of any plausible theory in human discourse.

Even in modern western philosophy thinker like Descartes, Leibniz, Kant, Frege, Quine and others have recognised the importance of the theory of identity meaning that an object is the same with itself. Identity notion implies one of the basic laws of reasoning [(x) (x=x)]. It is generally accepted view that G. Frege set the stage for modern researches into subject of identity in connection with semantics.

4. Logic of identity statements

In Indian logical theory it is possible to distinguish necessary identity and contingent identity based on the dual nature of identity as absolute and essential identity. For example, the sentence 'Devadatta is Devadatta' is an instance of absolute or necessary identity, and contingent identity is expressed through 'Devadatta is the eldest son of Aruna'. Since Indian conception of identity as non-difference (*abheda*) captures the sense of absolute identity in contemporary logic, the relation of identity bears certain important characteristics namely, symmetry, transitivity and reflexivity as expressed by the following formulas:

(i) (x) (y) (Rxy=Ryx) ... Symmetry of Identity,

(ii) (x) (y) (z) [(Rxy.Ryz)=Rxz] ... Transitivity of Identity,

(iii) (x) (Rxx) ... Totally Reflective Identity. (R is relation of identity).

Logic of identity makes use of the following principle of identity to test the validity of arguments containing identity statements.

$$[(\emptyset x).(x=y)] = \emptyset y.$$

Frege the founder of modern western logical theory deals with a puzzle about identity (=). He introduces the distinction between sense and reference of a proper name in an identity statement. If relation of identity holds good between objects then the statement 'a=b' is the same as 'a=a' [if (a=b) is true]. Even though a and b are the two names of the same object they differ in their cognitive contents. If a=b is true then it is highly informative. For example, the truth of the identity statement 'Morning star is evening star' is acknowledged through astronomical discovery. The cognitive difference between the two identity statements: 'Morning star = Evening star' and 'Morning star = Morning star' is due to Frege's distinction between sense and reference of proper names; the reference of an expression is the referent or the object named or denoted namely the planet Venus and sense of expression is mode of presentation; the sense of the expression 'Morning star' is the property of shining in the eastern sky early in the morning. According to Indian view the statement 'Morning star = Evening star' is analogous to the statement "this Devadatta is that Devadatta" which is implied by 'this is that Devadatta'.

An interesting aspect of Navya-Nyāya logical theory consists of the treatment of identity even in negative discourse. That is to say that *tādātmya-sambandha* as relation of identity functions in case of absential statements also. Following formulas of identity are implied in the Nyāya theory of identity.

(i) a = - -a (ii) -a = -a; (iii) - - -a = -a

Since absence (*abhāva*) has been recognised as one of the categories (*padārtha*), there is a necessity of identity for precise articulation of reality in relation to *abhāva* and *bhāva padārthās*. Consequently relation of identity plays a cardinal role in the explication of ontological, logical, epistemological and semantical categories.

Notes and References

1. In Indian philosophy, especially in Navya-Nyäya system we find clear formulations of different relations: relation of contact (*saṁyoga-sambandha*), relation of inherence (*samavāya-sambandha*), self-linking-relation (*sva-rūpa-sambandha*). *Tādātmya-sambandha* (relation of identity) has been accepted by many important systems like Navya-Nyāya, Advaita-vedānta, Viśiṣṭādvaita and Buddhism (Sautrāntika and Vaibhāṣika systems). Jhalkikar Bhimacharya: *Nyāya-kośa*, pp. 920-1; *Bhāṣāpariccheda* and *Siddhānta-muktāvalī*, *Tattva-cintāmaṇi*, Pt. I (700-1) of Gaṅgeśa; Matilal, B.K.: *The Navya-Nyāya-doctrine of negation*, pp. 48-9; Stcherbatsky: *Buddhist Logic*, Vol. I, 419, 443, Vol. II, pp. 65-6, Ingalls: *The Materials for the Study of Navya-Nyāya Logic*, pp. 74-76.
2. Following Leibniz, the founder of modern western logic, G. Frege (1879) gives a clear formulation of the law of identity which is subsequently used by modern logicians. According to the law of identity everything is identical with itself. That is to say that x and y are identical if and only if every attribute of x is also an attribute of y and conversely; this is called the classical version of absolute identity. Recently authors like Griffin (1977) are considering relative identity having the form 'x is relatively identical with y' if and only if x and y share certain relevant essential properties.'
3. (i) Gaṅgeśa: 700

   (ii) Mathurānātha: 701 in Gaṅgeśa

   (iii) Jhalkikar, Bhimacharya: 328

   (iv) Śaṅkarācārya: 2.2.38; Devaraja, pp. 44.
4. Bhatta, V.V. (1972: 59).
5. Guha, 1967: 77-9; Ingalls: 1957: 68-72; Jhalkikar: 1972: 720-1; Matilal: 1968: 48-9.
6. Guha, 1967:58; Matilal, 1968: 48-9.
7. Jhalkikar, B. 1972: Guha, 1967: 77, fn. 1.
8. Guha, 1967: 79; Jhalkikar, B. 1972: 327.
9. Satprakashananda, 1972: 48; *Vedānta-paribhaṣa* in Mādhavananda.
10. Datta, 1972: 319.
11. (i) Śaṅkarācārya, 2.2.38.

    (ii) Hiriyanna, 1973: 401.

Bibliography

1. Athalye, Y.V. and Bodas, M.R. (1972): *Tarka-samgraha*, Bhandarkar Oriental Research Institute, Poona.
2. Bhatta, V.V. (1972): *Siddhānta-muktāvalī*, Balaganapati, Mysore.
3. Copi, I.M. (1973): *Symbolic Logic*, Collier Macmillan, N.Y.
4. Datta, D.M. (1974): *Six Ways of Knowing*, Calcutta University.
5. Devaraja, N.K. (1972): *Śaṅkara's Theory of Knowledge*, Motilal Banarasidass, Delhi.
6. Frege, Gottlob: *Begriffsschriff, in Frege to Godel*, Ed. by Heijenort.
7. Gaṅgeśa (1974): *Tattvacintāmaṇi* with *Māthurī*, Pt. I, Motilal Banarasidass, New Delhi.
8. Griffin, N. (1977): *Relative Identity*, Oxford University Press, Oxford.
9. Guha, D. (1967): *The Navya-Nyāya System of Logic*, Bharatiya Vidya Prakashan, Varanasi.
10. Hiriyanna (1957): *Indian Philosophical Studies*, Vol. I & II, Kavyalaya Publisher, Mysore.
11. Hiriyanna (1973): *Outlines of Indian Philosophy*, George Allen and Unwin, London.
12. Ingalls, D.H.H. (1951): *The Materials for the Study of Navya-Nyaya* Logic, Harvard University Press, Canb. Mass.
13. Jhalkikar, B. (1972): *Nyāya-kośa*, Bhandarkar Oriental Research Institute, Poona.
14. Mādhavānanda, S. (1972): *Vedānta-paribhāṣā*, Advaita Ashrama, Calcutta.
15. Mādhavānanda, S. (1974): *Bhāṣā-pariccheda* with *Siddhāntamuktāvalī*, R.K. Mission, Howrah.
16. Matilal, B.K. (1968): *Navya-Nyāya Doctrine of Negation*, Harvard University Press, *Camb. Mass.*
17. Śaṅkarācārya (1972): *Brahmasūtra Bhāṣya*, Tr. by Swami Gambhirananda, Advaita Ashrama, Calcutta.
18. Satprakashanand, S. (1974): *Methods of Knowledge*, Advaita Ashrama, Calcutta.

5

The Paryāpti-Relation in Navya-Nyāya

V.N: Jha

0.0 Relation (*Sambandha*) like property (*dharma*) plays a great role in Navya-Nyāya Language which evolved out of a necessity to create a language of precise communication. The System of Navya-Nyāya identified that it is the qualified content (*viṣaya*) of a cognition that needs a structured analysis since the qualified content reflects a structure. No structure can be built without the involvement of relations. Thus, they tried to focus their attention on Relations, both general and particular. It is through the help of various relations and properties that the Navya Naiyāyikas created a language of philosophico-logical discourse. These relations and properties were used as delimitors (*avacchedaka*) in order to avoid ambiguity in a statement to the extent it was possible to avoid. This is how the discussion on relations assumed high importance.

The Navya Nyāya accepted three categories of relations: (1) *Saṁyoga* (contact) (2) *Samavāya* (inherence) and (3) *Svarūpa*. Of these, the first and the second categories belong to the distinct categories of entities (*padārtha*) and the third category is an open set of already admitted entities and not a separate category of entities. The first is *guṇa* (quality) and the second is a distinct category of *padārtha*. The third may be any thing out of the seven categories behaving like a relation. Therefore, *svarūpasambandha* is not treated as a distinct entity.

Thus, *kāryatā, kāraṇatā, sādhyatā, sādhanatā, viṣayatā, viśeṣaṇatā, avacchedyatā, avacchedakatā* etc. are treated as particular *svarūpasambandha* . Even the *kālika-sambandha* and *paryāpti-sambandha* are particular *svarūpasambandha* only.[1]

1.0 Here we are concerned with the *paryāpti-sambandha.* The word *paryāpti* means 'sufficiency' and *paryāpta* means 'being present or pervading sufficiently in a locus'. Thus if I say, —

(1) *vahnitvam ekaikasmin vahnau paryāptam,* it will mean 'fireness pervades sufficiently each of its locus i.e. the fire-individual (*vahni-vyakti*)'. To put it differently,

(2) *vahnitvam ekaikasmin vahnau paryāpti-sambandhena tiṣṭhati* 'fireness is present in each and every fire through the relationship of sufficiency'

Now let us see the following:

(3) *dvitvam dvayoḥ paryāptam* i.e., number 'two' is sufficiently present in both. To put it differently—

(4) *dvitvam paryāptisambandhena dvayoḥ vartate* 'number two is present in both through the relationship of sufficiency'.

Similarly, let us observe the following:

(5) *nīlatvam ghaṭatvam ca pratiyogitavacchedakam*

'Both nīlatva and ghaṭatva are the delimitors of the counterpositiveness'.

(5) needs little elaboration. (5) is used in the context of an absence of the blue jar. The blue jar is the counterpositive (*pratiyogin*) of the absence of the blue jar. The counterpositiveness, therefore, exists in 'the blue jar'. Naturally, both 'blue-ness and jar-ness' will act as the delimitors of the counterpositiveness. It is in this context that (5) is uttered. (5) may be paraphrased as:

(6) *nīlatva-ghaṭatvayoḥ pratiyogitāvacchedakatvam asti* 'there is *avacchedakatā* in *nīlatva* and *ghaṭatva* both.

If one wants to present these cases diagrammatically (2) will appear as follows:

(4) will appear as follows:

and (6) will look like the following:

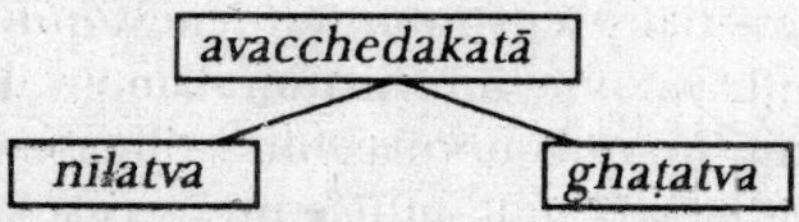

One point needs to be noted in this connection. In (2) *vahnitva* is sufficiently or completely present in its loci i.e. the individual *vahni.* In other words, it pervades its locus. Each locus of *vahnitva* is such that it is completely pervaded by *vahnitva.* But it is not the case with (4) and (6). In (4) *dvitva* exists in *ghaṭa* and *paṭa* together. That is, neither in *ghaṭa* not in *paṭa dvitva* can be said to be sufficiently existing. So is the case with (6). In (6) too the *avacchedakatā* exists in both *nīlatva* and *ghaṭatva* together and it does not exist either in *nīlatva* or in *ghaṭatva* sufficiently. And this is the reason why we cannot say the following in the above situations:

(7) *ghaṭaḥ dvau* '* the pot is two'

(8) *Paṭaḥ dvau* '*the cloth is two'

(9) *nīlatvam kevalam 'pratiyogitāvacchedakam* ' i.e. '*nīlatva* alone is the delimitor of the counterpositiveness.'

(10) *ghaṭatvam kevalam pratiyogitāvacchedakam*

i.e. '*ghaṭatva* alone is the delimitor of the counter positiveness'.

From all these examples and contexts it is clear that the idea of *paryāpti* is pervasion of locus, or sufficiency of locus. *Vahnitva* pervades its each locus, *dvitva* or a *vyāsajyavṛtti-padārtha* pervades its required loci and *avacchedakatā* pervades its required loci.

2.0 There is another point that needs consideration. Dvitva is a number that is a *guṇa* in the Navya-Nyāya Metaphysics. A *guṇa* exists in *dravya* by the relation of *samavāya*. Now, *dvitva* being a *guṇa* will exist in its locus by *samavāya*. And in that case what is the need of a relation called *paryāpti* for *dvitva*?

Similarly, *vahnitva* is *jāti* and a *jāti* exists in its locus by *samavāya* and so what is the necessity of accepting a relation called *paryāpti*?

Such questions have been asked. Let us examine these issues little more closely.

2.1 It is true that *vahnitva* exists in each of its loci by *samavāya*, but when one says that *ekaikasmin vahnau vahnitvam paryāptam,* the cognition reflects some information namely, that it completely pervades its locus, there is no place in its locus where it does not exist and it completely and sufficiently exists in its locus. This notion is not conveyed when we say *vahnitvam ekaikasmin vahnau samavetam,* and what is understood from it is that the fireness is not separable from its locus. Thus, *samavāya* and *paryāpti* convey two different notions. Therefore, there seems to be a need for establishing the *paryāpti-sambandha* over and above the *samavāya-sambandha.*

The same is the case with *dvitva* or a *vyāsajyavṛtti-padārtha*. The term *vyāsajya-vṛtti* itself indicates that such a *padārtha* can exist sufficiently or fully only in more than one locus. Number two onwards all numbers will exist completely not in one locus but in more than one locus. The relation through which a *vyāsajyavṛtti-padārtha* will completely or sufficiently exist in its locus is the *paryāpti-sambandha.* The *samavāya* will not serve that purpose.

Here, the following maxim raises its head:

If an entity does not exist in individual it cannot exist in the collection of individuals. Thus, unless *dvitva* exists individually in both *ghaṭa* and *paṭa*, it cannot exist collectively in both. To satisfy this condition, the Navya-Nyāya clarified that individually in both *ghaṭa* and *paṭa dvitva* exists by *samavāya*, but together it will exist in both *ghaṭa* and *paṭa* by *paryāpti*. So, *dvitva* is simultaneously present in both collectively by *paryāpti*, whereas individually it is present by *samavāya* in each.

There is another view that if something is not present by a particular relation in each of the collection, it cannot exist in the collection by the same relation. Thus, if *dvitva* is not present by *paryāpti-sambandha* in *ghaṭa* and *paṭa*, individually it cannot remain present by *paryāpti* in both collectively.[2] This view wants *dvitva* to be present in each, *ghaṭa* and *paṭa*, by *paryāpti* and so what is the need of *samavāya*? They may argue, therefore, that when their is no need of *paryāpti* as an additional relation since *samavāya* alone can explain all those logical points or let *paryāpti* alone be accepted since the purpose of *samavāya* can be served by it.

Samavāya is accepted in the following cases:

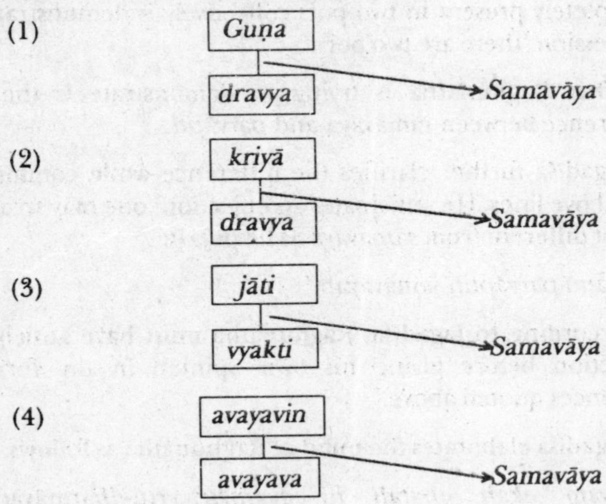

Now, if we replace *samavāya* in all these cases by *paryāpti*, what is the difficulty? *Guṇa* exist completely in *dravya*; so also *kriyā*, *Jāti* too exist completely in *vyakti; avayavin* in *avayava* and *viśeṣa* in *nitya-dravya*. Hence, the necessity of *Samavāya* is covered by *paryapti*.

But a close consideration will say that *samavāya* and *paryāpti* are different in notions and hence they are required to be posited differently as I have already pointed out earlier.

Raghunātha Śiromaṇi attempts to point out the experience of the notion of *paryāpti* as follows:

paryāptiś ca ayam eko ghaṭaḥ imau dvau iti pratīti-sākṣikaḥ svarūpa-sambandha-viśeṣaḥ. [3]

The relation of *paryāpti* is demonstrated in the verbalisation of the cognitions 'this is one pot' and 'these are two pots'. The expression 'this is one pot' clearly says that *ghaṭatva* is completely present even in one pot. Similarly, that the *dvitva* 'number two' is completely present in two pots collectively is demonstrated by the expression 'there are two pots.'

What Raghunātha is trying to demonstrate is the notional difference between *samavāya* and *paryāpti.*

Jagadīśa further clarifies the difference while commenting on the above lines. He anticipates an objection: one may treat *paryāpti* as not different from *samavāya* as he puts it:

Nanu paryāptiḥ samavāyaḥ [4]

According to Jagadīśa, Raghunātha must have anticipated this objection before giving his own opinion in the form of the sentences quoted above.

Jagadīśa elaborates the mind of Raghunātha as follows:

Ayam ekaḥ ghaṭaḥ iti ekamātra-vṛtti-dharmāvacchedena ghaṭatvasya paryāptim darśayitum, imau dvau iti ubhayamātra-vṛtti-dharmāvacchedena dvitvasya paryāptim darśayitum, anyathā dvau dvitvavān iti pratītyoḥ aviśeṣa-prasaṅgāt iti bhāvaḥ. [5]

The completeness of the presence of potness in one pot is determined in terms of the property of that single pot i.e. *tadghaṭatva* and the completeness of the presence of *dvitva* in two pots is to be determined in terms of the property existing in both the pots i.e. *ubhayatva*. If this is not accepted, Jagadīśa thinks, then one will not be in a position to distinguish between the two cognitions (1) *ayam ghataḥ dvitvavān* and (2) *imau ghaṭau dvitvavantau.*

The first cognition says that 'this pot has number two (as its quality) i.e. this pot is the locus of number two and the second cognition says that 'these two pots have number two collectively i.e. these two pots are the loci of number two collectively and simultaneously'.

These two are distinct two true cognitions reflecting two distinct notions. This is what Jagadīśa points out.

On this Jagadīśa anticipates the following objection:

Well, even if we agree to the necessity of having *paryāpti-sambandha* in order to account for the cognitions cited above, still one does not think it necessary to accept *paryāpti* for taking into account 'this is one pot', because the potness can exist in the pot by *samavāya* as *ekatva* will exist in the same pot by *samavāya*.[6]

To this objection, Jagadīśa replies that if we do not accept *paryāpti* in the above case, it is difficult to justify the true cognition of the following type:

idantvāvacchinne eva vahnitvam ekatvam ca paryāptam na tu dvitvam 'the fire-ness and number one completely exist i.e. pervade their locus delimited by this-ness, but not the number two'.[7]

Number two does not exist in one locus completely or sufficiently. In other words, a *vyāsajya-vṛtti-padārtha* does not pervade only one locus. Number one and a generic property, however, can pervade one locus. This is a true experience and on the basis of this experience one cannot deny the necessity of accepting a relation called *paryāpti* over and above *samavāya*.

2.2 Let us now consider the following context:

tatra nīlaḥ ghaṭaḥ nāsti 'there is no blue pot'.

If we translate it into Semi-Navya-Nyāya language it will read something like the following:

tatra nīlaghaṭābhāvaḥ asti.

Here, *nīlaghaṭa* is called *pratiyogin* of the *nīlaghaṭābhāva* in Navya-Nyāya, which implies that there is *pratiyogitā* in *nīlaghaṭa*. This *pratiyogitā* is required to be delimited by the properties of *nīlaghaṭa* i.e. by *nīlatva* and *ghaṭatva*.

Neither *nīlatva* alone nor *ghaṭatva* alone can be the delimitor of that *pratiyogitā*. *Nīlatva* and *ghaṭatva* collectively can act as the delimitor, which, again, implies that the delimitorness (avacchedakatā) is simultaneously present in both *nīlatva* and *ghaṭatva.* The delimitorness does not exist completely either in *nīlatva* or in *ghaṭatva* but it exists completely in both, *nīlatva* and *ghaṭatva.* This necessitates the postulation of a relation called *paryāpti*. It is through this relation the *avacchedakatā* is present simultaneously in *nīlatva* and *ghaṭatva.*

This approach also compels one to think that the *pratiyogitā-avacchedakatā* in even *ghaṭatva* in the context of ghaṭo nāsti should exist by the relation of *paryāpti* also. Because, in this context the *avacchedakatā* completely exist in *ghaṭatva* only. Thus, this gives rise to the following pictures:

(1)

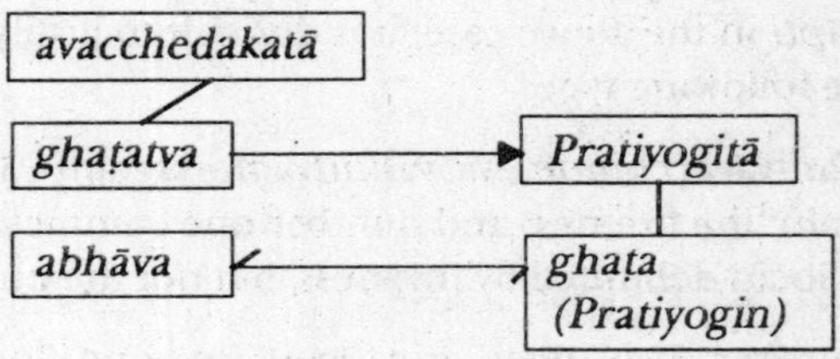

(2)

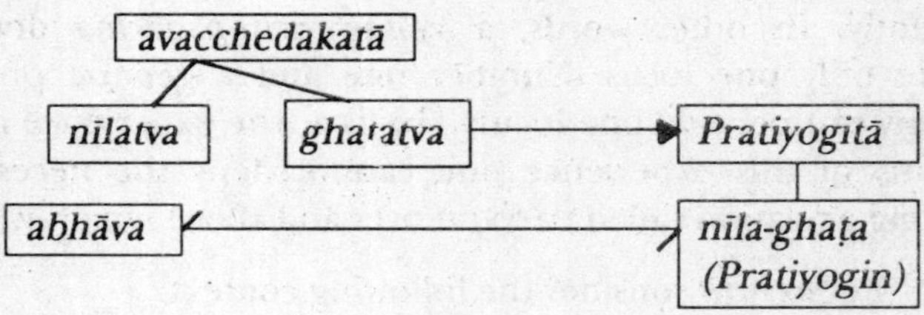

2.3 There is another aspect which requires our attention. *Paryāpti* is postulated as a relation and a relation has a *pratiyogin* and an *anuyogin* that determine the relation. Thus, when *ghaṭatva* is said to be *paryāpta* in each of its loci, it means *ghaṭatva* is *pratiyogin*, *paryāpti* is the relation and *ghaṭavyakti* is the *anuyogin* of the relation. This implies that there is *anuyogitā* in the *ghaṭa-vyakti* which determines the *paryāpti* in it. Thus, we can say that the ***tad-vyaktitva*** existing in *tadghaṭa* delimits the *anuyogitā* of *tadghaṭa*. Thus, we can describe the *paryāpti* here in the Navya-Nyāya language as follows:

tad-vyaktitvāvacchinna-anuyogitā-nirūpikā paryāptiḥ.

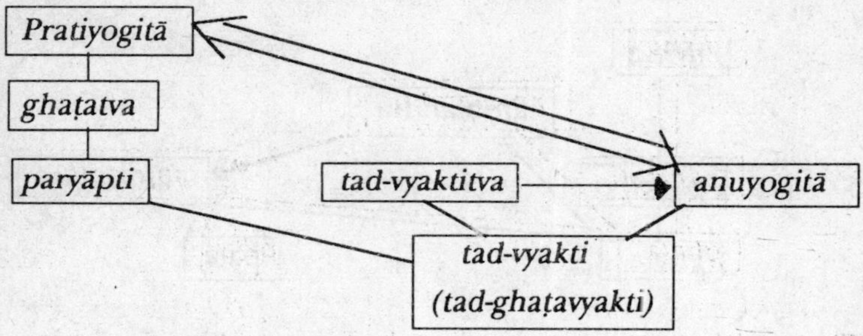

Similarly, when we say that *ghaṭatva* is the *avacchedaka* of the *ghaṭābhāvīya-pratiyogitā*, it implies that *avacchedakatā* completely exist in *ghaṭatva,* which means, the *avacchedakatā* exists in *ghaṭatva* by *paryāpti-sambandha*. This further implies that *ghaṭatva* has *anuyogitā* of *paryāpti* and the *avacchedakatā* is the *pratiyogin* of that *paryāpti*. In such cases, the *anuyogitā* is delimited by the *ekatva* of *ghaṭatva*. To put it diagrammatically—

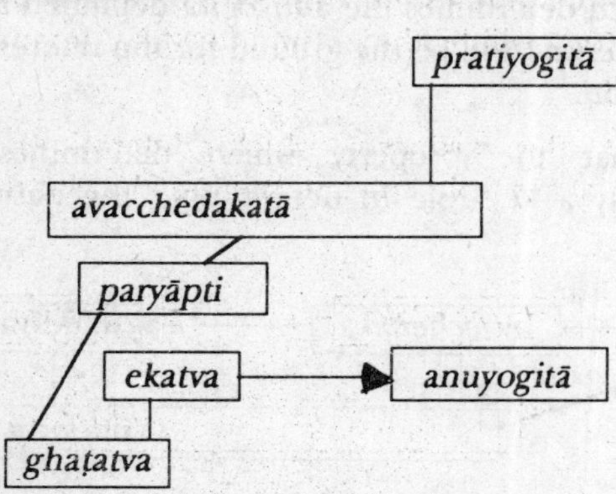

Thus, this *paryāpti* can be described as

ekatvāvacchinna - anuyogitānirūpikā

Likewise, when *dvitva* or any *vyasajya-vṛtti-dharma* will be said to be *paryāpta* in its locus, it will imply that such a *dharma* exists in its locus by *paryāpti-sambandha*. This will further imply that the *paryāpti* here has more than one entity as its locus. Here, the *anuyogin* of the *paryāpti* will be the loci of dvitva and the anuyogitā existing in those loci will be delimited by *anyataratva* i.e. the property (*dharma*) which is present in all those loci simultaneously. The following diagram may concretise the idea—

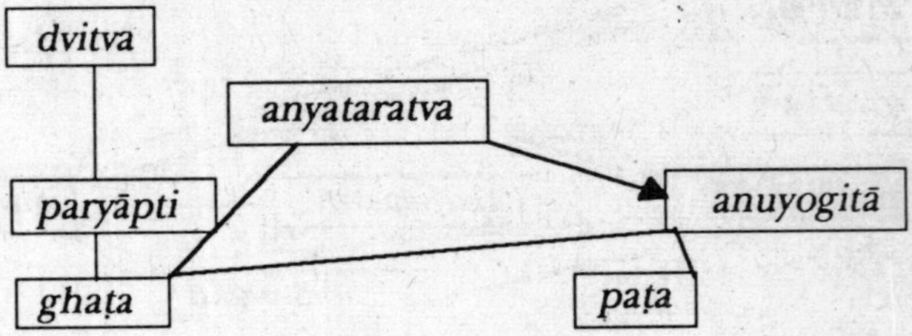

Thus, this paryāpti may be described as *anyataratvāvacchinna-anuyogitā-nirūpikā*.

In the context of the *vyāsajya-vṛtti-padārtha* like *tritva* etc. where the loci are more than two, the delimitor of the *anuyogitā* of *paryāpti* will be *anyatamatva*.

From all these one can generalise as follows:

The *paryāpti* which determines the *anuyogitā* delimited by the delimitor of the *uddeśyatā* will be the ground for the reference to the relation of *paryāpti*.

This implies that the property which determines the subjecthood will play a key role in determining the nature of *paryāpti*.

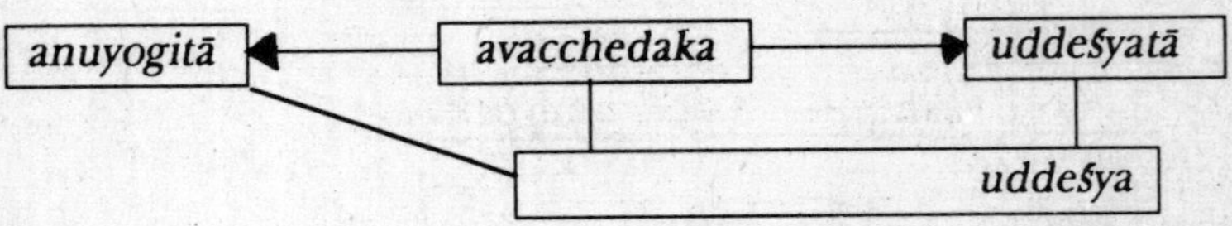

Such *anuyogitā* will be the describer of the paryāpti.[8]

3.0 To conclude, it appears that there were two views with regard to the existence of an entity in the sum and in its constituents. According to one view a *vyāsajya-vṛtti-padārtha* exists completely only in the sum, but not in the constituents. Thus, *dvitva* is present by *paryapti* only in *ghaṭa* and *paṭa* in the case of *imau ghaṭa-paṭau* 'these are pot and cloth,' but not in either *ghaṭa* alone or *paṭa* alone. That is why, one cannot say **ayam ghaṭau,** 'This are two pots'.

The other view takes objection to the above view and holds that unless by *paryāpti* a *vyāsajya-vṛtti-padārtha* exists in the constituents it cannot exist in the sum or the collection of the constituents. This view, therefore, allows *dvitva* to exist in each constituent by *paryāpti* so that it can exist in the collection of two by *paryāpti*. But this will invite a contingency. In this case, since *dvitva* is allowed to exist by *paryāpti* even in each of the collection, one may say **ayam dvau* '*this are two', which is absurd.

To avoid the absurdity, Jagadīśa suggested that let us focus our attention to subject part of the statement. The delimitor of the *uddeśyatā* will give us a clue to accept or reject a true or false statement. Let a *vyāsajyavṛtti-padārtha* exist in each of the constituents of the collection, still there will be no contingency of the type pointed out above. Because, the delimitor of the subjecthood will take care of it. Thus, if someone says *ayam dvau* it implies that *idantva* is the delimitor of the *uddeśyatā* here which is not a property sharing two loci and hence this statement will be declared as false. But *imau dvau* will be quite acceptable statement.

In addition, Jagadīśa points out that if the first view is accepted, there will arise another contingency, namely, one may say *imau na dvau* because in each *dvitva* is not accepted by *paryāpti* by the first view.

The above mentioned proposal of Jagadīśa avoids this contingency also, because here in *imau na dvau* the delimitor of the *uddeśyatā* is a property that exists collectively in both and hence one cannot say *imau na dvau.* It will be an absurdity if one says that *dvitva* exists in one locus the *anuyogitā* of which is delimited by a property sharing only one locus, but it is not at all absurd to hold that *dvitva* exists in even each locus the *anuyogitā* of which is delimited by a property which shares both the loci.

The same will be the test for other cases where the true experience of *paryāpti* arises.

Notes and ReferenceS

1. For a detailed study of various aspects of Relations see *The Philosophy of Relations* by V.N. Jha, Indian Books Centre, New Delhi, 1989.
2. cf. *Navya-Nyāya-bhāṣāpradīpaḥ* by Maheśa Chandra Nyāyaratna, Sanskrit College, Calcutta, 1973, p. 21 (Bengali commentary of Kalipada Tarkacharya).
3. *Avacchedakatvanirukti* with *vivṛti* of Vāmācaraṇa Bhaṭṭācārya, Master Kheladilal and Sons, Benaras City. p. 38.
4. *Loc. cit.*
5. *Loc. cit.*
6. *Ibid.*, pp. 38-39.
7. *Ibid.*, p. 39.
8. cf. *Navya-Nyāya-bhasāpradīpaḥ* with its Bengali Commentary, pp. 20-22.

6

प्रतिबध्यप्रतिबन्धकभावसम्बन्धः

D. Prahlada Char

सम्बन्धत्वं हि विशिष्टबुद्धिनियामकत्वम्। 'घटवद् भूतलम्' इत्यादिविशिष्टबुद्धिनियामकत्वात् संयोगादीनां सम्बन्धत्वसिद्धिः। प्रतिबध्यप्रतिबन्धक भावस्य- लोके यद्यपि विशिष्टबुद्धिनियामकता न दृष्टा। अथापि शास्त्रीयव्यवहारानुरोधेन प्रतियोग्यनुयोगिभावादेरिव प्रतिबध्यंप्रतिबन्धकभावस्यापि सम्बन्धत्वमभ्युपेयं भवति। सम्बन्धाश्च वृत्तिनियामकत्वेन वृत्त्यनियामकत्वेन च द्विविधाः प्रसिद्धाः। प्रतिबध्य-प्रतिबन्धकभावश्च वृत्त्यनियामकः कश्चन सम्बन्ध इति तु स्पष्टमेव।

[1]एवं स्थूलतया प्रतिबध्यप्रतिबन्धकभावस्य सम्बन्धत्वे सिद्धेऽपि तत्कस्येति शङ्का भवति। शङ्कितुश्चायमाशयः — किं मिलितयोः प्रतिबध्यत्वप्रतिबन्धकत्वयोः सम्बन्धत्वम्? अथ प्रत्येकस्य? उत प्रतिबध्यत्व प्रतिबन्धकत्वोभयसाधारणस्य एकस्याखण्डोपाधिविशेषस्यः? नाद्यः। तेन सम्बन्धेन विशिष्टबुद्धिं प्रति तस्य सम्बन्धस्य तत्र सत्त्वमावश्यकम्। घटसंयोगस्य भूतले विद्यमानत्वादेव हि संयोगेन भूतले घटवत्ताबुद्धिः। प्रतिबध्यत्वप्रतिबन्धकत्वयोश्च मिलितयोः कुत्राप्यसत्त्वेन मिलितयोस्तयोः विशिष्टबुद्धिनियामकत्वं नास्तीति तयोः सम्बन्धत्वानुपपत्तिः। न द्वितीयः। प्रतिबध्यप्रतिबन्धकभावस्य सम्बन्धत्वेन प्रसिद्धेः। प्रत्येकस्य तथात्वे च केवलं प्रतिबध्यत्वस्य प्रतिबन्धकत्वस्य वा सम्बन्धत्वेन प्रसिद्धिः स्यात्। प्रतिबध्यत्वेन प्रतिबन्धकत्वेनैव वा विशिष्ट-बुद्ध्युत्पत्तिसम्भवेन उभयसाधारणस्याखण्डोपाधिविशेषस्य कल्पनायां प्रमाणाभावात् तृतीयोऽपि पक्षः नाङ्गीकर्तुमुचित इति।

अत्रेदं समाधीयते—प्रत्येकस्य सम्बन्धत्वमेवाभिप्रेतं समुचितं च। न च प्रत्येकस्यैव सम्बन्धत्वेन व्यवहारापत्तिः। इष्टापत्तेः। निरपेक्षस्य प्रतिबध्यत्वस्य प्रतिबंधकत्वस्य वा

सम्बन्धत्वासम्भवेन प्रतिबध्यप्रतिबन्धकभावस्य सम्बन्धत्वेन व्यवहारः। एवं च प्रतिबध्यप्रतिबन्धकभावः सम्बन्ध इत्यस्य किञ्चिन्निष्ठप्रतिबध्यतानिरूपितप्रतिबन्धकत्वं, किञ्चिन्निष्ठ प्रतिबन्धकतामिरुपितं प्रतिबध्यत्वं वा सम्बन्ध इत्यर्थः। न च प्रतिबध्यत्वस्य प्रतिबन्धकत्वस्य वा प्रतिबध्ये प्रतिबन्धके वा केवले सत्त्वेन सम्बन्धिद्वयनिष्ठत्वाभावेन सम्बन्धत्वानुपपत्तिरिति वाच्यम्। प्रतिबध्यत्वस्य स्वरूपनिरूपकत्वाभ्यां प्रतिबध्यप्रतिबन्धको-भय संसृष्टत्वस्य, प्रतिबन्धकत्वस्यापि स्वरूपनिरूपकत्वाभ्यां प्रतिबन्धक प्रतिबध्योभय-सम्बद्धत्वेन सम्बन्धत्वाङ्गीकारेऽनुपपत्त्यभावात्।

प्रतिबध्यप्रतिबन्धकभावस्य सम्बन्धत्वेन व्यवहारस्य हेत्वाभाससामान्यलक्षणं निदर्शनं भवितुमर्हति। प्रकृतानुमितिप्रतिबन्धकयथार्थज्ञानविषयत्वं हि तल्लक्षणम्। तस्य चैवमनुगमः कर्तुं शक्यः। प्रकृतानुमितिविशिष्टविषयत्वं हेत्वाभाससामान्यलक्षणम्। विषयतायां प्रकृतानुमितिवैशिष्टयं च स्वविशिष्टयथार्थज्ञानीयत्वसम्बन्धेन। यथार्थज्ञाने स्ववैशिष्टयं च स्वनिष्ठप्रकृतानुमितित्वावच्छिन्नप्रतिबध्यतानिरूपितप्रतिबन्धकता-सम्बन्धेनेति।

[2]अवच्छेदकत्रैविध्येन प्रतिबन्धकत्वं चेदं त्रिविधम्। ग्राह्याभावत्वावच्छिन्न विषयताशालिनिश्चयत्वेन एकम्। यथा 'ह्रदो वन्हिमान्' इत्याकारकह्रत्वावच्छिन्नविशेष्यता-निरूपित वह्नित्वावच्छिन्नप्रकारताशालिज्ञानं प्रति ह्रदत्वावच्छिन्नविशेष्यतानिरूपित-वन्हित्वावच्छिन्नप्रतियोगिताकाभावत्वावच्छिन्नप्रकारताशालिनिश्चयत्वेन 'ह्रदो वन्ह्यभाववान्' इत्याकारकस्य निश्चयस्य ग्राह्याभावव्याव्यत्वावच्छिन्नप्रकारताशालि-निश्चयत्वेनापरम्। यथा 'ह्रहो वन्हिमान्' इत्याकारकज्ञानं प्रति ह्रदत्वावच्छिन्नविशेष्यता- निरूपितवन्ह्य-भावव्याप्यत्वावच्छिन्नजलनिष्ठप्रकारताशालिनिश्चयत्वेन 'ह्रदो वन्ह्यभाव्याव्यजलवान्' इत्याकारकस्य निश्चयस्य। तत्तद्वस्तुगतासाधारणधर्मरूपेण चान्यत्। यथा दाहं प्रति मणिमन्त्रादेः। मणिमन्त्रादेर्हि स्वगतेन मणित्वमन्त्रत्वादिना असाधारणधर्मरूपेण दाहप्रतिबन्धकता अभ्युपेयते। एवं 'साध्याभावद्वृत्तिर्हेतुः' इत्याकारकात्यन्ताभावगर्भ व्यभिचारग्रहस्य 'साध्यवदन्यावृन्तिर्हेतुः' इत्याकारकान्योन्याभावगर्भव्याप्तिग्रहविरोधित्वं च मणिमन्त्रादिन्यायेन साध्याभाववद् वृत्तित्वावगाहिनिश्चयत्वेनैवेति वाच्यम्। तस्य ग्राह्या भावानवगाहितया ग्राह्याभावावगाहिनिश्चयत्वेन प्रतिबन्धकत्वासम्भवाहिति मिश्राः। व्यभिचारग्रहस्यग्राह्याभावविषयकनिश्चयत्वेनैव प्रतिबन्धकत्वमिति दीधितिकाराणां मते तु साध्याभाववृत्तित्वं हेतौ साध्यवदन्यवृत्तित्वमनुमापयति। ततश्च साध्यवदन्यवृत्तित्वरूप व्यभिचारानुमितेः ग्राह्याभावावगाहिनिश्चयत्वेन साध्यवदन्यावृत्तित्वरूपव्याप्ति ग्रहप्रतिबन्धकतेत्याशयो वर्णनीयः। न चैवं साध्याभाववद्वृत्तित्वेन हेतुना साध्यवदन्यवृत्तित्वानुमितेः प्राक् साध्याभाववद्वृत्तित्वनिश्चयोत्तरं साध्यवदन्यावृत्तित्वरूप व्याप्तिग्रहापत्तिरिति वाच्यम्। साध्यवदन्यवृत्तित्वानुमितेरिव तादृशानुमितिसामग्र्या अपि साध्यवदन्यावृत्तित्वरूपव्याप्तिग्रहविरोधित्वाङ्गीकारादिति।

प्रतिबन्धकत्वं चेदं कारणीभूताभावप्रतियोगित्वस्वरूपमिति न्यायसिद्धान्तः। दाहकारणीभूतो यो मण्यभावः तत्प्रतियोगित्वेन मणेः अनुमितिकारणीभूतो यो हेत्वाभास विषयकज्ञानाभावः तत्प्रतियोगित्वेन हेत्वाभासज्ञानस्य दाहम् अनुमितिं प्रति च प्रतिबन्धकत्वमिति तेषामाशयः।

[3]केचित्तु प्रतिबन्धकत्वस्य कारणीभूताभावप्रतियोगित्वात्मकत्वं नानुमन्यन्ते। तेषामयमभिप्रायः-

१. अभावस्य कारणत्वासम्भवात् न प्रतिबन्धकत्वं कारणीभूताभावप्रतियोगित्वम्। अभावस्याकारणत्वे तस्य तुच्छत्वं हेतुः।

२. उत्तम्भकप्रतिबन्धकयोः समावेशस्थले असत्यपि प्रतिबन्धकाभावे कार्योत्पत्तेः व्यभिचारात् न प्रतिबन्धकाभावस्य कारणत्वं युक्तम्।

३. मणिप्रागभावादीनां पृथक् पृथक् कारणत्वे परस्परव्यभिचारः। अभावत्वेना नुगतरूपेण कारणत्वे तु प्रतिबन्धकमणिसत्तादृशायामपि मणिभेदरूपाभावस्य अग्नौ सत्त्वेन दाहापत्तिः।

४. प्रतिबन्धकत्वेनाभ्युपगतो मणिरग्नौ किंचित् करोति न वा? द्वितीये किमव्यकुर्वतस्तस्य प्रतिबन्धकत्वानुपपत्तिरेव। किञ्चित्करोतीत्याद्यपक्षे तु मणिनाऽग्नौ दाहजननशक्तिर्नाश्यित इत्यभ्युपगतमिति शक्तिनाशस्यव मणिजन्यस्य प्रतिबन्धकत्व सिद्धिर्नमणेः। अतः कार्यानुकूलशक्तिविघटकत्वमेव प्रतिबन्धकत्वम्। न तु कारणीभूता भाव प्रतियोगित्वमिति।

नैयायिकास्तु—प्रतिबन्धकत्वस्य कारणीभूताभावप्रतियेगित्वात्मकत्वे नैते बाधका अंशाः। तथाहि

यदुक्तं तुच्छत्वादभावोऽकारणमिति तत्र किं नाम तुच्छत्वम्? न तावदत्यन्तासत्त्वम्। अभावस्य तदभावात्। न हि शशविषाणादिरिवाभावो निरूपाख्यः। न चाभावस्य भाव त्वेनासत्त्वमस्तीति वाच्यम्। तस्याप्रयोजकत्वात्। तावन्मात्रेणाभावस्याकारणत्वे अभावत्वे नासतो भावस्याप्यकारणत्वप्रसङ्गनः। अन्वयव्यतिरेकाभ्यां दण्डादिभावस्य घटादिकारणत्वे तुल्ययुक्त्या मण्यभावादेरपि दाहादिकारणत्वसिद्धिः।

यदव्युक्तं उत्तेजकसमवधानदशायां असत्यपि मण्यभावे दाहजननात् व्यभिचार इति न प्रतिबन्धकाभावस्य कारणत्वमिति तदप्यसमचीनम्। केवलप्रतिबन्धकाभावस्य दाहकारणत्वानभ्युपगमात्। उत्तेजकाभावविशिष्टप्रतिबन्धकाभावस्यैव कारणत्वाङ्गीकृतेः। तादृश कारणाभावे कदाऽपि कार्योत्पत्त्यदर्शनान्न व्यभिचारः।

ननु उत्तेजकस्य प्रतिबन्धकमणेश्च सद्भावे भवन् उत्तेजकाभावविशिष्टमण्यभावः उत्तेजकाभावात्मकं यद्विशेषणं तदभावात्मकः। उत्तेजकाभावाभावश्च उत्तेजकात्मकः। ततश्च

दाहं प्रति कदाचिदुत्तेजकं कदाचिच्च मण्यभाव इति सामग्रीद्वयमुक्तं भवति। एवं च नानुगतः कार्यकारणभाव इति चेदत्रोदयनाचार्याः—विशिष्टाभावश्च न विशेषणाभावात्मकः। यतो हि दण्डाभावविशिष्टपुरुषाभावः दण्डाभावाभावात्मकः नैव भवितुमर्हति। दण्डविशिष्टे पुरुषे वर्तमाने दण्डाभावविशिष्टपुरुषो नास्तीति या प्रतीतिर्जायते तस्यामभावप्रतियोगितया दण्डाभावस्येव पुरुषाणामपि भानात्। तथा च दण्डाभावविशिष्टपुरुषाभावः केवलपुरुषाभावत्मकः। अयं चाभावः कदाचिद्विशेषणाभावात् कदाचिद् विशेष्याभावात् कदाचिच्च विशेषणविशेष्योभयाभावाच्च सम्पद्यमानः अतिरिक्तोऽभावः। तथाच विशिष्टाभावत्वेनानुगनेव रूपेण उत्तेजकाभावविशिष्टमण्यभावादेः कारणत्वाङ्गीकारे न काचित् क्षतिरिति।

मणिप्रागभावादीनां पृथक् कारणत्वे व्यभिचारः, अभावत्वेनानुगतरूपेण कारणत्वे च मणिभेदमादाय मणिसत्तादशायामपि दाहापत्तिरिति यदुक्तं तदपि संसर्गाभावत्वेनानुगतरूपेण कारणत्वोक्तया निराक्रियते। भेदश्च न संसर्गाभाव इति तस्य व्यावृत्तिः।

यदपि अकिञ्चित्कुर्वतः प्रतिबन्धकत्वानुपपत्तिरित्याद्युक्तं तच्च मण्यादेः सामग्रीवैकल्य रूपं प्रतिबन्धत्वं स्वीकृत्य मण्यादिसन्निधापकानां पुरूषाणामेव प्रतिबन्धकत्वमङ्गीकृत्य निराक्रियते।

एतावता प्रतिबन्धकस्य मणेः कारणीभूताभावप्रतियोगित्वसमर्थनार्थं या युक्तय उपपादितास्तासु सन्ति केचनांशा विचारणीया इति भाति।

[4]दण्डाभावविशिष्टपुरुषाभावः विशेष्ये पुरुषे सति प्रतीयमानः 'सविशेषणे हि विधिनिषेधौ सति विशेष्ये बाधे विशेषणमुपसंक्रामतः' इति न्यायानुसारेण विशेषणाभावात्मक इत्येवाङ्गीकर्तव्यः। एवमेव उत्तेजकाभावविशिष्टमण्यभावस्यापि, मणेः सत्त्वे, उत्तेजकाभावाभावरूपत्वम् अपरिहार्यम्। ततश्चाननुगमदोषस्तदवस्थः।

दण्डाभावविशिष्ट पुरुषाभावस्य केवलपुरुषाभावपरत्वे च विशेष्याभावरूपत्वमुक्तं स्यात्। किन्तु विशेष्यसत्त्वाविरोधिनस्तस्य विशेष्याभावरूपत्वं चिन्त्यम्। विशेषणसत्त्वविरोधिनस्तस्य विशेषणाभावत्वानङ्गीकारः अयुक्तश्च।

यदि च मण्युत्तेजकोभयसत्त्वकाले उत्तेजकाभावविशिष्टानां देशान्तरगतानां मण्यादीनां अभावो दाह हेतुः; अत्र च 'न हि दण्डिनि सत्यदण्डानामन्येषां नाभावः' इति कुसुमाञ्जलिवाक्यं प्रमाणमुच्यते तर्हि उत्तेजककान्लीनं दाहं प्रति विद्यमानमणेरभावः कारणं न स्यात्। तथाच विद्यमानस्य मणेः कारणीभूताभावप्रतियोगित्वरूपं प्रतिबन्धकत्वं न सिद्धयेत्।

[5]केचित्तु, विशिष्टाभावस्य क्वचिद् विशेषाणाभावरूपत्वं, क्वचिद् विशेष्याभावरूपत्वं क्वचिच्च विशेषणविशेष्यसम्बन्धरूपत्वमित्यभावत्रयात्मकत्वेऽपि नाननुगमो दोषः। विशिष्टविरोधित्वस्यानुगमकस्य सद्भावात्। तथा च विशिष्टविरोधित्वेन रुपेण विशिष्टाभावस्य

कारणत्वमित्याहुः।

तदपि चिन्तनीयम्। विशिष्टविरोधित्वं विशिष्टविरहात्मत्वं विशिष्टविरहव्याप्यत्वं वा वाच्यम्। तदुभयमप्यनुगतमेव। विशिष्टस्य प्रतियोगिनः विशेषणविशेष्य-तत्सम्बन्धानतिरिक्तस्याननुगमेन तदभावास्याप्यन नुगमात्।

[6]मणिकारस्तु—विशेषणविशेष्योभयसंबंधाभाव एव विशिष्टाभावः। स च विशेषणाभावे, विशेष्याभावे संबंधाभावे च विद्यमान इति विशेषणाद्यभावव्यापकः। तथा चानुगतेन तादृशाविशिष्टाभावत्वेन तस्य हेतुत्वमित्याह।

[7]तदपि विचारार्हम्। मण्युत्तेजकाभावरूपोभयसम्बन्धाभावोऽपि विशिष्टाभाव एव। यतो हि मण्युत्तेजकाभावरूपोभयं विशेषणम्। सम्बन्धश्च विशेष्यः। तादृशविशेषणविशिष्ट सम्बन्धरूपविशेष्याभावः विशिष्टाभावादन्यो न भवितुमर्हति। ततश्चायं सम्बन्धाभावः विशेषणद्वयेन सह सम्बन्धरूपविशेष्यस्य यत्सम्बन्धान्तरं तदभावो वाच्यः। एवञ्चानवस्था।

अपि च उत्तेजकाभावविशिष्टमण्यभावस्य उत्तेजकाभावमण्येतदुभय सम्बन्धा-भावात्मकत्वे तादृश सम्बन्ध एव विशिष्टमण्यभावस्य प्रतियोगी वक्तव्यः। ततश्च तादृश सम्बन्धस्यैव दाहकारणीभूताभावप्रतियोगित्वरुपदाहप्रतिबन्धकत्वं स्यात्, न तु मणेः।

यदि चानवस्थादिदोषपरिहाराय विशिष्टाभावस्य विशेषणाभावाद्यात्मकत्वं तर्हि पूर्वोक्तरीत्या अननुगमतादवस्थ्यमिति प्रतिबन्धकत्वं कारणीभूताभावप्रतियोगित्वरूपमिति नैयायिकवादश्चिन्तनीयो भाति।

आधारग्रन्थाः—

१. व्युत्पत्तिवादटिप्पणी गूढार्थतत्त्वालोकः। (व्यु.वा.गू)
Edited by Pt. Kirtyananda Jha.

२. प्रामाण्यवादगादाधरी। (प्रा. वा. गा.)
Edited by Sri Rajanarayana Shukla, Benaras.

३. न्यायकुसुमाञ्जलिः। (न्या. कु.)
Edited by Panditaratna T.Viraraghavacharya.

४. तत्त्वचिन्तामणिः। (त. चि.)
Published by Chowkhamba Sanskrit Series.

५. तर्कताण्डवम्। (त. ता.)
Edited by D. Srinivasachar, Published by O.R.I., Mysore.

६. तर्कताण्डवटिप्पणी भावदीपः—इत्यादयः।
Edited by D. Srinivasachar, Published by O.R.I., Mysore.

References

1 व्यु.वा.गू. P. No. 3

2 प्रा.वा.गा. P. No. 32

3 न्या.कु. P. No. 27-30

4 त.ता. P. No. 73

5 त.ता. P. No. 72

6 त.चि.

7 त.ता. P. No. 80

7

Theory of Nirūpya-nirūpaka-bhāva

V.P. Bhatta

Introduction

Indian Philosophers, especially Navya Naiyāyikas, have established various relations to explain the knowledge of possession or qualification (*viśiṣṭadhī*). Basically, a relation can be defined as an entity that causes the knowledge of possession (*viśiṣṭadhī-janakatvam*). That is to say that the relation is the cause of the knowledge that two different entities are related together[1] (*sambaddhavyavahārahetu*). For instance, consider the relation of contact (*samyoga*) in the case of the knowledge that 'the ground is the possessor of the pot' (*ghaṭavadbhūtalam*). Here, the contact is a relation between the pot and the ground since the same is the cause of producing the notion of related entities that the pot is related to the ground.

The relation, by its very nature, is a binary property that has a relational adjunct (which occurs through such a relation (*saṁbandha pratiyogi*) and also has a relational subjunct (in which something occurs through such a relation (*sambandhānuyogi*). For instance, consider the same relation of contact between the pot and the ground in *ghaṭavad bhūtalam* once again. Here, the relation of contact, when relating the pot with the ground, describes the adjunctness of the pot since the same is what is related to the ground, and also describes the subjunctness of the ground since the same ground is what is related with the pot. Thus, the contact in '*ghaṭavad bhutalam*' has the pot as its adjunct and the ground as its subjunct.

Two fold classification of relations

Generally speaking, relations are classified as those that are occurrence exacting (*vṛttiniyāmaka*) and also as those that are non-occurrence-exacting (*vṛttyaniyāmaka*). An occurrence exacting relation is that which determines the occurrence of a particular entity in a particular thing or a place. For instance, consider the relation of contact in 'the mountain is firy by contact' (*samyogena partvato vahnimān*). Here, the relation of contact is an occurrence-exacting relation since the same determines the occurrence of the fire in the mountain. Now, it should be noted that since an occurrence-exacting relation determines the occurrence of an entity in a place or a thing through such a relation, the same prevents the knowledge of the occurrence of the contrary, i.e. the absence of the entity in the same place. Thus, when the fire is perceived to occur in the mountain through the contact, the same relation of 'contact' prevents the knowledge of the occurrence of the contrary, i.e. the absence of the fire in the mountain.

The non-occurrence exacting relation is that which does not determine the occurrence (existence) of a particular entity in a thing or a place; for instance, consider the relation of contentness (objectness) '*viṣayatva*' in 'This is a pot' (*ayam ghaṭaḥ*). Here, in such a knowledge, the pot is the content (object) of the knowledge (*viṣaya*); and therefore, the contentness (objectness) (*viṣayatā*), which occurs in the content (object), namely the pot, is the relation between the content (object) such as the pot and the knowledge such as 'This is a pot'. Such an objectness, however, is not an occurrence-exacting relation because the same does not determine the occurrence of the item, namely, the pot in the knowledge through itself.

Explanation of the abstract properties

There are expressions such as (i) 'I know the pot' (*ghaṭam jānāmi*), (ii) 'He produces the pot with the stick' (*daṇḍena ghaṭam karoti*) and 'Pot occurs on the ground' (*bhutale ghaṭaḥ*). In the first expression, the pot is the object (content) of the knowledge since the same is being known; in the second expression, the stick is the cause of the pot since the same produces the pot; and in the third expression, the pot is the superstratum of occurrence since the same occurs on the ground. That is to say that when someone has the knowledge of the pot, the same pot becomes the object of his knowledge; when the stick produces the pot, the stick becomes the cause of the pot and when the pot occurs on the ground, the pot becomes the superstratum of occurrence.

Nyāya explains these facts by proposing certain abstract properties such as the objectness or contentness (*viṣayatā*), causeness or causation (*kāranatā*) and superstratumness or occurrent-ness (*ādheyatā, vṛttitva*). According to Naiyāyikas, such abstract properties as the superstratumness (or occurrent-ness) explain (regulate) the knowledge such as 'Pot is the superstratum (occurrent) on the ground' (*ghaṭaḥ bhūtalasya ādheyaḥ*). Similarly, the objectness (contentness) explains (regulates) the knowledge that 'The pot is the object (content) of the knowledge of the pot' (*ghaṭaḥ ghaṭajñānasya viṣayaḥ*) and the causeness or causation explains (regulates), the knowledge that 'The stick is the cause of the pot' (*daṇḍaḥ ghaṭasya kāraṇam*).

Now, such abstract properties, according to logicians, occur in the entities which are visualized as the object, the cause, the superstratum etc. through the relation of inherence. Thus, the objectness occurs in the object (pot) through inherence, the causeness occurs in the cause (stick) through inherence and the superstratumness occurs in the superstratum (pot) through the inherence.

Dependent nature of the knowledge of the abstract properties

The knowledge of the abstract properties such as the superstratumness (*ādheyatā*), the effectness (*kāryatā*) etc. is dependent on, i.e. conditioned by the knowledge of their corresponding relational abstract properties such as the substratumness (*ādhāratā*), the causeness (causation) (*kāraṇatā*), etc. For, to understand certain entity as the being the superstratum of the effect, one must understand some other entity as the being the substratum or the cause of the entity. For instance, consider the knowledge of the superstratumness of the pot and also that of the effect of the pot in the statement 'The pot occurs on the ground' (*bhūtale ghaṭaḥ*) and 'He produces the pot through the stick' (*daṇḍena ghaṭam karoti*) respectively. Here, in the first instance, the pot is superstrated on the ground, and therefore, the same is the superstratum on the ground; whereas, the ground is where the pot is superstrated; and therefore, the same ground is the substratum of the pot. In the second instance, the pot is produced by the stick, and therefore, the same is the effect of the stick; whereas the stick is what produces the pot and therefore, the same stick is the cause of the pot.

Now, the knowledge of the abstract property, the superstratumness of the pot is dependent on the knowledge of its corresponding abstract property, namely, the substratumness of the ground. For, to understand the pot as the being the superstratum on the ground, one must understand the ground as the being the substratum of the pot. In the second instance, the knowledge of the effectness of the pot is dependent on the knowledge of its corresponding abstract property, namely, the causeness of the stick. For, to understand the pot as the being the effect of the stick, one must understand the stick as the being the cause of the pot. Thus, it is established that the knowledge of the abstract properties such as the superstratumness, the effectness etc., is dependent on the knowledge of their corresponding abstract properties such as the substratumness, the cause-ness etc.

Conditioned occurrence of the abstract properties

If the knowledge of the relational abstract properties is dependent on, i.e. conditioned by the knowledge of their corresponding abstract properties, the existence (occurrence) of the abstract properties such as the objectness[2] (*viṣayatva*), etc. is conditioned by the existence (occurrence) of their corresponding abstract properties such as the object-referring-ness (*viṣayitva*) etc. For, to occur for the abstract properties such as the objectness, etc. in the object etc., the same object etc. must be referred to by a knowledge; and therefore, the object-referring-ness must occur in the knowledge etc. For instance, consider the occurrence of the objectness in the object 'pot' in 'I know the pot' (*ghaṭam jānāmi*).

Here, the pot is what is known, and therefore, the same is the object of knowledge; whereas the knowledge is what refers to the pot, and therefore, the same is object-referring (*viṣayi*). Now, the occurrence of the abstract property, the objectness of the pot, is conditioned by the occurrence of its corresponding abstract property, namely the object-referring-ness of the knowledge. For, to occur for the objectness of the pot in the pot, the same pot must be referred to as the object by the knowledge; and thereby the object-referring-ness must occur in the knowledge. Thus, it is established that the occurrence of the abstract property such as the objectness is conditioned by the occurrence of its corresponding abstract property such as the object-referring-ness.

The reason for the dependent (or conditioned) knowledge and also the conditioned occurrence of the abstract properties such as the superstratumness and the objectness etc. lies in the very nature of such abstract properties. The abstract properties are assumed by the Naiyāyikas to explain the different capacity or function of different entities. The abstract property, for instance, the superstratumness of the pot in 'Pot occurs on the ground' (*bhūtale ghaṭaḥ*) is supposed to explain the capacity or function of the pot in being the superstratum on the ground; and such a capacity or function of the pot is dependent on the fact that the ground functions as the substratum of the pot. Similarly, for instance, the objectness of the pot in 'I know the pot' (*ghaṭam jānāmi*) is supposed to explain the capacity or function of the pot in being the object of the knowledge; and such a capacity or function of the pot is conditioned on the fact that the knowledge refers to it as its object. Thus, it can be stated that the dependent (conditioned) knowledge and also the conditioned existence of the abstract properties is the very nature of such abstract properties as the superstratumness, the objectness etc.

Nature and function of *Nirūpya-nirūpakabhāva*

To explain precisely such dependent nature of the knowledge of the abstract properties such as the superstratumness, effectness etc. and also to explain the conditioned occurrence of the abstract properties such as the objectness etc., logicians have proposed the theory of the relation of the described and describer or the theory of the relation of the conditioned and the conditioner (*nirupya-nirūpaka-bhāva*).

Now, in the case of 'Pot occurs on the ground' (*bhūṭale ghaṭaḥ*) and 'He makes a pot with the stick' (*daṇḍena ghaṭam karoti*) the superstratumness and the effectness are the 'describeds' and the 'substratumness' (ādhāratā) and the causeness (*kāraṇatā*) are the describers respectively. That is to say that in such cases, the substratumness occurring in the ground and the causeness occurring in the stick describe the superstratumness and the effectness of the pot by being conducive to the knowledge of the same abstract properties, (the superstratumness and the effectness). Also, in the case of 'I know the pot' (*ghaṭaṃ aham jānāmi*), the objectness (of the pot) is the conditioned and the object-referring-ness (of the knowledge) is the conditioner. That is to say that in such cases, the object-referring-ness occurring in the knowledge conditions the objectness of the pot by being conducive to the occurrence of the abstract property of the objectness in the pot. Therefore, the relation of the described and the describer or the relation of the conditioned and the conditioner (*nirūpya nirūpaka khāva*), as envisaged by the logicians, explains exactly the dependent nature of the knowledge of the abstract properties such as the superstratumness etc., and also the conditioned existence of the abstract properties such as the objectness etc. Thus, the *nirūpya nirūpaka bhāva* is a relation between a set of two corresponding abstract properties such as the superstratumness and the substratumness etc. wherein one is described or conditioned by the other.

The abstract property which is described or conditioned (*nirupya*) describes or conditions (*nirūpaka*) in turn the describing or conditioning abstract property

The most significant characteristic of described and the describer or conditioned and the conditioner relationship is that the abstract property, which is described or conditioned by its corresponding abstract property, describes, or conditions in turn, 'the corresponding abstract property' (*yannirūpitam yad bhavati, tannirūpakam tat*). For instance, the abstract property, namely, the superstratumness (or the effectness), which is described by the substratumness (or the causeness), describes the corresponding abstract property, namely, the substratumness (or the causeness). Also, for instance, the abstract property, namely, the objectness, which is conditioned by the object-referring-ness, conditions the corresponding abstract property, namely the object-referring-ness.

The reason for this interesting phenomenon is not far to seek with. As explained earlier, if the knowledge of a particular abstract property such as the superstratumness is dependent on the knowledge of its corresponding abstract property, namely, the substratumness, then the knowledge of the substratumness too is dependent on the knowledge of its corresponding abstract property, namely, the superstratumness. Thus, since the knowledge of a pair or a set of abstract properties is mutually dependent on the knowledge of their own corresponding abstract properties, the abstract property, which is described by its corresponding abstract property, can itself be claimed to describe the corresponding abstract property in turn.

Also, similarly, if the occurrence of a particular abstract property such as the objectness is conditioned by the occurrence of its corresponding abstract property, namely, the object-referring-ness, then the occurrence of the object-referring-ness too is conditioned by the occurrence of its corresponding abstract property, namely, the objectness. Thus, since the occurrence of a pair or set of abstract properties is mutually conditioned by the occurrence of their own corresponding abstract properties, the abstract property, which is conditioned by its corresponding abstract property, can itself be claimed to condition the corresponding abstract property in turn.

Nirūpya-nirūpaka-bhāva is svarupa saṁbandha

It should be noted here that the described and the describer or the conditioned and the conditioner relationship (*nirupya-nirūpaka-bhāva*) of such a pair of corresponding abstract properties as the superstratumness and the substratumness is the very own nature (*svarūpa*) of such a pair of abstract properties. When the abstract properties are considered as the described and the describer or as the conditioned and the conditioner, the same or the state of being the conditioned and the conditioned; and therefore, the *nirūpya-nirūpaka-bhāva* which actually represents such a state of being the described and the describer or the state of being the conditioned and the conditioner, must be analysed as the very nature or the state of the abstract properties such as the superstratumness and the substratumness which function as the described and the describer or as the conditioned and the conditioner.

In view of such a fact, the Naiyāyikas have established that the *Nirūpyanirūpaka-bhāva* is a self-linking, i.e. self-nature or self-form-relation (*svarūpa-sambandha*). According to the Naiyāyikas, self-nature or self-form-relation is supposed where the qualificative cognition is impossible to explain due to any other conventional relation (*sambandhāntareṇa viśiṣṭapratītijañānāyogyatvam—Tattvacintāmani*). For instance, the relation between the absence of a pot and ground is *svarūpa* since the qualificative cognition, namely, 'pot is absent on the ground' cannot be explained through any other relation. Now, such a *svarūpa* relation is two fold: (i) merely self-nature or self-form (*svarūpa*) or (ii) qualification (*viśeṣaṇatā*). Self-nature or self-form is a relation between either positive or negative entities (*bhāvābhāvānyatara pratiyogika*). For instance, the relation between the superstratumness and the substratumness or that between the counter-positiveness and the absence. Qualification is three fold: (i) Temporal qualification, (*kālika viśeṣaṇatā*), (ii) regional qualification (*dikkṛta viśeṣaṇatā*) and (iii) special qualification (*daiśika viśeṣaṇatā*). While the qualification is a relation between any absence and its locus or between any positive entity and its region or time, the self-nature or self-form, unlike other conventional relations, is a peculiar relation which can be analysed as the nature or form of either the relational adjunct or that of the relational subjunct (*anuyogipratiyogi anyatarasvarūpaḥ sambandha viśeṣaḥ*). That is to say that such a self nature-relation is not a distinct entity as such and can be analysed as either the relational adjunct or the relational subjunct or both. Thus, when Naiyakas state that the *nirūpya-nirūpaka* bhāva is a *svarūpasambandha*, what they mean is that the same is the very nature of the abstract properties. According to Naiyāyikas, abstract properties such as the superstratumness and the substratumness possess the *Nirūpya-nirūpaka bhāva* relation—

mean that they function as the describeds and the describers or function as the conditioned and the conditioners; consequently, the abstract properties possess the *nirūpya-nirūpaka bhāva* relation means that such abstract properties have the nature of being the described and the describer or the nature of being the conditioned and the conditioners.

Alternative explanation of Nirūpya nirūpaka bhāva

However, Gadādhara proposes an alternative explanation of *Nirūpya-nirūpaka bhāva* which may be rendered as the indicated and the indicator relationship of the epistemological entities such as the delimiting property of the limit of the 'separation' (*vibhāga*) in instances like 'The leaf separates from the tree' (*vṛkṣād vihajate*). According to him, *nirūpakatvam* should be defined as the state of being the object of the knowledge conducive to the awareness of the entities (*taj jñāna janaka jñāna viṣayatvam*), i.e. the indicatorness. And, in the statements such as 'The leaf separates from the tree' (*vṛkṣād vibhajate*), the separation (*vibhāga*) is the indicator (*nirūpaka*) since the same is the object of the knowledge, namely, 'The leaf separates from the tree' which is conducive to the awareness of the delimiting property of the limit (*avadhitā*) occurring in the tree.

Now, on the basis of such a definition of the *nirūpakatva*, we can suppose that *nirūpyatva*, according to Gadādhara, is the state of being the entity known by the knowledge referring to the indicator i.e. the indicatedness. And the delimiting property of the limit (avadhitā) is the (nirūpya) since the same is the entity known by such a knowledge. Thus, according to Gadādhara's explanation, *Nirūpya-nirupaka bhāva* can be taken to represent the indicated and the indicator relationship of the epistemological properties such as the delimiting property of the limit (*avadhitā*) of the separation (*vibhāga*).

It should be noted here, that such an analysis of the terms *nirūpakatva* and *nirūpyatva* implies that the *nirūpya-nirūpaka bhāva* (indicated and indicator relationship) must be extended to cover even the non-abstract properties, i.e. the epistemological properties. For, the separation (*vibhāga*) etc. in (*vṛkṣād vibhajate*) etc. cannot be considered to be the abstract properties like the etc. cannot be considered to be the abstract properties like the superstratumness, the substratumness etc. In such cases, the separation which is the indicator of the delimiting property of the limit occurring in the tree, is not an abstract property like the substratumness or the substractumness etc. which describe or condition each other. On the other hand, the same (separation) is merely an epistemological property cognized as the object of such a knowledge and thus, indicates the *avadhitā* of the tree.

Further, it should be noted that unlike, the abstract properties which describe or condition mutually each other, the epistemological entity, namely, the separation indicates the '*avadhitā*' but is not, in turn, indicated by the '*avadhitā*'; and hence, the indicated and the indicator relationship is not mutual like the described and describer relationship or the conditioned and the conditioner relationship.

Conclusion

Navya-Nyāya has explained the different capacities or relations of different entities such as 'the being (i.e. the becoming) the object, (*viṣaya*)' 'the being the superstratum' (*ādheya*), and 'the being the effect' (*kārya*) etc. by proposing the abstract properties such as 'the object-ness' (*viṣayatva*), 'the superstratumness' (*ādheyatā*), and 'the effectness' (*kāryatā*) etc. However, while the knowledge of such abstract properties is dependent on the knowledge of their corresponding abstract properties such as 'the object-referring-ness' (*viṣayitā*)', 'the substratumness', (*ādharatā*) and 'the causeness' (causation) (*kāraṇatā*) etc., the existence (occurrence) of such abstract properties is conditioned by the existence of the corresponding abstract properties. To explain the knowledge of such properties dependent on the knowledge of their corresponding abstract properties, and also to explain the existence of such abstract properties conditioned by the existence of their corresponding abstract properties, the Nyāya has proposed the theory of the described and the describer relationship or the theory of the conditioned and the conditioner relationship (*nirūpya-nirūpaka-bhāva*).

Such described and describer relationship or conditioned and conditioner relationship is considered to be a type of *svarūpa* nature of the described and the describer or the conditioned and the conditioner. However, Gadādhara, defines the *nirūpakatā* as the being the object of the knowledge conducive to the knowledge of the entities (*tajjñāna janaka-jñānaviṣayatvam*). And, such a definition of the *nirūpakatā* should be explained by extending *nirūpyanirūpaka bhāva* to include even the non-abstract properties such as the 'separation' (*vibhāga*) etc. in 'The leaf separates from the tree' (*vṛkṣād vibhajate*) etc.

Thus, the *Nirūpya nirūpaka bhāva* represents the two most fundamental concepts of the Navya-Nyāya analysis of relations, namely, the described and describer (or conditioned and conditioner) relationship of abstract properties and the indicated and the indicator relationship of the non-abstract properties, i.e. epistemological entities.

Notes

1. This definition applies to the occurrence-exacting (*vṛtti niyāmaka*) relations more aptly and not to non-occurrence-exacting (*vṛtty aniyāmaka*) relations as such.
2. It can be the existence of an abstract property such as the superstratumness; however, I have chosen the objectness for variety.

References

Ingalls, D.H.H.: Materials for the Study of Indian Logic, Harward Oriental Series, 40, 1951.

Jha, V.N.: Sambandha Parīkṣā.

Jhalkikar, Bhīmācārya: Nyāyakośa, B.O.R.I., Poona, 1978.

Matilal, B.K.: The Navya-Nyāya Doctrine of Negation, Harward Oriental Series, 46, 1968.

8

Jñāpya-Jñāpaka-bhava Relation

Raghunath Ghosh

The present paper deals with the notion of '*sambandha*' (i.e. relation) in Navya-Nyāya system of Logic, because it occupies a prominent role in clarifying the logical and philosophical concepts of Indian Philosophy in general and Navya-Nyāya in particular. In the first part of the paper an effort has been made to throw some light on the concept of *sambandha* and its importance and significance in explaining the philosophical theories. The second part deals with the concept of *jñāpya-jñāpaka-bhāva* relation. I have tried to represent the nature and functions of this relation and its various types in a clear non-technical language as far as practicable. The concluding part consists of some observations and evaluative remarks. By way of evaluating the view of the Navya Naiyāyikas sometimes the view of Bhartṛhari is put forward to substantiate the Navya-Nyāya-view.

I

'*Sambandha*' is a kind of contact (*sannikarṣa*). It is promoter to determine the property of being the qualificand and qualifier between two different objects.[1]

Some Navya Naiyāyikas have defined '*sambandha*' as a special determinant of a qualified knowledge (*viśiṣṭapratīti* or *viśiṣṭadhī*). That is, the knowledge which has got a qualified knowledge as its content is called a relation.[2] The same concept has been beautifully explained by Jagadīśa Tarkālaṁkāra as '*viśeṣya-viśeṣaṇatvānya-viśiṣṭadhīviṣayatva*'. That is, *sambandha* has its *viṣayatā* or contentness qualified by the difference of the qualificandness and qualifierness of a qualified knowledge (*viśiṣṭadhī*). The *viṣayatā* in the form of *Saṁsargatā* which is different from the *viṣayatā* in the form of *viśeṣyatā* and *viśeṣaṇatā* is *sambandha*.[3] In the case of the qualified knowledge in the form "*rūpavān ghaṭah*" (the coloured jar) there are three objects that have become the content of knowledge. Three objects are *ghaṭa* (jar) as qualificand, *rūpa* (colour) as qualifier and the relation in the form of *samavāya* existing between jar and colour. In these three cases there are *viṣayatā* or contentness. Among these, the contentness existing in a jar is in the form of qualificandness, the contentness existing in colour is in the form of qualifierness. The contentness existing is *samavāya* which is different from the above-mentioned two is in the form of *saṁsargatā* which is called *sambandha*. The *viṣayatā* in the form of *avacchedakatā* (i.e. the property of being a limitor) existing in colourness, jarness and in the property being inherence (*samavāyatva*), as Jagadīśa observes, is not different from that existing in *viśeṣaṇatā* and hence, there is no question of being over-extensive (*atiprasaṅga*) of the definition of relation in colourness.[4]

Western thinkers have classified relation into (a) monadic, diadic, triadic etc., (b) into symmetrical, asymmetrical etc. This has been done by them for the sake of mathematical logic. Indian thinkers are not directly interested in formal logic. The outlook of the Indian thinkers is confined to empiricistic and positivistic world as far as possible.[5] Hence, regarding monadic relations like 'A is identical with itself' they would reformulate the situation as 'A has its identity' or simply as 'A's identity'. Here there is not even any real difference between A and the identity. If there is any difference, it is nothing but verbal. This linguistic usage puts forth an object as different though it is actually *not*. From the very use of language a difference which is not real is posited.

Relation according to the West, may be dyadic, triadic etc. in accordance with the terms they contain. The diadic relation is that which exists between two 'different' objects (but not the same object appearing two as in the case of identity). When one substance simultaneously comes in contact with two or more substances, the contact is triadic. Regarding triadic relations or the relation occurring in three or more terms, the Naiyāyikas generally reduce them to the diadic relation of known types. The triadic relation is accepted by the western logicians when A comes in contact with C through B. In this case A and B simultaneously come in contact with C or A simultaneously comes in contact with B and C. The former case is explained by the Navya Naiyāyikas as follows. In the former case A and B are the adjuncts of the relation (*saṁsarga-pratiyogi*) and C is the subjunct (*anuyogī*). On the latter case A is the *anuyogī* and B and C are the adjuncts.[6] Otherwise, there would be no end to such complications like multiterm-relations. In this connection we may recall the comments of Late Professor Kalidas Bhattacharya—"If mathematical logic or a computer machine could tackle such complicated propositions directly without in any way breaking them into simple diadics, for the purpose of combining them with other such propositions and deducing newer propositions, one could with some justification recognise such multi-term relations though even this by itself need not be logical justification proper...... But apart from that, all such consideration is purely formal in which the Indians had little interest. They would never favour any formal (purely logical) solution of metaphysical problems."[7]

II

The *Jñāpya-jñāpaka-bhāva-sambandha* apprehends the relation between a *jñāpya* (indicated) and *jnapaka* (indicator). *Jñāpakatva* may be defined as 'being a limitor in the form of an object existing in the knowledge which has become the cause (*karaṇībhūtajñāne viṣayavidhayā avacchedakātva*). The knowledge in the form of an indicator has become a cause of knowing an indicated (*jñapya*). Hence, *jñāpaka* always remains in the knowledge which has become a cause and is regarded as one of the forms of Hetu (*jnapakahetu*). When an object has become a limitor in this type of knowledge, it is called *jñāpaka*. For being a *jñāpaka*, object should occur as a limitor in the knowledge which has become a cause.

The definition of *jnapakatva* may otherwise be defined as '*jñāpakatvaṁ nāma jñānajanakajñānaviṣayatvaṁ* ' following the line of Mahāmahopādhyāya Mahesh Chandra Nyāyaratna.[8] This definition may be elucidated in the following manner. *Jñāpakatva* is the property of being an object (*viṣayatva*) of the knowledge which has caused another knowledge (*jnānajanakajñāna*). In the case of the syllogistic argument in the form—'The mountain is fire-possessing as it has got smoke', 'smoke' has become an object of the knowledge which has caused the inferential knowledge of fire. In this case of inference the knowledge of *vyāpti* in the form 'smoke pervaded by fire' (*vahnivyā-pyodhūmaḥ*) and the knowledge in the form of *parāmarśa* (in the form '*vahnivyāpyadhūmavan parvataḥ* , i.e., mountain is endowed with smoke pervaded by fire) have generated the knowledge of *sādhya* (i.e. fire). As the knowledge of *vyāpti* and *parāmarśa* are grounded on the knowledge of hetu (i.e. smoke), 'smoke' in this case is a *jñāpakahetu*.[9] That which is known through this *hetu* is called *jñāpya* (i.e. Sādhya). Between them there is *jñāpya-jñāpakabhāva* relation through the strength of the knowledge of *vyāpti* (*vyāptibalena*) and *parāmarśa* (*parāmarsavalena*).

In the light of the above-mentioned definition we may consider a few cases to see whether there is the said relation or not. In the case of *lakṣaṇā* (indirect signifying power) there I think, is *jñāpya-jñāpaka-bhāva* relation because the *śakyārtha* (direct significance) of a term gives rise to the knowledge of *lakṣyārtha*. That's why, *lakṣaṇā* is defined as '*śakyasambandho lakṣaṇā*' [10] i.e. *lakṣaṇā* is a relation of a term to what is directly signified (*śakya*) by it. In the example '*Gaṅgāyāṁ ghoṣaḥ*' the term '*Gaṅgā*' has been employed to mean the bank of the river *Gaṅgā* indirectly, but not the river. Here the direct sense of the term '*Gaṅgā*' gives rise to the knowledge of the bank of it. Because the direct sense of the term cannot be taken into the account in this particular case on account of the fact that the milkmen's hamlet cannot remain on the stream of the river. The direct meaning of the term '*Gaṅgā*' becomes *jñāpaka* of the bank of it (i.e. *jñāpya*) through the strength of *lakṣaṇā* (*laksanābalena*).

In the same way, the direct sense of *Gaṅgā* may be *jñāpaka* of *śaitya-pāvanatva*' i.e. coolness and purity of the river (which is *jnapya* here) on the strength of *vyañjanā* (suggestive meaning). In the case of knowledge attained through *upamāna* (e.g. '*gosadṛśo gavayaḥ*'), the *saṁjñā* i.e. definition (here '*gosadṛśo*') becomes *jñāpaka* of the *saṁjñī* (definatum or object which is defined i.e., *gavaya* in this case which is *Jñāpya* here). Here there is the said relation through the cognition of similarity (*sādṛśyajñānavaśāt*). The *jñāpya-jñāpaka-bhāva* relation may remain between objects directly (*sākṣātsambandhena*) as in the case of smoke and fire, cow and *gavaya*.

Sometimes an object becomes *jñāpaka* indirectly (*paramparāsambandhena*) as in the case of *vyañjanā*. The direct sense of the term fails to indicate the desired meaning i.e. suggestive meaning. In the previous example the term '*Gaṅga*' becomes *jñāpaka* of its bank which again becomes *jñāpaka* of *saityapāvanatva*.

It may be argued that the said relation may exist between a word and its denotation. In other words, a word has got some 'power' of indicating its denotation. Here potency or *śakti* of a term is a medium which can favour us by way of making us recollected its meaning or denotation (*padārthasmaraṇānukūlavyāpāra*). Hence one can say that between *pada* and *padārtha* there is the relation called *jñāpya-jnapaka bhāva*. Because without the utterence or usage of the term one cannot have a clear meaning of it. Bhartṛhari is in favour of this view. According to him, word is expressive (*vācaka*) as well as indicative (*dyotaka*).[11]

The above-mentioned view is not acceptable. For the *jñāpakatva* is taken here as a specific sense as indicated in its definition. In a word there is no *jnanajanaka-jñānaviṣayatva*. In other words, an object of a knowledge cannot give rise to the knowledge of another object in this case. When the term 'cow' (*go*) is uttered, it is a meaningless word at the initial stage and hence it is not an object of a knowledge so that it can give rise to another knowledge. If it is said that at this stage a few alphabet is the object of the knowledge which can give rise to its meaning, it is not also supportable. For, the term '*jñānaviṣayatva*' means the term which is under consideration (i.e. cow) should become the object of knowledge as a whole but not the alphabet. It should come to our awareness as a capacity of word, but not as alphabat. If a particular term being an object of knowledge becomes the indicator of another one, there is *jñāpakatva* in the restricted sense of the term. This alphabet may be described as *jñāpaka* through indirect relation. That is, it can give the meaning through the formation of a term.

Where there is a proposition, there is prediction. The predicate-term is predicated of the subject-term. In this sense the relation of Identity (Tādātmya) as in the case 'Ghaṭa is Kalaśa' also bears the *jñāpya-jñāpaka-bhāva sambandha.* Through the knowledge of the two terms (*ghaṭa* and *kalaṣa*) and their identity, the *bhedābhāva* (i.e., the absence of *anyonyābhāva*) between the entities is indicated. Some thinkers are interested to make an artificial difference between two identical objects after using the term '*iva*'. In *Vākyapadīya* Bhartṛhari has said that two objects, though identical, are demonstrated in such a way that one will think of their difference. But this difference is artificial in order to show the absolute sameness of the object. In '*Indra iva dasyuhā bhava* ' (like Indra become the dasyu-killer) which is addressed to Indra, the term '*iva*' shows the relation of standard and the object of comparison on the basis of an artificial difference. It is a case of another type of identity which is also *jñāpaka* of incomparability. Where a really different object is not avilable as standard of comparison, the object of comparison is itself used as the standard in order to bring out its incomparability. As for example '*Rāmarāvaṇayor yuddhaṁ rāmarāvaṇayoriva* ' (i.e., Rama-Ravana-fight is like Rāma-Rāvaṇa fight).[12] It is also a case of identity, though there is an artificial difference. This type of demonstration is a *jñāpaka* of 'incomparability' which is *jñāpya* in this case.

III

So far we have seen various forms of *jñāpya-jñāpaka-bhāva-sambandha.* From the foregoing discussion it can be said that *jñāpakatva* is to be taken as of generic and specific type. In other words, an object may be indicator of an object which is completely unknown to someone. On the other hand there might be some object which may give us information of an object which is not as new as the earlier one. In the former case the *Jñāpya-jñāpaka-bhāva* relation may be described as of specific type while in the latter case it is of generic. Let us try to elucidate this point with the help of an example. When a particular object (i.e., smoke existing in mountain) gives a 'new' information of another object (i.e., fire), there is *jñāpya-jñāpaka-bhāva* which is of specific type. In this case *hetu* is something which is the indicator (*jñāpaka*) of something which is not available after analysing the *hetu* and hence it is 'informative' in the true sense of the term.

In the case of *tādātmya* there is also *jñāpya-jñāpaka-bhāva-sambandha* which may be described as of generic type. One can easily understand the identity or *bhedābhāvatva* of the two objects (i.e. *ghaṭa* and *kalaśa*) after looking at the very structure of the sentence—'*Ghaṭa* is *Kalaśa*'. The knowledge of *bhedābhāva* of the two cannot be denied here, and hence, the said relation cannot be denied. But the information we get from the sentence is not as new as the knowlege of fire from smoke. In the case of syllogistic argument—'*ghaṭanyonyābhāvavān paṭatvāt*' (i.e., it is endowed with the mutual absence of a jar, as it has got clothness), the cloth is the *jñāpaka* of its difference from jar. In this case also, one can understand the difference of cloth from a jar after looking at the cloth. Hence it cannot be described as 'informative' in the true sense of the term. On account of this the *jñāpya-jñāpaka-bhāva-sambandha* of generic type is to be accepted here, as the *jñāpakatva* of the *hetu* is not completely denied.

Let us consider what type of *jñāpya-jñāpaka-bhāva* relation exists in the knowledge attained through *jñānalakṣaṇā pratyāsatti* (i.e., super-normal connection through knowledge). In the case of the knowledge in the form—'*Surabhi candanaṁ*' (i.e. the sandal-wood is fragrant), we have the knowledge in the form 'This is *candana*' (*idaṁ candanaṁ*) due to the contact of our eye with the sandal-wood which is capable of being perceived. In order to perceive fragrance (*saurabha*) the super-normal connection in the form of *Jñānalakṣaṇa* is to be accepted. Through this *saurabha*, though not actually known through eye, is to be imagined as having grasped through eye, because 'fragrance' (surabhitva) is manifested as a qualifier in the sandal-wood, the object of our visual perception through the recollective knowledge. The knowledge attained through recollection (*smṛti*) makes *saurabha*, the object of it, a qualifier of sandal-wood existing in front and makes it associated with the eye. Hence, in this case we get the knowledge of sandal-wood having fragrance as its qualifer.[13] As the knowledge of sandal-wood attained through normal connection can give rise to the knowledge of *saurabha* as a qualifier of sandal-wood through *jñānalakṣanā*, there is *jñāpyā-jñāpaka-bhāva-sambandha* of generic type. This relation cannot be described as specific because the knowledge of both sandal-wood and fragrance are taken as identical due to the fusion of the two. As this type of perception may otherwise be called by the Modern Psychologists as an undivided or complicated perception, there is no scope for thinking of the *jñāpya-jñāpaka-sambandha.* That is, the perception of the two objects occurs so spontaneously that we overlook the said relation between them though actually it is there. Hence, it is better accept the said relation of generic type, but *not* specific.

When an object is to be determined as *jñāpaka*? In reply it can be said that *hetu* is of two types: *jñāpakahetu* and *kārakahetu.*[14] *Hetu* is a general term which indicates an object or objects producing an effect. (*Janako hetuṣca kāraṇarūpaḥ*) Sometimes a *hetu* also can make us something known. According to Bhartṛhari, an object which makes us something known is called *lakṣaṇa*. To him sometimes a *hetu* is also *lakṣaṇa* (*Janakaśca heṭuh, no lakṣaṇamitiheturevātra jñāpakatva-sāmānyalakṣaṇaśabdenokta ityavirodhah*).[15] Hence, the definition of an object may be called as an *jnāpaka* of the definatum (i.e., the object defined). That *hetu* sometimes becomes *jñāpaka* has been shown with the help of the following expression '*vrkṣamanu vidyotate vidyut* (i.e., the lightning flashes off the tree). Here, the tree is taken as a *lakṣaṇa* as it is taken as a point of indication of the lightning as pointed out by Bhartṛhari. In the example, '*sākalyasya saṁhitaṁ anu prāvarṣat* (i.e., it rained after the reaction of the *saṁhitā* by Sākalya), the *saṁhitā* is not only the point of indication (*lakṣaṇa*) but also the cause or *hetu.* It is called *lakṣaṇa* because this *hetu* is something which makes something known (*jñāpaka*). In the like manner, smoke can be taken as a sign (*lakṣaṇa*) of fire due to having *jñāpakatva* in it. It the Mahābhāṣya the *hetu* sometimes is described as *lakṣaṇa.*[16] '*Saṁhitā*' in the previous example is both cause (*hetu*) and *lakṣaṇa* of rain.[17] In order to determine whether there is *jnapya-jñāpaka-bhāva-sambandha* between two objects or not, we have to see whether an object bears *jñāpakatva* in it or not in that particular context. If it is really there, we conclude that there is the said relation. It is very much immaterial whether an object having *jnapakatva* is described as a *jñāpaka-hetu* or *lakṣaṇa*, though sometimes the coinage of particular technical term or terms are essential for accuracy or preciseness of expression or for the removal of confusion.

Notes and References

1. "*Sambandhaḥ sannikarṣaḥ. Sa ca vibhinnayorvastunor-viśeṣaṇaviśeṣyabhāvaprayojakaḥ*"
   Navya-Nyāyabhāṣāpradīpaḥ Edited by Kalipada Tarkacharya, Sanskrit College, 1973, p. 9.
2. "*Viśiṣṭadhīniyāmakasyaiva tathātvāt*."
   Siddhāntalakṣaṇa Jāgadīśī, Chowkhamba, p. 252.
3. "*Viśeṣyaviśeṣaṇtvānyaviśiṣṭadhīviṣayatvaṁ eva sambandhatvamiti bhāvaḥ*"
   Ibid., p. 256.
4. *Suprabhā* on *Navya-Nyāyabhāṣāpradīpaḥ,* 9, Edited by Kalipada Tarkacarya.
5. Dr. Kalidas Bhattacharya: On *the Concepts of Relation and Negation in Indian Philosophy*, Sanskrit College, Calcutta, 1977, pp. 9-10.
6. Dr. D.C. Guha: *Navya-Nyāya system of Logic*, Varanasi, (Old Edition), 1968, p. 60.
7. Dr. Kalidas Bhattacharya: On *the Concepts of Relation and Negation in Indian Philosophy*, pp. 10-11 (Same Edition).
8. Navyanyāyabhāṣāpradipaḥ, p. 78 (Same Edition).
9. "Jñāpakatvaṁ nāma jñānajanaka-jñānaviṣayatvaṁ. Udāharaṇaṁ yathā vahnimān *dhūmāt ityādau vahnyādyanumitirū-pajñānajanaka jñānaviṣayo dhumaḥ ... Vahnimān dhūmādityādau vahnivyāpyo dhumaḥ iti vyāptijñānasya vahnivyāpyadhūmavān parvata iti parāmarśasya ca vahnyanumitirūpasādhyaj-ñānajanakatvāt dhūmādirupahetu viṣayakatvācca dhumāder jñāpakatvarū-pahetutvaṁ.*"
   Ibid., p. 78.
10. *Dīpikā on Tarkasaṁgraha* (with seven commentaries), Edited by Satkāri Sarmā Vaṅgīya, Chowkhamba, p. 323.
11. *Vākyapadīya* - III/14/253-254.
12. Ibid., III/14/563-566.
13. *Bhāṣāpariccheda*, verse no. 63, *Siddhāntamuktāvalī* on the same.
14. "*Hetupadārtho dvividhaḥ-jñāpako janakaśca*."
    Navya-Nyāya bhāṣāpradīpaḥ, p. 78 (Same Edition).
15. *Vākyapadīya*, III/Pt. I/1/15-17/p. 251, Edited by K.V. Abhyankar and V.P. Limaye, University of Pune, Sanskrit & Pali Series, Vol. II.
16. *Mahābhāṣya*, 1, p. 347, 1, 10.
17. K.A. Subramania Iyer: *Bhartṛhari*, Poona, 1969, pp. 294-295.

9

The Qualifier and Qualificand Relation

K.N. Hota

0.0 When we talk about a qualified cognition or *viśiṣṭajñāna*, it has to have at least three entities: the qualifier, the qualificand and the relation between them. (1) *Daṇḍī puruṣaḥ* 'man is with a staff' is a qualified cognition, where *daṇḍa* is a qualifier and *puruṣa* is a qualificand, and their relation. Let us take up another example of this cognition viz. (1) *ghaṭābhāvavad bhūtalam* 'the ground is with the absence of pot'. This cognition equally contains the qualifier—the absence of pot, and the qualificand—the ground, and the relation between them. One may want to know in this connection that whether the relation in the first case is the same as that of the second. Obviously its answer would be no. If we compare the above stated two examples, it appears, the relations in both the cases are different. The relation in the first case, is a contact (*saṁyoga*), whereas in the second, it is a relation called the qualifier-and-qualificand (*viśeṣaṇa-viśeṣyabhāva*). The Naiyāyikas give another name to this as *svarūpasambandha* 'self-linking relation'. The present paper is concerned with the qualifier-and-qualificand relation in the sense of self-linking relation. In this paper, I shall deal with the nature and the classification of the said relation.

0.1 Nature

While showing the different relations between the sense-organs and the objects in the process of perceptual cognition,

Uddyotakara names the sixth relation as *viśeṣaṇaviśeṣyabhāva* with the help of which the Naiyāyikas perceive two categories namely, the absence and the inherence.[1] Vācaspati denies any other relations like the contact and the inherence (*samavāya*) between the inherence and its locus, i.e., halves. He objects the applicability of inherence in this case and says, if inherence would be accounted for as a relation between the inherence and its locus, it will lead to the endless regression (*anavasthā*) which never allows one to attain its goal. Nor it can be a relation contact, since the inherence is not a substance, and hence, inherence cannot subsist in the halves by the relation contact. Nor can one also claim that something, i.e., inherence, is established even without being associated with, because it is an accepted view that the sense-organs reach their objects and reveal them. So, it must be associated with some relation *viśeṣaṇa-viśeṣyabhāva*.[2] Further, he refuses to accept any other relations to establish the *viśeṣaṇaviśeṣyabhāva,* only because that to know this relation if one depends upon other relation, he cannot ignore the fault of *anavasthā* again. Moreover, it is also not true that the object viz. inherence, which does not come into the contact of the sense-organ is known, but it is known in those circumstances where the object is connected with the sense-organ. So, it can be concluded that without resorting to the help of any other relation, there exists a *viśeṣaṇa-viśeṣyabhāva* relation between the inherence and its locus. Similarly, in the case of absence, by the same relation one can perceive the absence of pot (i.e., *viśeṣaṇa*) on the ground that is connected with the sense-organ, and also perceive the absence *anudāttasvara* in the sound 'a'.[3] This is the opinion of Vācaspati Miśra.

0.2.0 Jayanta Bhaṭṭa propounds some arguments in this connection. In the Nyāya system we have generally recognized two relations: (1) the contact and (ii) the inherence. They are treated as the direct relations on the basis of which we have also formed some other relations which are said to be the indirect. They are enumerated as *saṁyukta-samavāya* 'inherence with the contacted object', *saṁyukta-samaveta-samavāya* 'inherence with the inherent in the contacted object' and so on. With the help of those relations we perceive the objects. 'The ground is with the absence of pot', is a qualified cognition. This cognition cannot be attained through the perception only because that none of the *sannikarṣat* or relations between the sense-organ and the object (i.e., absence of pot) is applicable here.[4] If we say, there exists some other relation called *saṁyukta-viśeṣaṇatā* 'the qualifierness with the contacted object', it is also not true, because the absence of pot itself is not a qualifier of ground. Something can be understood as *viśeṣaṇa* if it is related by the relations like the contact and the inherence. As for example, when *daṇḍa* and the quality white colour (*śuklaguṇa*) are known through the relations, contact and inherence with the contacted object respectively, we then can only say their absence as the qualifier of their loci. But, the present case of absence is different from it. The absence cannot be related with anything by the relation contact, since it is not a category coming under the substance (dravya). Nor can it be related by the inherence with the contacted object, since it is not belonging to the class of quality (*guṇa*). So, question does not arise here for the perception of absence by the relation *saṁyukta-viśeṣaṇatā* or *samaveta-viśeṣaṇatā.*[5]

Replying to the above objections Jayanta says, it is not wise to hold a view that in the case of absence since neither the contact nor the inherence exists, the absence cannot be a qualifier of its locus ground. Because, there we can very well show another relation that is quite different from the relation contact and inherence and that relation is known as *viśeṣaṇa-viśeṣyabhāva.*[6]

0.2.1 It can be asked again that if it is a relation then does it require any other relation to explain it? Obviously its answer would be positive which will correspond to that it is dependent on other relation. And in such a case, the object which is related either by the contact or by the inherence, will be treated as the qualifier as in the case of *daṇḍī puruṣaḥ* and *nīlotpalam* respectively. In those circumstances, in fact, this relation cannot be accounted for as an independent relation. Moreover, since the desire varies from person to person, according to the desire, the qualifier and the qualificand will also be changed and in that case the qualifier will be treated as the qualificand, and the qualificand would be regarded as the qualifier. Not only that, in such a case, one will hold this relation as an imaginary one (*Kālpanika*).[7]

Jayanta gives a clarification to the above objection. He says that we do accept the *viśeṣaṇa-viśeṣyabhāva* in the context viz. *daṇḍī puruṣaḥ,* but at the same time, so far as the principle of this relation is concerned in the case of absence, it requires no other relation to explain it. This norm is applicable only in the case of the positive entity (of course, excluding the *viśeṣaṇa-viśeṣyabhāva* between the inherence and its locus), but not in the case of the negative. With the above answers the opponent should be convinced that there exists a relation *viṣeṣaṇa-viśeṣyabhāva* of the absence of pot with the ground independently.[8]

It cannot also be held that the object being related (*sambaddha*) should necessarily be the qualifier. Let us take the instance of *daṇḍī.* When we say *daṇḍī, daṇḍa* stands for a qualifier of a man. But, in some other situation when *daṇḍa* is connected with the feet of a person, or *daṇḍa* is carried by him on his head, though there, some contact relation exists between the two relata, we do not have the notion of *daṇḍī*, or in other words, we do not say *daṇḍa* is a qualifier of *puruṣa*.[9]

It is also not true that whatever is a qualifier, that must be treated as being related (*sambaddha*) by some relation, i.e., either contact or inherence. Inherence is a category and it exists in its locus viz. halves. Though inherence is a qualifier to its qualificand halves, it is related to the qualificand not by any other relation other than the viśeṣaṇa-viśeṣyabhāva. So, in such a case, without resorting to any other relation, we will have to establish viśeṣaṇa-viśeṣyabhāva as an independent relation like the other relations such as *pratibandha* 'the invariable concomitance', *vācyavācakabhāva* 'expressed-expresser relationship'. This is what we know through our observations.[10]

In other objection, it is asked that in this relation how do the qualifier and the qualificand change their natures, i.e., from qualifier to qualificand and from qualificand to qualifier. Jayanta appreciates this argument and suggests that since both, the qualifier and the qualificand are treated as of the forms of both (*ubhayātmakatvāt*), sometimes the qualifier can become a qualificand, and the qualificand can become a qualifier, and if this act of interchanging their natures occurs, it will not amount to any fault. Accordingly, the absence of pot and the ground in different state, sometimes become the qualifier and qualificand as in the expression—*ghaṭābhāvavad bhūtalam* and sometimes they are called as qualificand and qualifier as in the case of *bhūtalavṛttitāvān* ghaṭābhāvaḥ respectively.[11] Finally, he concludes that the relation of absence of pot with the space (deśa) like the ground cannot be anything else than the *viśeṣaṇa-viśeṣyabhāva*. Similarly, the relation of the object which is produced (*janyadravya*) with *kāla* is to be understood.[12]

0.3 The relation between the sense-organ ear and the absence of sound is held by Udayana as *viśeṣaṇa-viśeṣyabhāva* and he describes this relation as a natural relation (*svābhāvika-sambandha*).[13] Natural relation here is considered in the sense that it is a relation that exists without depending upon any other relation like the contact and inherence.[14] The said relation as has been intended by him is a cause of perceptual cognition of *śabdābhāva*.

Let us focus some objections on the present issue. Something can be called as a qualifier only when it proves some object, i.e., *viśeṣya* which is different from any of the objects. Thus, we can say, x is a qualifier if it substantiates that y is different from any other objects namely, A, B, C etc. *Śabdābhāvavad śrotram* 'ear is with the absence of sound', is a qualified cognition in which śrotra is a qualificand and *śabdābhāva* is a qualifier. Here, if one claims that *śabdābhāva* is a qualifier then it must establish that śrotra in which sound remains, is different from the *śrotra* where *śabdābhāva* resorts to. But the *śabdābhāva* does not do so. The reason is, the qualificand *śrotra* is beyond the reach of our sense-organs and hence, it is not perceptible. When *śrotra* is unknown we cannot also have the said qualified cognition and so also *śabdābhāva* cannot also be maintained as a qualifier.[15]

Udayana does not say how *śrotra* is known. But it is his commentator, *Vardhamānopādhyāya*, who contends that though *śrotra* is beyond the reach of our sense-organs, still we can cognize it through some other source of valid knowledge that is inference, with the help of which one can infer *śrotra* by the probans (*hetu*) sound.[16] If this is ascertained, there will be no difficulty to show the said qualified knowledge wherein *śabdābhāva* can very well demonstrate that *śrotra* (where *śabdābhāva* exists) is different from any other *śrotra* where sound remains.

He further contends that it is true that the establishment of differentiating the qualificand (*viśeṣya-vyavasthāpanam*) from other objects is the result of qualifier. But at the same time, it is also not true that whatever is called *viśeṣyavyavasthāpanam,* that is *viśeṣaṇatā*. If that would be taken into account, it will lead to the fault of *ātmāśraya* 'dependance on self'. To explain: if we accept *viśeṣyavyavasthāpanam* as *viśeṣaṇatā,* by the relation *viśeṣaṇatā* one will have the knowledge of absence and inherence and that same knowledge is here treated as the qualifier. Hence, it is a fault of *ātmāśraya.*[17]

At this point the following question may be raised. It is clearly known that, that can be called as *viśeṣaṇatā,* if it proves the object, i.e., *viśeṣya* as different from others; if this is so then one may have a querry that does this *viśeṣaṇatā* require other relation for its accomplishment. In fact, it needs no other relation to serve the purpose. The *viśeṣaṇatā* as a self-linking relation, being existing in *viśeṣaṇa*, itself satisfies the requisite condition of relation. It is not like the relation between *daṇḍa* and *puruṣa* (in *daṇḍī puruṣaḥ*) where the *viśeṣaṇa-viśeṣyabhāva* is based on some other relation, i.e., the contact. *Śabdābhāvavad śrotram,* in this cognition *viśeṣaṇatā* as a relation remains in its *viśeṣaṇa* viz. *śabdābhāva.* Udayana explains this *viśeṣaṇatā* as having the compatibility of producing the qualified cognition (*viśiṣṭa-pratyayajananayogyatā*). The compatibility (*yogyatā*) is unchallengable in the case of the absence of sound only because that the absence of sound is naturally related to the locus of counterpositive, i.e., sound.[18] While establishing *viśeṣaṇatā* as a self-linking relation *Gaṅgeśa* supports Udayana and says that something (x) can be regarded as a self-linking relation if and only if x without depending upon any other relation is capable of producing a qualified cognition.[19]

1.0 Classification

Bhāsarvajña classifies this relation into two: *viśeṣaṇatā* 'qualifierness' and *viśeṣyatā* 'qualificandness.' This classification is based on the desire of a person. Thus, when the absence is perceived as a qualifier, it is a relation called *viśeṣaṇatā,* and when it is perceived as a qualificand, it is a relation named as *viśeṣyatā.*

The Naiyāyikas have recommended six *sannikarṣat* or relations for the perceptual cognition. On the basis of the first five *sannikarṣat, viśeṣaṇatā* and *viśeṣyatā* are again sub-divided into five each, and combining the varieties of both, the *viśeṣaṇa-viśeṣyabhāva* relation has got ten varieties. They are enumerated with the examples in the following:

(1) *Saṁyuktaviśeṣaṇatā* 'the qualifierness with the contacted object': *ghaṭābhāvavad bhūtalam* 'the ground is with the absence of pot'.

(2) *Saṁyuta-samaveta-viśeṣaṇatā* 'the qualifierness with the inherent in the contacted object': *toyasparṣaḥ uṣṇatvābhāvavān* 'touch of water is with the absence of hotness'.

(3) *Saṁyukta-samaveta-samaveta-viśeṣaṇatā* 'the qualifierness which is related by inherence with the inherent in the contacted object: *nīlatvaṁ śuklatvābhāvavat* 'the blueness has an absence of whiteness'.

(4) *Samaveta-viśeṣaṇatā* 'the qualifierness with the inherent': *vīṇāśabdaḥ tīvratvābhāvavān* 'the sound of lute is with the absence of strongness.'.

(5) *Samaveta-samaveta-viśeṣaṇatā* 'the qualifierness with the inherent in the inherent' : *śabdatvaṁ bhedābhāvavad* 'soundness is possessed of an absence of variation'. Similarly, all the five varieties of *viśeṣyatā* can be understood.[20]

Jānakīnātha does not classify this relation as has been done by Bhāsarvajña. According to him, *viṣeṣaṇa-viśeṣyabhāva* includes the *viśeṣaṇatā* relation alone and he divides it into two: (i) *indriyaviśeṣaṇatā* 'qualifierness in the sense-organ' and (ii) *indriyasannikarṣaviśeṣaṇatā* 'qualifierness in the related object of sense-organ'. By the former relation the absence of sound is perceived in the sense-organ ear, and by the latter, the absence of pot is perceived on the ground. He does not further sub-divide *indriyaviśeṣaṇatā*, but does hold a view that since *sannikarṣat* are many, *indriyasannikṛṣṭaviśeṣaṇatā* has to have its many varieties.[21]

Gaṅgeśa's view on this point does not differ from Jānakīnātha. But instead of saying *indriya-viśeṣaṇatā* and *indriyasannikṛṣṭaviśeṣaṇatā* he calls them as *viśeṣaṇatā* and *indriyasambaddhaviśeṣaṇatā* respectively,[22] of course, conceptually he does not have any disagreement with Jānakīnātha.

Viśvanātha accepts only one type of *viśeṣaṇatā,* i.e., *indriyasambaddhaviśeṣaṇatā* , under which he subsumes all its varieties. In earlier discussion we observed that *viśeṣaṇatā* is classified on the basis of first five *sannikarṣat.* But *Viśvanātha* classifies it with the help of sixth *sannikarsa,* i.e., *viśeṣaṇatā* even, and the example he cites for it, is *ghaṭābhāvādau* paṭābhāvaḥ 'there is an absence of cloth in the absence of pot etc.' Here, one perceives the absence of cloth in the absence of pot that exists on the ground by the relation *cakṣuḥsaṁyuktaviśeṣaṇaviśeṣaṇatā* .[23]

2.0 Conclusion

Neither Gautama nor Vātsyāyana talks about this relation in terms of sixth *sannikarṣa.* The process of perceptual cognition as has been presented by Gautama is very common, (i.e., *indriyārthasannikarṣotpannam jñānam*). Vātsyāyana though develops Gautama's idea, he specifically does not give any information about what should be the relation between the absence and the *indriya* or between the inherence and the *indriya.* It is Uddyotakara who for the fi-st time enumerates all the six varieties of *sannikarṣat* in which viśeṣaṇa-viśeṣyabhāva is also mentioned. He says that the absence and the inherence are to be perceived by the *viśeṣaṇa-viśeṣyabhāva* relation. Vācaspati Miśra elaborated Uddyotakara's idea and substantiated that no other relation is required to explain this relation. Jayanta Bhaṭṭa and Udayana follow Vācaspati and tried to establish this relation from different angles. In addition to that Jayanta had also the notion of *Kālikaviśeṣaṇatā*[24] or temporal relation and *daiśikaviśeṣaṇatā* which has been developed in the later stage of Nyāya-vaiśeṣika system.

As regards the classification of this relation, it seems that there was no such classificative idea of this relation in Prācina-nyāya though Bhāsarvajña is an exception to it. Bhāsarvajña classifies it in terms of *viśeṣaṇatā* and *viśeṣyatā,* but the later Naiyāyikas do it in terms of *indriyaviśeṣaṇatā* and *indriyasambaddhaviśeśaṇatā* .

Notes and References

1. *Nyāyadarśanam* (*Nyāyavārttikam*), ed. by Tārānātha Nyāya-Tarkatīrtha, Munshiram Manoharlal Publishers Pvt. Ltd., New Delhi, 2nd edn., 1985, pp. 95-96.
2. *Sa cāyutasiddhy ādisampattyā samavāyaḥ, na cāsyānyaḥ samavāyo 'navasthānāt. Na cendriyeṇāsya saṁyogo 'dravyatvāt Na cāsaṁbaddhasya grahaṇam, indriyāṇāṁ prāpyakāritva samarthanāt. Tasmāt viśeṣaṇa-viśeṣyabhāvaḥ pariśiṣyate Nyāyavārttika-tātparyaṭīkā*, Ibid., p. 96.
3. *Ibid.*
4. *Tatra tāvad idaṁ nāstīti jñānaṁ na pratyakṣajanitam, indriyārtha-sannikarṣābhāvāt. Sannikarṣo hi saṁyoga-samavāyasvabhāvaḥ, tat prabhavabhedo vā saṁyukta-samavāyādir iha nāstyeva, Nyayamañjarī*, ed. by K.S. Varadacharya, Oriental Research Institute, Mysore, 1969, Vol. I, p. 132.
5. *Ibid.*
6. *yad uktaṁ saṁyoga-samavāyayor abhāvāt abhāvo na bhūpradeśasya viśeṣaṇam iti—tad apy asādhu—saṁyoga-samavāyābhyām anyasyaiva viśeṣaṇaviśeṣyabhāvanāmnaḥ sambandhasya adūra eva pratītibalena darśayiṣyamāṇatvāt, Ibid.*, 40.
7. *Ibid.*, pp. 145-46.
8. *Tathā, sambandhābhāvād iti yad uktam—tatra deśena saha tāvad abhāvasya viśeṣaṇa-viśeṣyabhāvaḥ sambandhaḥ sa tu sambandhāntaramūla iti bhāve'yam niyamaḥ, nābhāve , Ibid.*, p. 159.
9. *Na hy evaṁ bhavati—yat sambandhaṁ tat viśeṣaṇam eva.*

   Pādapīḍite, śirasi vā dhāryamāṇe daṇḍe 'daṇḍī' iti pratyayānupādāt, Ibid., p. 160.
10. *Ibid.*
11. *Ibid.*
12. *Ibid.*
13. *Asti hi śrotraśabdābhāvayoḥ svābhāviko viśeṣaṇa-viśeṣyabhāvaḥ, Kusumañjali*, ed. by P.P. Upadhyaya, Chowkhamba Sanskrit Series Office, Varanasi, 1957, p. 239.
14. *Svābhāvikaḥ = saṁyogasamavāyādisambandhāntaranirapekṣa iti, Bodhanī*, a commentary on *Kusumañjali, Ibid.*
15. *Ibid.*, p. 240.

16. *Prakāśa*, a commentary on *Kusumāñjali, Ibid.*
17. *Tathā viśeṣyavyavasthāpanāyāḥ- phalatvāt. Na tu tad eva viśeṣaṇatvam, ātmāśrayaprasaṅgāt, Ibid.*
18. *Saiva ca viśiṣṭapratyayajananayogyata viśeṣaṇatety ucyate. Sā cātra durnivārā, pratiyogy adhikaraṇena svabhāvata evābhāvasya militatvāt, Ibid.*, p. 291.
19. *Tattvacintāmaṇi*, ed. by N.S. Ramanuja Tatacharya, Kendriya Sanskrit Vidyapeetha, Tirupati, Vol. I (*Pratyakṣakhaṇḍa*), 1973, p. 764.
20. *Nyāyabhūṣaṇam* of Bhāsarvajña, ed. by Swami Yogindrananda, Ṣaḍdarśana Prakāśana Pratiṣṭhānam, Varanasi, 1968, p. 168.
21. *Nyāyasiddhāntamañjarī*, ed. by Gaurinath Sastri, Sri Satguru Publications, Delhi, Second edition, 1990, p. 44.
22. Tātācārya, *op. cit.*, p. 613.
23. *Nyāyasiddhāntamuktāvalī*, ed. by Narayanacarana & Shvetavaikuntha Shastri, Chowkhamba Sanskrit Samsthan, Varanasi, 4th edition, 1990, p. 205.
24. For the details about *Kālikaviśeṣaṇatā*, see *The Philosophy of Relations*, by Dr. V.N. Jha, Indian Books Centre, Delhi, 1990, p. XXX.

10

Jayanta on the Relation Between Word and Meaning

Ujjwala Panse

0.0 Naiyāyikas from the time of Gautama have two prominent opponents in addition to the Buddhists namely, the Vaiśeṣikas and the Mīmāṁsakas so far as verbal testimony as a means of valid cognition is concerned. Three controversial aspects of the issue are:

(1) Whether verbal testimony is an independent means of valid cognition, (2) Whether there is any relation between a word and its meaning and (3) What is the nature of that relation i.e. whether it is an eternal one or otherwise?

As we know, Vaiśeṣikas do not accept that verbal testimony is an independent means of valid cognition; they include the same in the inference. Buddhists did not accept that there is any relation between word and meaning. Similarly, Mīmāṁsakas held that the relation between the two is eternal.

In this paper we are mainly concerned with the last controversy.

0.1 Presuppositions

(1) Verbal Testimony is a means of valid cognition,

(2) There is a relation between a word and its meaning, and

(3) The knowledge of this relation is necessary for verbal understanding. In other words, the knowledge of the relation between word and meaning is necessary for verbal testimony to play the role of a means of valid cognition.

With these presuppositions in mind we shall now first see what Jayanta has to say on the relation between word and meaning in his *Nyāyamañjari* (*NM*).

1.0 Jayanta on *Pada-padārtha-sambandha*

At the very outset Jayanta declares that unless there is a relation between a word and its meaning in the form of *samaya* i.e. convention formed by somebody (*puruṣa*) a word does not produce an understanding of the meaning. (पुरूषपरिघटित-समयसम्बन्धव्यतिरेकेण शब्दादर्थप्रत्ययानुत्पत्तेः। (सम्बन्धकरणे पुरूषानपेक्षत्वमघटमानम्) *NM* P. 220)

Thereafter he begins the discussion at the very beginning, and states that the relation between a word and its meaning cannot either be *saṁyoga* like that between a pot and berry or *samavāya* like that between a cloth and threads because we do not perceive it. Neither can it be inferred because we do not experience the cutting of or filling up of mouth with sweets as soon as the words like *kṣura* (knife) or *modaka* (sweets) are uttered. Since the word exists in mouth and the referent on earth there is no invariable concomitance or co-locus-ness between the two.

The relations like *kāryakāraṇabhāva*, *nimittanaimittikabhāva* or *ādhārādheyabhāva* are not possible in case of these two, but we cannot also say that there is no relation at all between them as word is the reason of the regular understanding of certain meaning. (न नास्ति शब्दस्यार्थेन सम्बन्धः प्रत्ययनियमहेतुत्वात्, धूमादिवत्। NM P. 221) But the relation is also not of the nature of *hetu-hetumad-bhāva*. Then what is the nature of that relation? The relation, Jayanta states is called *samaya* and it is defined as: *abhidhāna abhidheya* -niyama-*niyogaḥ samayaḥ* (NM, p. 221) which means: Convention of the regularity between a word and a meaning. If one asks what is the exact nature of this *samaya* then Jayanta answers it is actually nothing but *saṁjñā-saṁjñi-sambandha* of the Mīmāṁsakas.

Unless this *samaya* is known the nature of a word as a revealer is not understood and hence, he adds, the relation between the word and the meaning is not natural. In other words, words do not possess any natural power or capacity that denotes their meanings (संज्ञासंज्ञिसम्बन्धो हि समय एवोच्यते तदुपयोगमन्तरेण प्रत्यायकत्वानवगमान्न स्वाभाविकी शक्तिः। NM P. 223).

1.1 Thus, to sum up the stand of Jayanta,

(1) There is a relation between the two

(2) That is named as *samaya*

(3) This *samaya* is defined as: abhidhāna-abhidheya-niyama-*niyoga* which means: regular application of the consistent relation between word and meaning, which ultimately may take the form of desire be it of the God or of the man.

(4) Unless this *samaya* is known verbal understanding will not take place.

From this it seems to me that, this *samaya* is nothing but what is later called *saṁketa* and *lakṣaṇā,* or *śakti* or *vṛtti* by the later authors on Navya-Nyāya like Gadādhara, Viśvanātha etc.

Nature of the *saṁketa* is, as Gadādhara states: the desire of God or that of man that may be expressed in words as: Let this word denote this particular meaning or let this meaning be understood from this particular word. (vide *Śaktivāda*, pp. 1-5).

Let us now look at the stand of the Mīmāṁsakas in brief and then see how Jayanta has answered them.

2.0 Mīmāṁsakas' Position

(1) Words possess a natural power/capacity (*śakti*) to denote meanings and it is known through the behaviour of elderly persons. This power of words is as natural as the power of burning in the fire and hence there is no concern of a human being so far as the relation between word and meaning is concerned.

(2) Knowledge of this natural relation is necessary for knowing the meaning just as the natural property existing in smoke, namely, *analāvinābhāvitva* has to be known for an inferential cognition. In

other words, as inferential cognition of fire does not arise unless you know the relation between smoke and fire so also verbal understanding does not take place unless the relation be it natural—is known.

(3) All words are capable of expressing all meanings. This explains different meanings of the same word in different regions.

2.1 Jayanta's Answer to Mīmāṁsakas

Jayanta refutes all these arguments one by one and does not accept that the relation is eternal or natural.

(1) Natural relation cannot be accepted because, as we perceive the words and meanings we do not perceive any third entity namely the relation between them. If Mīmāṁsakas intend that this relation being of the nature of a capacity or potentiality in words cannot be perceived separately, then this capacity which is different from the nature of a thing has already been refuted by Jayanta on the ground that it is not perceptible because it is not a substance. It is not inferrable because effects come into existence even otherwise. And most important is, even if this relation between word and meaning in the form of capacity among words is accepted, still one cannot do away with *samaya*, because unless *samaya* is known one cannot understand the meaning (of a word). Thus, one has to accept *samaya* on the top of the natural power and it is already established how *samaya* itself is sufficient to make one understand the meaning, then why unnecessarily should one go for the natural relation between the two?

(2) On the second argument of the Mīmāṁsakas which explained the necessity of the knowledge of the natural relation between a word and a meaning by giving an analogy of smoke and fire, Jayanta says, this argument is not sound because though *analāvinābhāvitva* (i.e. the state of not existing without fire) is natural to *dhūma* its *pratyāyakatva* (i.e. the state of being a revealer) is not natural and hence unless we know it no inferential knowledge of fire is possible but in the present context, the Mīmāṁsakas contention is that the capacity to denote the meaning (*pratītiśaktiḥ:*) i.e. *pratyāyakatva* or capacity to reveal itself is natural to the word then why on earth is there any necessity of knowing the relation?

(3) The third point that all words denote all meanings is also difficult to accept because it is not possible to differentiate among different *śaktis* of a word - because this *śakti* is nothing but the nature of the word itself. One cannot infer this *śakti* on the basis of the difference in the effects because that difference can be explained even otherwise. Moreover, if all *śaktis* are present in one and all words then all meanings will be understood from any word. Here, if one says that the knowledge of *samaya* will come for help then Jayanta says that let there be *samaya* alone and not the natural relation.

Lastly, Jayanta adds that the behaviour of common man also goes in favour of *samaya* as people say in common parlance, 'Devadatta has said that let this meaning be understood from such and such a word'.

This is how Jayanta has dealt with the concept of relation between word and meaning. Now let us see in brief what his predecessors viz. Gautama, Vātsyāyana and Udyotakara have to say on this issue.

3.0 Gautama, Vātsyāyana and Udyotakara

Gautama has established the relation by the rule *śabdārthavyavasthānādapratiṣedhaḥ: Nyāyasūtra* 2.1.54, which means: since there is a regularity or consistency between a word and a meaning we cannot deny (the relation between the two). Vātsyāyana explains: since we understand a particular meaning from a particular word regularly we have to infer that there is a relation between them. If there is no such relation all words would denote all meanings.

(शब्दादर्थप्रत्ययस्य व्यवस्थादर्शनादनुमीयते अस्ति शब्दार्थसम्बन्धो व्यवस्थाकारणम्। असम्बन्धे हि शब्दमात्रादर्थमात्रे प्रत्ययप्रसङ्गः।

Nyāya Bhāṣya on *Nyāyasūtra*, 2.1.54).

Udyotakara offers the form of inference: A word denotes a meaning being related to it because whatever is a cause of regular understanding reveals an object (or meaning) being related to it, like a lamp,—word is of such type. Therefore it also reveals the meaning being related to it

In the next rule namely *Na, sāmayikatvāt śabdārthasampratyayasya. Nyāyasūtra,* 2.1.55 Gautama says that the understanding of a meaning of a word is *sāmayika* i.e. depends upon *samaya* and not on the relation.

Vātsyāyana explains: The convention that 'such and such a meaning is the connotation of such and such a word' is what is called *samaya*. When this is known a meaning is understood from a word and vice versa. Those who favour the natural relation between word and meaning also have to accept this. And knowledge of *samaya* can be had from the application of the same by the elderly persons.

To quote him: न सम्बन्धकारितं शब्दार्थव्यवस्थानम्। किं तर्हि? समयकारितम्। यत्तदवोचाम अस्येदमिति षष्ठीविशिष्टस्य वाक्यस्यार्थविशेषो ऽनुज्ञातः शब्दार्थयोः सम्बन्ध इति, समयं तमवोचाम इति। कः पुनरयं समयः। अस्य शब्दस्य इदमर्थजातमभिधेयमिति अभिधान-अभिधेय-नियम-नियोगः। तस्मिन्नुपयुक्ते शब्दादर्थसम्प्रत्ययो भवति। विपर्यये हि शब्दश्रवणेऽपि प्रत्ययाभावः। सम्बन्धवादिनोऽपि चायमवर्जनीय इति। प्रयुज्यमानग्रहणाच्च समयोपयोगो लौकिकानाम्।

Nyāyabhāṣya on *Nyāyasūtra*, 2.1.55, pp. 543-44).

It will not be out of place to remember here that Kaṇāda also says *sāmayikaḥ śabdādarthapratyayaḥ* in his *Vaiśeṣika-sūtra*, 7.2.20.

We can observe from this that what Jayanta is trying to defend is the stand of Vātsyāyana. He fully agrees with the Bhāṣyakāra and hence pleads for it by elaborately explaining the matter. Udyotakara, following the same stream of argument only adds: (कश्चिच्च सम्बन्ध अनुज्ञातः इति यदवोचाम समयं तदवोचाम इति। अयं च वाच्य-वाचक-भावलक्षणः सम्बन्धः स्वाभाविक-शब्दार्थ-सम्बन्ध-वादिना ऽप्यनुज्ञेयः। न हि स्वाभाविक-सम्बन्धवादिनो ऽनुपयुक्तशब्दार्थ सम्बन्धस्य शब्दग्रहणाद् विशेषप्रत्ययो भवति। स पुनः समयः कुतः प्रत्येतव्यः? पदज्ञानाल्लोकतश्चेति। ......मात्रादींस्तेषु तेषु अर्थेषु तांस्तान् शब्दान् प्रयुञ्जानानुपलभ्य सोऽपि तथैव शिक्षितः तांस्तानेव शब्दांस्तेषु तेष्वर्थेषु प्रयुङ्क्ते न पुनरेनं लिपिमिव कश्चित् शिक्षयतीति।

Nyāyavārtika on *Nyāyabhāṣya* on *Nyāyasūtra*, 2.1.55).

He has made it clear that if we say sometimes that we approve of the relation what we actually intend is nothing more than the *samaya*.

To refute the argument of the Mīmāṁsakas that all words are capable of expressing all meanings Gautama cites the rule *jātiviśeṣe cāniyamāt* (*Nyāyasūtra,* 2.1.56) which means: there is no regularity in a particular word and a particular meaning in different people or regions. Vātsyāyana explains: Understanding of meaning from a word depends upon *samaya* and it is not natural. Because *ṛṣis, āryas* and the *mlechhas* use the words arbitrarily, for denoting certain meanings. If the relation between the two is natural then there cannot be such arbitrariness, because the cognition of colour on the basis of light does not vary from person to person. It (light) reveals the colours of things to all alike.

सामयिकः शब्दादर्थसम्प्रत्ययो न स्वाभाविकः। ऋष्यार्यम्लेच्छानां यथाकामं शब्दविनियोगोऽर्थप्रत्यायनाय प्रवर्तते। स्वाभाविके हि शब्दस्य अर्थप्रत्यायकत्वे यथाकामं न स्यात्। यथा तैजसस्य प्रकाशस्य रूपहेतुत्वं न जातिविशेषे व्यभिचरति, इति। (*Nyāyabhāṣya* on *Nyāyasūtra*, 2.1.56). Udyotakara simply repeats what Vātsyāyana has stated and adds that the word *jāti* here stands for a region.

3.1 Conclusion:

From whatever we have discussed so far the following points emerge:

(1) Jayanta is in total agreement with Gautama, Vātsyāyana and Udyotakara so far as this issue is concerned. He has as though revived their views by elaborating their arguments and by refuting systematically all the arguments of Mīmāṁsakas occurring in the *Śābarabhāṣya* on Jaimini 1.1.5.

(2) Gautama has used the word *samaya* in the rule 2.1.54. We shall not be able to say for the first time so confidently as *Kaṇāda* has also used it in his *sūtra* 7.2.20.

(3) The word *jāti* was first used by Gautama and was taken to mean caste or different cultural levels among human beings by Vātsyāyana. Udyotakara took it in the sense of 'region' or 'province' in this particular context.

Jayanta has explained the necessity of accepting *samaya* taking both the meanings of the word *jāti* namely caste and region.

(4) The difference among meanings of a particular word as per different people or places can be explained only if *samaya* is accepted, as the convention depending upon the desire of human being may change person to person or place to place.

In this context Jayanta reminds the Mīmāṁsakas that they have accepted a particular meaning as per the usage of the *mlecchas* in case of the words *pika* or *nema* or *tāmarasa* etc. in the पिकनेमाधिकरण of Jaimini as well as the meaning of the word *rājya* as per the usage in the Āndhra region in the अवेष्टयधिकरण of Jaimini. And hence, he says *samaya* is the only solution to the problem.

(5) Thus, while commenting on the *Nyāyasūtras* in his own poetic style, Jayanta, many a time has shown his independent opinions regarding various issues of philosophical importance but there are also many pleasant occasions like this one when he has agreed with the tradition in toto and as if has revived the rich system in his lucid style.

Select Bibliography

1. *Nyāyamañjarī* of Jayantabhaṭṭa, Ed. by S.N. Shukla, The Kashi Sanskrit Series—106, Chowkhamba Sanskrit Series Office, Varanasi, 1971.

2. *Nyāyasūtra* of Gautama, (*Nyāyadarśana*) with *Bhāṣya, Vārtika* and *Tātparyaṭīkā,* Ed. by A.M. Tarkatīrtha, Munshiram Manoharlal Publishers, New Delhi, 1985.

3. *Nyāyabhāṣya* of Vātsyāyana,

   Edition as (2) above.

4. *Nyāyavārtika* of Udyotakara,

   Edition as (2) above.

5. *Vaiśeṣikasūtras* of Kaṇāda, with *Upaskāra* of Śaṅkara Miśra, Ed. by S.N. Mishra, Kashi Sanskrit Series—195, Chowkhamba Sanskrit Series Office, Varanasi, 1969.

6. *Praśastapādabhāṣya* of Praśastapāda with *Kiraṇāvalī* of Udayana, Ed. by J.S. Jetly, Oriental Institute, Baroda, 1971.

7. *Vaiśeṣika-Upaskāra* of Śaṅkara Miśra

   Edition - as (5) above.

8. *Śaktivāda* of Gadādharabhaṭṭa, Ed. by Harinath Bhaṭṭācārya, Kashi Sanskrit Series—77, Chowkhamba Sanskrit Series Office, Varanasi, 1929.

9. *Śābarabhāṣya* of Śabaraswamin, (*Tarkapādaḥ*), Ed. by K.A. Abhyankar & G.A. Joshi, Anandashram Sanskrit Books Series—97, Poona, 1976.

10. *Bhāṣāpariccheda* (*Kārikāvali*) of Viśvanātha Nyāyapañcānana, Ed. by Pañcānana Bhattacharya, 9, Rajakrishna Lane, Calcutta-6, 1884.

11

Lakṣaṇā in Nyāya System

Subas Chandra Dash

1.0 Introduction

In the process of verbal understanding when the words are uttered and the listener listens to those words, at that time he is reminded of the respective meanings of those words. This remembrance of meaning is possible through the knowledge of the relationship existing between them. That relation is called *vṛtti.* It is defined as "the relationship existing between the word and its meaning which is capable of generating the remembrance of the word meaning which is essential for the verbal understanding".[1]

This *vṛtti* is of two types in the Nyāya system namely—(i) *śakti* and (ii) *lakṣaṇā.*[2] *Śakti* is the primary relation and *lakṣaṇā* is the secondary relation between the word and its meaning. In this paper I have restricted the discussions of *Lakṣaṇā* to the Nyāya system only. How the concept of *lakṣaṇā* was introduced in Nyāya system and why at all it is necessary or treated as a relation in a verbal understanding requires a proper study.

1.1 History and development of the concept of *Lakṣaṇā.*

In the *Nyāya sūtra* (*Nyā sū.*), we get the reference of the terms like *bhākta* and *upacāra.* In the *sūtra* 2.2.15—*tattvabhāktayornāmātvasya vibhāgādavyabhicārah,* the term *bhākta* is used. In the *Bhāṣya* we do not get any elaborate discussion of the term *bhākta*. In another context under *sūtra* 4.1.16, the Bhāṣyakāra uses the term *bhākta* and *bhakti.* Here the discussion starts on the words denoting the case-relations which are used with regard to past as well as future things. In one instance he mentions that there are many *bhākta prayogas* in a language. To quote, *putro janiṣyate, janiṣyamāṇam putramabhinandati... ajātāḥ putrāḥ pitaram tāpayantīti bahulam bhāktāḥ prayogā dṛśyante.*

And then the question arises—what is this *bhakti*? The answer is given as—immediate sequence. *Kā punariyam bhaktiḥ. ānantaryam bhaktiḥ. ānantarya-sāmarthyādupamṛdya prādurbhāvārthaḥ.* This problem is raised to establish the agenthood of *aṅkura* from a *bīja.* Neither the Vārttikakāra nor the Tātparyaṭīkākāra add anything in this connection. But this much is clear that as the sprout comes into existence immediately after the seed has been destroyed, the meaning of destruction is immediate sequence and the sprout not yet born is purely secondary or a figurative use.

Gautama[3] and Vātsyāyana use the term *upacāra* in the sense of usage. Vātsyāyana clearly states that *upacāra* is *prayoga*.[4] In another place while discussing the types of *chala,* Gautama mentions *upacārachala* which he defines as—*dharmavikalpanirdeśe'rthasadbhāvapratiṣedha upacārachalam* (1.2.14). The word *dharma-vikalpa* means the use of any word for some reason in a particular meaning as different from its common meaning. This clarification is given by Vātsyāyana—*dharmavikalpo'nyatradṛṣṭasyānyatra prayogaḥ. Yathā mañcāḥ krośantīti arthasadbhāvena pratiṣedhaḥ. mañcasthāḥ puruṣāḥ krośanti - na tu mañcāḥ krośanti.* Here, the term *dharma* means *yathārthaprayoga*. But sometimes this usage becomes subject to option in the form of secondary usage as *mañcāḥ krośanti.* Here the word *mañca* is used in the sense of the people sitting on the erected platform and not mere the *mañca*. So here we see the words being used in the secondary sense which is a valid usage.

Upacārachala is defined as follows: *bhaktyāprayoge prādhānyena kalpanam upacāraviṣayam chalamupacārachalam.* Here also the word *bhakti* is used. Then the question arises what is *upacāra*? The Bhāṣyakāra explains—*upacāro nītārthaḥ sahacaraṇādinimittena. atatbhāve tadvadabhidhāna-mupacāra iti.* To explain it *upacāra* is applicable when we do not use a word in its primary sense, but on the basis of proximity or nearness etc., it gives another meaning. *Upacāra* is therefore treated not only as the usage, but also the transference of meaning to a word to which it does not belong primarily. As we have seen above the erected platforms don't make noise, but the people sitting on it make noise. Vātsyāyana also passingly mentions that there are two types of usages namely (i) *pradhāna* and (ii) *bhākta*. *pradhānabhūtasya śabdasya bhāktasya ca guṇabhūtasya prayoga ubhayorlokasiddhaḥ.*

Now let us come to Uddyotakara and examine what he has to say about *upacāra* and *bhakti*. He says that the usage (*abhidhānadharma*) is of two types namely—primary and secondary. He is very clear in explaining the above example *mañcāḥ krośanti* and says that the word *mañca* primarily refers to the erected seat made of wood. But the seat is unable to make noise of its own. Therefore, we accept *bhakti* in order to connect the persons those are sitting on the *mañca*.[5]

Then coming to Vācaspati Mishra under the same *sūtra* we find that he also accepts two types of usages. He says *śabdasya dharmaḥ prayogaḥ tasya vikalpo dvaividhyam dvividhaḥ prayogaḥ pradhāno bhāktaśca.* He also points out that *upacāra* is *prāpitārthaḥ*—which means the meaning which is obtained afterwards (figuratively). And this *upacāra* has ten instances to operate as it is given by another *sūtra* 2.2.62, starting from *sahacaraṇa* etc. This fact has also been mentioned by Vātsyāyana while he says—*upacāro nītārthaḥ sahacaraṇādinimittena* on the *sūtra* 1.2.14. And if some one asks how does this *upacāra* operate and on what basis? The answer is given as-this operates on the basis of the primary meaning and that transference or shifting of meaning takes place in the usage which is accepted by people or which is in the usage. *bhāktasya etāvati vaktavye pradhānagrahaṇam siddhatayā dṛṣṭāntalābhāya. lokasiddha evopacāraḥ kartavyo...... lokasiddhaścāyamupacāro mañcāḥ krośantītyarthaḥ.*

He also narrates in how many ways *prayoga* takes place just like his earlier authors. He records—there are two types of usages (i) *pradhāna* and (ii) *bhākta*. The *prayoga* is of the nature of *abhidhāna* (expresser) and *abhidheya* (expressed). Commenting upon the *abhidhānābhidheya vyavahāra* which incorporates two types of usages mentioned by Uddyotakara, Vācaspati clarifies further and says—*abhidhānam sabdaḥ abhidheyo gamyaḥ. sa ca kvacidvācyaḥ kvacidbhākta iti subodham.* Thus, here it is clear that words express meanings in two ways. Meanings are thus called as (i) *vācya*—primary on expressed (ii) *bhākta*—secondary or figurative.

In Visvanātha's *vṛtti*, we find again a better picture. He uses the term *śakti* and *lakṣaṇā*, since he belongs to a latter period. He enumerates—*dharmaḥ śabdasyārthena sambandhaḥ tasya vikalpaḥ vividhaḥ kalpaḥ śaktilakṣaṇānyatara rūpaḥ tathā ca śaktilakṣaṇayorekataravṛttyā prayukte śabde tadaparavṛttyā yaḥ pratiṣedhaḥ sa upacāra chalam yathā mañcāḥ krośanti.*

Regarding the various causes of *upacāra* (one thing is spoken of as another) there is a long discussion in the *sūtra* 2.2.62. Earlier thè problem arises whether the word expresses an individual or not? The question is raised by the opponents if the individual is not denoted by the word, how is it that the word is applied to it?

The answer is given as—in actual usage we find that for certain reasons one thing is spoken of as another, even though it is not usually the same as the latter. The *sūtra* runs as—*sahacaraṇa sthāna-tādarthya-vṛtta-māna- dhāraṇa-sāmīpya-yoga-sādhanādhipa-tyebhyo brāhmaṇa-mañca-kaṭa-rāja- saktu-candana-gaṅgā-śāṭakānna-puruṣesvatadbhāve'pi tadupacāraḥ.*

Here, the Bhāṣyakāra explains what is *upacāra*. It is a thing which is expressed by means of a word which is not directly expressive of it. For example, there are ten ways:

(1) ***Sahacaraṇa*—'Association'**

Sahacaraṇād-yaṣṭikām bhojayeti. yaṣṭikāsahacarito brāhmaṇo'bhidhīyata iti. Here in the example *yaṣṭikām bhojaya,* the word *yaṣṭikā* 'stick' stands for the holder of the stick and not merely 'stick'.

(2) ***Sthāna* —'Location'**

Mañcāḥ krośanti 'The platforms make noise'. Here the term *mañca* is used in the sense of the persons sitting on the erected platform but not the erected seat or platform.

(3) ***Tādarthya*—'purpose'**

Kaṭam karoti 'he makes a mat'. In this case, the sentence means 'He collects reeds for the purpose of making a mat'. Here also the reeds stand for the mat for which they are collected.

(4) ***Vṛtta*—'Behaviour'**

Yamo rājā—'The king is the God of death'. Here, the word *yama* is used in the sense of a king who acts like *yama*.

(5) ***Māna*—'Measure'**

Āḍhakasaktava 'one *āḍhaka* (measure) of flour'. Here the word *āḍhaka* expressing the measure is used in the sense of that which is measured *āḍhakena mitāḥ saktavaḥ*.

(6) ***Dhāraṇa*—'Weighing or containing'**

Tulācandanam— 'one *tulā* of sandal wood'. Here *tulā* is used in the sense of that which is weighed in the balance *tulāyām dhṛtam candanam*.

(7) ***Sāmīpya*—'Proximity'**

Gaṅgāyām gāvaścaranti 'The cows are grazing on the Ganges'. Here the word *Gaṅgā* is used in the sense of 'the bank of Ganges'.

(8) ***Yoga*—'Inherent connection'**

Kṛṣṇaḥ śāṭakaḥ—'The black cloth'. Here the term black refers to the thing having blackness. *Kṛṣṇena rāgeṇa yuktaḥ śāṭakaḥ kṛṣṇa ityabhidhīyate*.

(9) ***Sādhana*—'Cause'**

Ānnam vai prāṇāḥ—'food is life'. Here the word *annam* is used in the sense of life. Actually speaking it is the cause of life.

(10) ***Ādhipatya*—'Prominence'**

Ayampuruṣaḥ kulam—'This person is the family'. Here the word *kula* is used in the sense of the prominent person in the family.

Thus, *upacāra* stands for the transference of meaning for any one of the above ten reasons.

Now coming to Jayanta Bhaṭṭa, while discussing *upacārachala* in his *Nyāyamañjarī*, he mentions that there are various types of the *dharma* of *śabda-vyāpāra*. He mentions them as—*mukhya vṛtti* or *gauṇī* or *lakṣaṇā* through which one gets the meaning. Here, for the first time in the Nyāya system the term *lakṣaṇā* has been used.[6] Regarding *upacārachala* he says—when the primary meaning does not apply to a case, for the transference of a meaning whatever *chala* is introduced is called *upacārachala* like—*mañcāḥ krośanti*.[7]

He further says that on the basis of *vṛddhavyavahāra* the words are used in a particular sense. And not only the words are seen used in the primary sense but we find words used in a different sense by different *vṛtti*. It is clearly seen that by the time of Jayanta the word *vṛtti* is used to convey the word-meaning relation in general.[8] He also refers to the *sūtra* enumerated by Gautama as—ten reasons of *upacāra* starting from *sahacaraṇa* etc. He further makes a distinction between *gauṇa* and *lakṣaṇā* for the first time within the system. Jayanta says in case of a *gauṇa* usage there is *sāmānādhikaraṇya*—as we see the example—*gaurvāhikaḥ*. But in the case of *lakṣaṇā* we do not see *sāmānādhikaraṇya* as in the instances like *gaṅgāyām ghoṣaḥ* etc. We can see that Jayanta uses the word *lakṣaṇā* here to convey the secondary relation. The earlier authors used *upacāra* and *bhakti* for *lakṣaṇā*. After Jayanta we find, *lakṣaṇā* is treated as a separate *vṛtti* by the *prācīna* and *Navya-Naiyāyikas.*

In the text *Nyāyasāra*, Bhāsarvajña while discussing on the same topic—*upacārachala* mentions like his earlier authors. He also cites the same example for *upacārachala* - *mañcāḥ krośanti* and says—the sentence means 'the people sitting on the platform make noise' but not the platform itself, because it is not a sensient being who can make noise.[9]

He does not differ from the tradition. He further mentions that—in ordinary language and *śāstric* language, there are two types of usages found. Here, he does not say anything more. But in his commentary he makes it clear that—we observe that, the words are used in two types namely—primary and secondary in both the ordinary and *śāstric* usages.[10] The primary words are used to convey primary meanings and the secondary words are used in secondary meanings. Here, we find that, the author uses the terms like, *mukhya, pradhāna, upacāra, gauṇa* and *bhākta* frequently. In this case, he has not used the term *lakṣaṇā* to convey a secondary relation. However, he uses other synonyms. He also accepts ten methods of *upacāra* occurring in different instances as mentioned earlier.

Gaṅgeśa devotes a separate chapter on *lakṣaṇā* and discusses thoroughly the views of the opponents and finally establishes his own theory in his text—*Tattvacintāmaṇi.* Here, Gaṅgeśas arguments are not discussed.

1.2 Definition and the necessity of accepting *Lakṣaṇā*.

Lakṣaṇā is called the secondary relation between a word and its meaning. It is conceived by the Nyāya-Vaiśeṣika system as a relation with the primary sense of the word—*lakṣaṇā śakyasambandhaḥ* (*Nyāyasiddhāntamuktāvalī* (*Nyā si mu*) *Kārikā*-82). That means the knowledge of the secondary relation depends upon the knowledge of the primary relation. Let us take an example—*siṁha māṇavakaḥ.* Here the meaning of the sentence is 'man is a lion'. This is the primary meaning of the sentence. But in this context, this is not the meaning desired. The speaker wants to say that—the man has the strength equal to that of a lion. And then the question arises how does one understand this meaning? The simple answer is in such case the primary meaning is obstructed (*bādhita*). So when the primary meaning is not applicable or does not fit into the context, there is *mukhyārthabādhā,* and then we go for the secondary meaning. This is the position of *lakṣaṇā* in all the systems which accept it as a distinct relation.

But what is the ground for accepting *lakṣaṇā*? There are two alternative reasons namely—*anvayānupapatti* and *tātparyānupapatti.*

(i) The Mīmāṁsakas and the Ālaṁkārikas claim that *anvayānupapatti* 'inexplicability of the relationship with the primary meaning' is the reason for resorting to *lakṣaṇā.*

(ii) But the neo-logicians say that the reason for accepting *lakṣaṇā* is *tātparyānupapatti*—'inexplicability of the intention of the speaker' and not *anvayānupapatti.*

In the text *Nyā si mu,* we have a long discussion given by Viśvanātha regarding this problem. He gives the stock example *gaṅgāyām ghosaḥ* for *lakṣaṇā*. In this sentence, when the speaker utters it, the word *gaṅgā* stands for river Gaṅgā. Through the primary relationship, we get *pravāha*, this is the expressed sense of the word. And *ghoṣaḥ* means the village. Finally, we get the meaning—the village is in the river Gaṅgā, which is not intended. So, here we have *anvayānupapatti* 'inexplicability of the relationship with the primary meaning'. That is why we go for *lakṣaṇā* and through that we get 'the bank' from the word Gaṅgā through *pravāha*. Then we understand village from the word *ghoṣaḥ* and finally—we get the verbal understanding 'the village is on the bank of Ganges'. Thus *lakṣaṇā* takes place here and the reason for accepting it is *anvayānupapatti*. This is the view of the opponents.

As a matter of fact, the primary relationship (*śakti*) works between a *pada* (*śakta*) and a *padārtha* '*śakyārtha*'

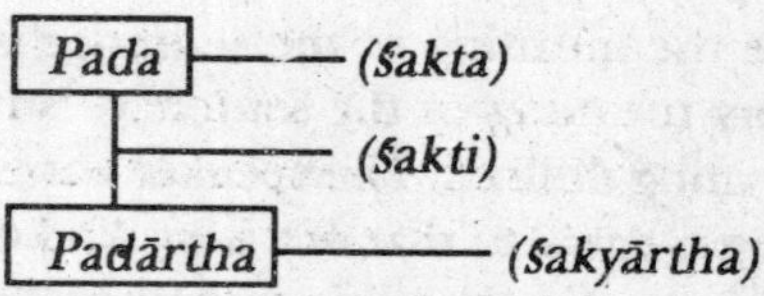

The verbal understanding arises after the *vākyārtha* stage. The secondary relation (*lakṣaṇā*) functions between a primary meaning of a word and a secondary meaning.

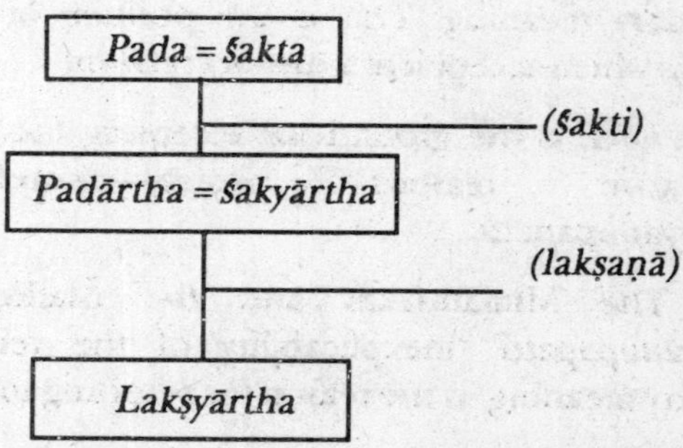

That is the reason why lakṣaṇā is defined as *śakyasambandha* 'the relation with the primary meaning'.

But if *anvayānupapatti* is accepted as the ground for acepting *lakṣaṇā*, then there will not be *lakṣaṇā* applicable in the case of the sentence—*yaṣṭiḥ praveśaya*, is the view of the neo-logicians. They argue that in this case, the primary meaning of the word *yaṣṭiḥ* is not intended by the speaker when he utters that sentence with an intention that, 'the holders of the stick' should be asked to enter in the dining hall. Because, the 'stick' cannot enter into the dining hall by itself. Of course, it is not difficult to throw it inside the hall, still the purpose of eating is not served as intended by the speaker. That is why from the word *yaṣṭiḥ* what is intended is that 'a holder of the stick' should be asked to enter into the dining hall.

Therefore, the ground for resorting to *lakṣaṇā* is *tātparyānupapatti* and not *anvayānupapatti*, is the view of the neo-logicians.

2.0 Classification of Lakṣaṇā

The Naiyāyikas have accepted two types of *lakṣaṇā* namely—(i) *jahatsvārthā* and (ii) *ajahatsvārthā*. (i) *Jahatsvārthā*: When the primary meaning is abandoned fully and a new meaning is substituted in its place, then it is a case of *jahatsvārthā lakṣaṇā*.[11] For example, *mañcāḥ krośanti.* In this example, the word *mañcāḥ* stands for the persons sitting on that erected seat but not only the seat. In the example, *Gaṅgāyām ghoṣaḥ,* the word Gaṅgā means the bank of the river Gaṅgā and not *prāvāha*. (ii) *Ajahatsvārthā*: In this type of *lakṣaṇā*, the word retains its own meaning and conveys something more. The primary sense is not totally excluded. When the secondary sense includes the primary sense it is called *ajahatsvārthā lakṣaṇā*.[12] For example, *chatriṇo yānti*, *kākebhyo dadhi rakṣatām* etc., here the word *chatriṇo* stands for a group of people with and without umbrellas. So also the word *kāka* stands for the crow as well as the birds other than crow who eat curd.

3.0 Conclusion

From the above discussions we can conclude:

(i) Gautama and Vātsyāyana use the word *upacāra* in the sense of *śabdaprayoga* and every kind of secondary usage emerges out of *upacāra*. At the sametime Vātsyāyana gives a special status to the word *upacāra* as—*upacāro nītārthaḥ.* It is an extension of meaning when the primary meaning is not applicable.

(ii) The term *bhākta* is used in the sense of figurative usages since the time of Gautama. At the time of Vātsyāyana *bhakti* and *bhākta* are used frequently in the secondary sense.

(iii) On the basis of usage, the words and their relations are determined. So the *vṛddha-vyavahāra* is treated as the cause for various categories of words and their relations.

(iv) By the time of Jayanta Bhaṭṭa, the word *lakṣaṇā* is used for the first time in Nyāya system. Before him the words—*bhakti, upacāra, gauṇa* etc. were used to convey secondary relation. He has also used these above terms simultaneously in his text *Nyāyamañjarī*. He also used the word *vṛtti* frequently which stands for a word-meaning relation in general like the neo-logicians. He for the first time differentiates between *gauṇa* and *lakṣaṇā*.

(v) After Jayanta Bhaṭṭa, the word *lakṣaṇā* has been used frequently to convey a secondary relation by the *prācina* and *Navya-Naiyāyikas*.

Notes and References

1. (i) *Vṛttiśca śābdabodhahetu padārthopasthityanukūla padapadārthayoḥ sambandhaḥ. Tattvacintāmaṇi (Śabdakhaṇḍa),* Ed. by Pt. Kāmāmkhyānāth Tarkavāgīśa, Bibliotheca Indica, p. 627, 1897, Calcutta.

   (ii) *Vṛttyā padapratipādya eva padārtha ityabhidhīyate, Śaktivāda,* Kashi Sanskrit Series No. 77, Varanasi, 1929, P. 5.

2. *Vṛttiśca śaktilakṣaṇānyatarasambandhaḥ. Nyāyasiddhānta-Muktāvalī,* Ed. by Pt. Hariram Sukla, Chaukhamba Sanskrit Series Office, Varanasi, 1951, P. 264.

3. *Vyaktyākṛtijātisannidhāvupacārāt saṁśayaḥ,* 2.2.59.

   Yāśabda-samūha-tyāga-parigraha-saṅkhyā vṛddhyapacaya-varṇa samāsānubandhānām vyaktāvupacārād vyaktiḥ, 2.2.60.

4. *Nyāya bhāṣya*, Ibid, *upacāraḥ prayogaḥ.*

5. *Dharmavikalpaśabdenābhidhānadharmo dvedhā'bhidhīyate pradhānam bhāktaśca mañcāḥ iti kāṣṭhasaṁghāteṣu pradhānam mañcaśabdaḥ krośanakriyāyā asambhavamīkṣitvā sthāniṣu puruṣeṣu bhāktaḥ.* On *sūtra* 1.2.14.

6. *Abhidhānasya dharmaḥ anekaprakāraḥ. mukhyayā vṛttyā, gauṇyā vā lākṣaṇikayā vā yat arthe pratyāyanam. Nyāyamañjarī,* Oriental Institute, Mysore, Vol. II, 1983, p. 641.

7. *Gauṇena lākṣaṇikena vā nirdeśe prayoge kṛte yaḥ arthasadbhāvapratiṣedhaḥ mukhyārthaniṣedhaḥ, sa upacāranimittam chalam upacārachalam.* Ibid.

8. *Vṛddhavyavahārācchabdārthavyutpattiḥ tatra na kevalayaiva mukhyayā vṛttyā śabdāḥ pravarttamānāḥ dṛśyante. vṛttyantara vyavahārasyāpi suprasiddhatvāt.* Ibid, p. 642.

9. *Upacāraprayoge mukhyārthakalpanayā pratiṣedha upacārachalam yathā mañcāḥ krośantītyukte chalavādyāha-puruṣāh krośanti na mañcāḥ.* Ed. by Swami Yogindrananda, Ṣaḍdarśana Prakashan Pratisthanam, Varanasi, 1968, p. 337.

10. Ibid, p. 338.

11. (i) *Yatra vācyārthasyānvayābhāvastatra jahatī. Tarkasaṁgraha Dīpikā* (*Tar Dip*) Ed. by Athalye and Bodas, Bombay Sanskrit Series, No. LV, BORI, Poona, 1930, p. 51.

    (ii) *Nyāya-Bodhini* (*NyāBo*) Ibid, p. 52.

12. (i) Yatra - *vācyārthasyānvayastatrājahatī, Tar Dip* , p. 51.

    (ii) *NyāBo*, p. 52.

12

Causality in Indian Philosophy: A Brief Survey

M.K. Gangopadhyay

In Indian Philosophy, we have evidences of speculations about causality quite early. It is generally accepted that the philosophical gropings of the Indians started in the Upaniṣads, which are generally held to be anterior to Buddha and are assigned to roughly the sixth century B.C. One of the Upaniṣads provides us with a clear hint about the fact that there were indeed different views regarding causality among the ancients. There was one view which really amounted to a denial of causality, and there were again views which though unanimous in accepting causality differed among themselves as to its exact nature.

The Śvetāśvatara Upaniṣad begins with a question as to the First Cause of the world. While giving the answer in the next verse, it records a number of views, stating that the First Cause has been conceived as time (*kāla*), inherent nature (*svabhāva*), fate (*niyati*), chance (*yadṛcchā*), the material elements (*bhūta*) and the male principle (*puruṣa*).[1]

For our present discussion, the two most relevant theories would be *yadṛcchā-vāda* and *svabhāva-vāda*. So let us try to have some idea about their implications. There, again, we have nothing to help us in the ancient text itself; we have to depend on what the later writers and commentators say. We should be careful about another point also. It is found that among some of these commentators there is a tendency to equate the former with the latter, claiming that both are simply a denial of the causal law and some modern scholars too seem to do the same.[2] But it hardly appears to be logical. The two terms *yadṛcchā* and *svabhāva* carry quite different implications, and the former alone can be interpreted as a denial of causality. That is perhaps why most of the later writers refer to it by the name *ākasmikatva-vāda*.

There is no doubt that the Upaniṣad differentiates between the two doctrines and most of the traditional Indian philosophers also accept the fact. Thus, Śaṅkara says, 'by *svabhāva* is meant the power invariably or specifically belonging to an object, e.g., heat as belonging to fire; by yadṛcchā is meant purely fortuitous origin'.[3] Śaṅkarānanda comments, 'by *svabhāva* is meant the inherent nature of the respective objects, i.e., their unique causal efficacy, e.g. burning in the case of fire or flowing downwards in the case of water; by *yadṛcchā* is meant a certain power which brings about coincidence in the manner of the crow and the palm-fruit (*kāka-tālīya*)'.[4] Amalānanda Sarasvatī (commentator on the *Bhāmatī*) tries to emphasise the difference by saying 'yadṛcchā means random occurrence without regard for the law of fixed causation; by contrast, *svabhāva* is a property which exists as long as the thing exists, e.g., respiration in the case of a living being'. Some of the modern scholars, therefore, render the two names *yadṛcchā-vāda* and *svabhāvavāda* respectively as 'accidentalism' and 'naturalism'.[5]

Of the traditional writers, Guṇaratna, a Jaina philosopher of c. 15th century A.D., is perhaps the only one to offer the clearest and most detailed exposition of the two doctrines pointing to the basic difference between them. We may quote him at some length.

Referring to accidentalism he says:[6] 'According to the view of the Yadṛcchāvādins, the word *yadṛcchā* means the obtainment of objects without any prior deliberation (*abhisandhi*) (i.e., by chance or accidentally). But, then, who are these advocates of accidentalism? The answer is as follows. The advocates of accidentalism are those who, in this world, do not admit to any fixed cause-effect relation in respect to objects, but (maintain such a relation to be due to) accident.

'They contend in the following manner. There is no fixed cause-effect relation among things, because it is not ascertained to be there by any *pramāṇa*. Thus, for example, a frog may be born of a frog, and again, it may also be born of cow-dung. Fire may be produced from fire and again, it may be produced from kindling wood (*araṇi*). Smoke may be produced from smoke and again, it may also be produced from putting fuel into the fire. The plantain tree may grow from the bulb and also from the seed.... Therefore, there is nowhere any fixed cause-effect relation. It is to be concluded that wherever any thing is produced, it is only due to accident. People with critical judgement do not tire themselves in vain by imagining otherwise, when they actually find the order of things to be different. As it has been said, all these varied multitudes of pleasure and suffering experienced by people come about only accidentally, just as the striking of the *tāla* fruit by the crow (resulting in its subsequent fall on the ground) is not an action preceded by intention (i.e., is accidental)'.

Again, referring to naturalism he says:[7] 'The naturalists argue as follows. Here, it is the essential nature of a thing that it undergoes transformation by itself (*svataḥ*). All entities are born due to the influence of *svabhāva*. Thus, for example, from clay, a jar is produced and not cloth, and from yarn, a cloth is produced and not the jar. But this production according to a fixed rule cannot be explained to take place without it being characterised by such specific *svabhāva*. Therefore, it is to be concluded that all this is due to svabhāva. Thus, it has been said: Who produces sharpness in thorns? (Who creates) different dispositions in animals and birds? All this has proceeded from *svabhāva*. There is no scope for action according to one's will. What is the use of effort? Of the many thorns of a jujube tree, one is sharp, another is straight, yet another is crooked. But its fruit is round. Say, who has made all this.

Moreover, let alone the talk of other forms of effects, even the cooking of *mudga* would not be possible without *svabhāva*. For example, even when all the necessary things, the cooking pot, fuel, and others have been assembled, the cooking of *Kaṅkatuka mudga* is not observed to take place. Therefore, (on the principle that) when the one is present in the presence of the other, the one follows the agreements in presence and in absence of the other, and the one is produced by the other, even the cooking of *mudga* is to be accepted to be due to *svabhāva*. Therefore, it is to be concluded that all these things are due to *svabhāva*'.

Associating the doctrine of naturalism with the Lokāyatas, Mādhavācārya explains it in the first chapter of the *Sarvadarśanasaṅgraha*: 'But an opponent will say, if you thus do not admit *adṛṣṭa*, the various phenomena of the world would be just fortuitous (*ākasmika*). However, answer the Lokāyatas, this is not properly said, inasmuch as the causation of all phenomena is adequately explained by *svabhāva*. As it has been said, fire is hot, water is cold and air is neutral to touch. By whom are all these varieties created? It is only because of *svabhāva* that all these are so'.

Among the modern scholars, Hiriyanna discusses the main points of the two doctrines at some length. He also tries to make a clear distinction between them. First he comments:[8] 'Both the doctrines are at one in rejecting the idea that nature reveals a divine power working behind it or indeed any transcendental being which controls it or is implicated in it. Nor does either school seek for its views any supernatural sanction'. Then, not overlooking their difference, he points out, 'While the one maintains that the world is a chaos and ascribes whatever order is seen in it to mere chance, the other recognises that things are as their nature makes them. While the former denies causation altogether, the latter acknowledges its universality, but only traces all changes to the thing itself to which they belong ...... Hence, according to *svabhāvavāda,* it is not a lawless world in which we live; only there is no external principle governing it. It is self-determined, not undetermined'.[9]

Coming to the period of the philosophical systems and their Sūtra literature, we find just a few cryptic references to causality in the *Vaiśeṣikasūtra* of Kaṇāda, generally considered to be one of the earliest works. Of course, it is difficult to be certain about Kaṇāda's implications. His work is not a systematic one like the *Nyāyasūtra* of Gautama. Correct readings of the *sūtras* are not always available. There is scope for doubt about the genuineness of many. No early commentary has come down to us. Later commentators are eager more to read later theories into them than to bring out their original implication. Still, he seems to refer to causality at least on two occasions.

First, we have two *sūtras* in the first chapter (VS i. 2.1-2) which state that absence of cause implies absence of effect, but absence of effect does not imply absence of cause. Neither the context nor the significance is clear. But later commentators try to show that Kaṇāda is giving here an argument for establishing causality as a general principle. Thus, Śaṅkara Miśra explains: 'It is observed that even when a lump of clay, a potter's wheel, water, a potter, thread and others have been brought together, there is absence of a pot due to the absence of a staff. (It is also observed that) even when earth, water and others have been brought together, there is no sprout due to the absence of the seed. This relation between the staff and the pot, and between the seed and the sprout, cannot be explained without (assuming) a cause-effect relation between them; for otherwise there would have been the absence of the pot even in the absence of a loom or the absence of the shoot even in the absence of a fragment of a stone ... If there would have been no fixed rule (*niyama*) in the form of the cause-effect relation, then, there would have been the absence of cause due to the absence of effect. But the absence of effect is not a determinant (*tantra*) for the absence of cause; the fact is otherwise, the absence of cause is a determinant for the absence of effect'.

Yet another important point which is no doubt recognised by all the advocates of causality in Indian philosophy seems to be implied here. The real cause of an effect is not any individual cause, but the collocation of causes (*sāmagrī* or *kāraṇakūṭa*).[10]

Secondly, Kaṇāda refers to the cause-effect relation in the context of inference, which for the Indian logicians is a quite familiar and relevant occasion in the sense that the ultimate justification for an inductive generalisation or *vyāpti* is generally sought by appealing to the principle of causality. Enumerating the possible cases of inference, he says, an effect may lead to the inference of a cause (e.g., we infer fire from smoke or light) and also, a cause may lead to the inference of an effect (e.g., a deaf man infers sound from the striking of the drum with a stick).[11]

Of the three varieties of inference mentioned in the *Nyāyasūtra* of Gautama (i. 1.5) which is not much later than Kaṇāda's work, the first two are known as *pūrvavat* and *śeṣavat*. That there was some controversy about the interpretation of their nature is beyond doubt, for even Vātsyāyana, the author of the earliest extant commentary, offers for each two different explanations. According to his first interpretation, the first two varieties represent respectively an inference of effect from cause (e.g., of future rain from the rising cloud) and an inference of cause from effect (e.g., of past rain from the fullness of the river). The terms *pūrva* (antecedent) and *śeṣa* (consequent) are significantly taken to mean the cause and the effect in recognition of the basic idea involved in the notion of causality that the cause is a prior event, while the effect is a posterior event.

However, in the same work, there is also a small section in the fourth chapter (iv. 1. 22-24) comprising only three *sūtras* which is more relevant to our present discussion. But here also one is confronted with a great deal of difference of opinion as regards the actual implications of the *sūtras.* Vātsyāyana's interpretations indicate that the section is designed to refute the view that effects have only material causes (*upādāna-kāraṇa*), but no efficient cause (*nimitta-kāraṇa*). But later commentators like Uddyotakara and Vācaspati significantly name the section *ākasmikatva-prakaraṇa* or the one on accidentalism and think that the opponent's thesis here is that an effect has no invariable or fixed (*niyata*) cause.

We shall first try to understand the position following Vatsyāyana.

The first one of the three *sūtras* represents the opponent's view. The opponent argues that effects (*bhāva*) are produced from no efficient cause (*animitta*), because the sharpness of a thorn and the like are observed to be so.[12] The sharpness of a thorn implies nothing but a peculiar pointed shape resulting from a specific form of arrangement amongst the minute component parts of a thorn. That the material cause of such a peculiar shape is constituted by these minute component parts is proved by perception and hence, there can be no denial of the material cause. However, no efficient cause of the sharpness of a thorn, in the form of a conscious agent or something else, is ever observed. Similar is the case with the variegated colour of the minerals in the mountain and the hardness of the rock. It follows therefore, that effects have no efficient cause.

The next *sūtra* records a criticism of the above as made by 'some'. It has been claimed that effects are produced from no efficient cause. It follows, therefore, that the production of an effect is always preceded by no-efficient-cause or the absence of efficient cause, which itself then should be regarded as an efficient cause. How does the opponent contend that there is no efficient cause for effects?

But it is easy to see that it is only a kind of verbal jugglery having little logical value and in the third and last *sūtra* of the section, Gautama points out the fact. Thus, he says that there is a difference between 'efficient cause' and 'non efficient cause'. A denial is a denial and it cannot be turned into an admission. As Vātsyāyana comments, 'A denial can never imply the admission of what is actually sought to be denied, just as, when the possibility of water is negated by saying that the vessel does not contain water, it can in no way be construed as implying that there is water in it. The admission of an efficient cause and the denial of an efficient cause are but quite different things.

But then, it may be asked, what is Gautama's own argument against the opponent's view in the first *sūtra*? Vātsyāyana admits that here there is none and explains the reason for the omission. Earlier, in the last section of the third chapter, Gautama has shown that *adṛṣṭa* is a cause for the production of the body. But *adṛṣṭa* can only be an efficient cause. The arguments establishing that *adṛṣṭa* is a cause suffice to prove also that an effect must have an efficient cause.

On the other hand, as Viśvanātha, the author of the *Nyāyasūtravṛtti*, records, the modern commentators (*navyāḥ*) offer a different explanation. According to them, the first *sūtra* refers to the opponent's view, no doubt, but the next two *sūtras* represent Gautama's own view, two arguments being given in two *sūtras*.

The second *sūtra* points out that the opponent's position involves self-contradiction. He contends that an effect has no cause. But how does he arrive at this conclusion? Obviously, he does so on the basis of an inference. Thus, it follows that his conclusion, the inferential knowledge, is produced by the inference and he has to admit a causal connection at least between the knowledge and the inference. If he admits it, he accepts causality, and if he does not, he cannot prove his contention.

The third *sūtra* states that the opponent's view goes against uncontradicted experience and valid general usage. People do distinguish between a cause and a non-cause. They categorically assert, for example, that for a particular effect "p", "q" is a cause, but "r" is not a cause. If there be no specific cause for a specific effect, how can such experience or usage be justified?

Among the advocates of causality in Indian philosophy, Udayana, the great Nyāya-Vaiśeṣika philosopher of tenth century A.D., may be considered the champion. The fact is that the entire metaphysical system of Nyāya-Vaiśeṣika realism is founded upon the principle of causality. Causality is held to be a categorical and universal feature of reality. 'The principle of causality is that every event has a cause, that whatever happens is made to happen by a cause. It is believed by common sense to be a necessary and self-evident principle, and the Nyāya-Vaiśeṣika does not hesitate to accept the position'. It is not only a school of staunch realism, but also a great defender of the common-sense view. In the first chapter of one of his major independent works, the *Nyāyakusumāñjali*,[13] he criticises the position of the sceptics and defends causality in his characteristic style, terse, not so perspicuous and polemical. As a modern scholar points out, in his writings we find the fully developed form of the Nyāya theory of causation and his treatment is accepted as definitive by practically all subsequent Naiyāyikas, including those of the new school.[14]

The sole basic argument of Udayana in defence of causality is that effects are all conditional (*sāpekṣa*), for their existence they are dependent upon something else. This is easily proved from their occasionality (*kādācitkatva*), the fact that they are *sometimes* present and *sometimes* absent. It is a fact, palpable and indisputable. Had their existence been unconditional they would have been either ever-present or ever-absent, but not so periodically. Things which are unconditional are either eternal, e.g., *ākāśa* or totally non-existent, e.g., *śaśaśṛṅga*. But effects are of the nature of neither. Therefore, they must be conditional or produced by causes.

Now, the opponent may say, there is no need to admit a cause, for an effect is produced only accidentally, *akasmād eva bhavati*. Udayana, just like the extraordinary dialectician he was, critically examines the statement. Analysing specially the term *akasmāt*, he contends that the statement may at best be interpreted in five different ways yielding five different propositions,[15] but none of them can be logically justified.

Initially, the term *akasmāt* may be taken as a combination of two elements, the negative particle a and an inflected form of the pronoun *kim*.

Thus, in the first instance, we may take the pronoun *kim* in the sense of cause and the negative particle as related to it. Then the statement would be the negation of a cause: an effect is produced without a cause.

Secondly, we may take the pronoun *kim* in its usual sense, and the negative particle as a separate element and as related to the verbal form *bhavati*. Then the statement would be the negation of the production of an effect: an effect is never produced from anything.

Thirdly, we may take the pronoun *kim* in the sense of something other than the effect itself and the negative particle as related to it. Then the statement would mean that an effect is produced from nothing but its own self, the effect itself is its cause.

Fourthly, we may take the pronoun *kim* in the sense of what is real or existent and the negative particle as related to it. Then the statement would mean that an effect is produced by an absolute non-entity.

Fifthly, the term *akasmāt* may be considered a single, unanalysable term, with a distinct meaning. If we take it in the sense of *svabhāva* or essential nature, the meaning of the statement would be that the occasionality of an effect is only due to its inherent nature.

Let us now see how Udayana treats these alternatives. (I quote mostly from Sadananda Bhaduri.)[16]

"The first proposition makes the happening of an event independent of a cause and thus, cannot offer any explanation as to why the event should not happen always. If it is possible for an event to happen at any time without a cause exercising a positive influence upon its happening, there is nothing to prevent the event from happening at any other time, or, for the matter of that, at all other time. In fact, that an event happens at a particular time (and place) and not at any other, can be explained only by pointing out that there is a cause antecedent to it, which being a determinate fact makes the event determinate.

The second proposition simply denies the problem. If there be no happening, there need be no cause. But the happening of an event is a fact testified to by perceptual experience. We observe an event as coming into existence at some time, and not existing previously to that time ... What makes the previous non-existence cease? Why should there be a transition from non-existence to existence? If it be the nature of the event not to happen (and this was admittedly its nature in the past), it cannot be supposed to happen at any time—not even at the time when it is actually found to come into existence.

"The third proposition also fails to make the occurrence of an event intelligible to our reason. If an event were to be produced by itself, it would not be produced at all, because, being non-existent before being produced, it could not conceivably exert any causal influence upon its production. A cause again is held to be necessarily antecedent to its effect. A self-caused thing, thus, would have itself as its own antecedent—which is certainly an inconceivable position, for a single self-identical thing cannot be both the antecedent and the consequent. Besides, such an assumption of absolute identity of cause and effect obviously militates against the common experience that for the *production* of a piece of cloth it is the yarns (existing before the production of the cloth) that are requisitioned, and not the cloth itself".

It is also out of the question to subscribe to the fourth alternative according to which an effect would be produced from an absolute non-entity. An absolute non-entity can in no way specifically determine any particular point of time. Thus, all the points of time would be the same in the absence of a determinant factor and there would be nothing to prevent the appearance of the effect at all points of time or always.

According to the commentators, the fifth alternative is advanced by Svabhāvavādins, who again are generally identified as the Cārvāka sceptics. Their contention is that the postulation of any external condition is not necessary for explaining the occasionality of an effect. It is true that an effect comes into being at a particular moment only. But, why? Because it is the very nature of the thing to be so. There are things which are eternally existent, such as, time and space. There are things which are eternally non-existent, such as, a horn growing on the head of a hare and a flower blooming in the sky. There are also others which are existent and non-existent, existent in their time, and non-existent before and after that time. 'It is not open to us to question why there should be such a diversity of things. But if we still press the question, the only answer is that it is the nature of things to be what they are and behave as they do'.

Even the advocate of causality has ultimately to take refuge in the doctrine of *svabhāva*. Thus, although a weaver or his apparatus is as necessary to the production of a cloth as a number of yarns, yet such is the *nature* of the cloth that after being produced it inheres only in the yarns and not in the weaver or his apparatus. The cloth is held to be incapable, by its very nature, of being related by means of inherence, to any of its causal antecedents except the yarns'. If the specific rule regarding the spatial aspect of an effect is to be explained by *svabhāva,* why should it not be so even for the specific rule regarding the temporal aspect of an effect?

Repudiating the above, Udayana reiterates that in spite of all this there is no escape from the fact that the denial of cause fails to explain the observed occasionality of effects. So he concludes that the contingency (*kādācitkatva*) of an event cannot be explained if the event were independent of a previous limit (*avadhi*) in the shape of an antecedent fact, or were to follow promiscuously from any antecedent fact. Contingency consists in the subsequent existence of a thing which was not existent before. It does not mean mere relation to a particular (subsequent) time, because even eternal things being existent for all time have necessarily a relation to that time. Thus, being in relation to a subsequent time, as qualified by previous non-existence, constitutes the contingency of an event. And such contingency requires a sufficient reason for its being, which is found only in a previous limit, i.e., in an antecedent fact which by existing prior to an event determines when it should begin to be. This antecedent fact is styled the cause of the event'.[17]

Of course, the opponent may still say that what he means by saying that an effect comes into being of its own nature is that there may be a limit, but the limit is not something the effect depends on. To this, Udayana asks, what does the opponent mean by saying that the effect does not depend on the limit? Is it that the limit is not necessary? Surely it is necessary, since in the absence of any regularity of succession a donkey might be the limit of smoke as easily as fire. Or is it that though the relation between limit and effect is necessary, still it is not effective in producing the effect? But what further does the opponent want? Causation just means regular connection between something prior to the effect and the appearance of that effect.

However, without in any way undermining the value of Udayana's contribution, it may be pointed out that the credit of first introducing this argument based on occasionality in defence of causality should go most probably to the Buddhist logician Dharmakīrti. In the third chapter of the *Pramāṇavārtika* (verse 35), while claiming that one of the means for arriving at an inductive generalisation (*avinābhāva-niyama*) is to establish a cause-effect relation between two, he says: 'A thing without a cause (*ahetu*) would be either eternally existent or eternally non-existent since it does not depend on anything else. It is only because of dependence on some condition (*apekṣā*) that it is possible for things to be characterised by occasionality' (*nityaṁ sattvam asattvaṁ vā'hetor anyānapekṣaṇāt/apekṣāto hi bhāvānāṁ kādācitkatvasambhavaḥ //*). The same idea has been expressed in a similar language also in another verse of the first chapter (verse 181) while explaining that *duḥkha* or suffering is something caused and not eternal. The former verse particularly has often been quoted, in the context of the defence of causality, by later commentators, although, as we shall presently see, doubts have been raised about Dharmakīrti's final stand on the acceptance of causality.

In Indian philosophy, the denial of causality is often associated with the school of the Cārvāka sceptics. Unfortunately, no work belonging to this school has come down to us. To form any idea about the views held by it we are dependent upon the summaries of them given in the works of other schools generally for the purpose of showing their illogicality. Vācaspati Miśra, in his *Tātparyaṭīkā* (on NS i. 1.5), while criticising the Buddhist view that causality is one of the means for arriving at an inductive generalisation, has given an account of the stand of the deniers of causality, which may be taken as illustrative of the Cārvāka view.

Thus, the sceptic asks, what is meant by saying that smoke is the effect of fire?

Does it mean simply that smoke appears after the appearance of fire? Then, smoke may be the effect of even an ass, for, in some case, smoke may be found to appear after the appearance of an ass.

Or, the statement may mean that smoke appears after the appearance of fire and fire only. Such is not the case with an ass. Even when an ass is present, but fire is absent, there is no appearance of smoke. Also, even when an ass is absent, but fire as accompanied by wet fuel is present, there is appearance of smoke.

But such as position too is not logically tenable. It is possible to observe in some instances that the appearance and disappearance of smoke agree with the appearance and disappearance of fire. But what guarantee is there that it is so even in other instances, in different places and different times? It is possible to observe, in many instances, that there is an ass and there is smoke, and that there is no ass and there is no smoke. But, still, smoke is not considered an effect of the ass. Why?

Because, in some instance, smoke appears even in the absence of the ass, if there is fire. Thus, even when an ass is present, smoke is considered to be caused by fire. Now, in the same way, it may be argued that though in many instances smoke and its absence are preceded by fire and its absence, in some instance, in spite of the presence of fire, smoke is caused by something else, for example, a goblin (*piśāca*). So long as no determinant is available there is bound to be the scope for a doubt.

Of course, one defending causality may protest and say that wherever smoke has been observed it has been observed to be followed by only fire accompanied by wet fuel, but never by a goblin. Smoke is something occasional and for its presence it must be dependent upon some condition (*nimitta*). It is only proper that it should have for its condition only that after the appearance of which it is observed to appear, that with which it has not been observed to have any deviation (*vyabhicāra*); it would be improper to take for its condition something with which it is observed to have deviation (e.g., an ass) or something by which it is never observed to be preceded (e.g., a goblin). If fire be not its condition, how is it that smoke is not observed in any instance to be without fire? Thus, if fire be its condition, how can there be a doubt to the effect that smoke may be present without fire? If an effect be without a condition, it would be either eternally present or eternally absent, since it would have to depend on nothing for its presence, but it would never be occasional. When it is said that smoke is the effect of fire it is meant that smoke appears only and only (eva) after fire. If it could appear even after something else (than fire), this condition of 'only and only after' could not be satisfied, and smoke would not be the effect of fire. But it could neither be the effect of something else, for it would not be something appearing only and only after something else as it is observed to be appearing after fire. Thus, in fact, smoke would be something without a cause. But then, its occasionality would remain unexplained.

To the above, the sceptic replies that all this could be acceptable only if it could be proved that smoke is the effect of fire, that smoke is followed by only and only fire. It is true that smoke is observed to be neither without fire nor preceded by a goblin. Still, it is possible that smoke is really the effect of a goblin; in the instances concerned, fire is present not as the cause of smoke, but only due to some accidental circumstances of its own, just like the ass in some instances. Thus, there is no means to dispel the doubt that in some instances smoke may be occasional, in spite of the absence of fire, being due to some other cause.

But the most scathing criticism of causality comes from the uncompromising Yogācāra idealists, specially the commentators of Dharmakīrti. Dharmakīrti's own position is somewhat difficult to assess, for he seems to assume a dual personality. As a logician he is a Sautrāntika believing in the reality of the external world, and as he defends induction he also defends causality. But as a metaphysician he is a Yogācāra believing in the reality of only consciousness (*vijñāna*) and has no hesitation in criticising the notion of causality. The subject has been excellently dealt with in an article by my teacher Prof. H.K. Ganguli.[18] I shall quote from him the observations of Manorathanandin, a commentator of the *Pramāṇavārttika*:

"It is generally supposed that the causal relation between the seed and the sprout is grasped through the cognition of *anvaya* and *vyatireka,* that is, the positive relation between the sprout and the seed and the contrapositive relation between the absence of the seed and the absence of the sprout. But the cognition of any relation between the two is impossible. One perceives A and also perceives B. There are two separate perceptions and two separate percepts. There is no cognition of relation between the two perceptions or between the two percepts. Neither the perceptions nor the percepts bear any stamp of togetherness (*jñānayoḥ jñeyayoś ca sāhityābhāvāt*). It should not be argued that what is relevant to the causal relation is not togetherness, but sequence, and that we perceive the sequence all right. One cannot perceive sequence which means perceiving 'before and after'. When we perceive A it is presented as present, when we perceive B it is also presented as present. It is only after perceiving B that we say 'A happened before'. But this 'happening of A before' is not at all a constituent of the given percept B. Neither is the "happening of B after A" a part of the percept B. Nor is the "coming after of B" a part of the percept A. One cannot resurrect the dead past and infuse it into the pure 'given' of the perceptual present. One cannot also stretch one's hand to the unborn future and drag it into the 'given' of the moment. So 'before' or 'after' cannot belong to the perceptually given which is always presentable only as the present. So it is not possible to have any occasion to perceive the *before* and the *after*".

Prajñākaragupta, the celebrated author of *Vārtikālaṅkāra,* the vast commentary on the *Pramāṇavārttika*, also tries his best to demolish the notion of causality, subjecting it to vigorous criticism from various standpoints. Thus, for example, he argues:

"If the advocates of causality stick to the notion of necessity, this relation can be shown as working both ways, that is, the cause is as much necessarily related to the effect as the effect is to the cause. Just as there is no effect without the cause, so there is no cause without the effect. A cause is a cause only in so far as there is an effect caused by it .... This relation of reciprocal inviolability between the cause and the effect imposes on them some sort of mutual indebtedness for their being. Hence, what one is pleased to call the effect, coming after what one is pleased to call the cause going before, may be equally legitimately considered as the future cause responsible for the past effect. Since in the structure of sequence both the cause and the effect are necessarily related to each other, one is amply justified to equally claim that what comes after causes what goes before. In a flowing time series, if there be at all such a thing, notions of 'before' and 'after' are only matters of convention, so that the series may be easily conceived as moving in the reverse order".

One of his arguments showing the failure of *anvaya* and *vyatireka* in determining the causal relation is:

"Moreover, the *vyatireka* 'if there is no fire, then there is no smoke' is by implication equivalent to the *anvaya* 'there is smoke, if and only if there is fire'. Unless this relation of 'if and only if' is established by any instrument of cognition, the *vyatireka* or the exclusive contrapositive, involving the 'if then' relation between two negations, also cannot be established. Thus, *vyatireka* depends on *anvaya*. Again, the *anvaya* involving the relation 'if and only if' is logically equivalent to 'if not, then not', which is the expression of *vyatireka* relation. Hence, the relation of 'if and only if' cannot be established without establishing the relation of 'if not, then not'. Thus, both *anvaya* and *vyatireka* sink together being vitiated by the fallacy of mutual dependence".

As is well known, in the philosophy of the West, the view of Hume on causality has been much discussed. He argues that no necessary or real connection can be established between two events. Experience shows nothing more than the coexistence and succession of phenomena and events. It provides us with no ground for transforming perceived succession in time into causal succession, for substituting *must* for *is*, for interpreting the observed connection of fact into a necessary connection which always eludes observation. "From the fact that I have seen a given apple fall ten times to the ground, I infer that all the apples in the world do the same when loosened...... I infer further that this has always been the case, and will continue to be so to all eternity. Where is the intermediate link between the proposition 'I have found that such an object has always been attended with such an effect' and this other, 'I foresee that other objects which are, in appearance, similar, will be attended with similar effects? "From the habitual perception of two events in connection (sunshine and heat) arises the mental determination to think of the second when we perceive the first, and, anticipating the senses, to count on its appearance".[19]

Thus, it has been pointed out that, on the Indian side, the denial of causality as ascribed to the Cārvāka sceptics has a close resemblance to this position. "The Cārvāka, therefore, like Hume, has sought to make out that the commonsense demand for a cause with regard to an event is only due to the habit of connecting two events in thought which happen to be found conjoined in experience in a large number of instances. There is no logical or ontological *nexus* between the two events. ... With the Cārvāka, therefore, as with Hume, the so-called causal relation is the empirical result of association; it is grounded in our thought, and not in the things".

On the other hand, the Yogācāra critics of causality seems to go a step further. We shall again quote from Prof. Ganguli's article:

"It is clear from the above that Hume challenges others to show how the reality of a necessary relation can be discovered by experience. Experience can give only contiguity and succession and not the so called necessity. The difference from Manorathanandin is obvious. Not to speak of a necessity, he challenges the very possibility of contiguity and succession being observed in experience. Moreover, if we have followed his arguments carefully, constancy or regularity too cannot be experienced. Hume says, 'I have found that such an object has always been attended with such an effect'. But Manoratha's arguments are directed both against *always* and *attended with*. One perceives A and also perceives B. But there is nothing in the pure object of perception which may correspond to the meaning of *always*. It has already been shown by Manoratha that succession cannot be a matter of perception. Hence, to be attended with in the sense of temporal contiguity cannot be found in experience.

This extremely defiant radicality of the Buddhists, in some cases at least, shows that they have gone further than merely anticipating Hume regarding the problem of causal relation".

We have already remarked that in Indian philosophy the Nyāya-Vaiśeṣikas are the most ardent defenders of causality. Their final argument in defence of causality is an appeal to uncontradicted, universal, human behaviour (*loka-vyavahāra*).

"The belief in causation is almost an instinct with the human mind. Without it, all practical activity would become impossible. Whatever we do, we do with a purpose, and a purposive action implies a belief or an expectation that a particular course of action will never fail to be followed by a particular result" (*evaṁ kārya-kāraṇabhāvābhāve pravṛtti-nivṛttī na syātām, tathā ca nirīhaṁ jagaj jāyeta, na hiṣṭa-sādhanatājñānam antareṇa pravṛttiḥ, aniṣṭa-sādhanatā-jñānam antareṇa nivṛttiḥ*).[20]

"Scepticism, however, ingenious and powerful, cannot break down this belief. The sceptic is a professional disbeliever, but he gets involved in self-contradiction when he seeks to apply his disbelief universally. As Udayana rightly points out, one can doubt or disbelieve only so long as one does not contradict or stultify one's position as a rational being. It is not legitimate for any one to question the necessity of causal relation when he *invariably* kindles fire to produce smoke, or takes food to satisfy hunger, or uses arguments to carry conviction to the minds of others. The fact is that even the sceptic lives and acts as any rational being does; he, thus, commits himself to the acceptance of a world in which no event can happen except under conditions with which its happening is necessarily connected"[21] (*tad eva hy āśaṅkyeta yasminn āśaṅkyamāne sva-kriyā-vyāghātādayo doṣā nāvatarantīti loka-maryādā. na hi hetuphala-bhāvo na bhaviṣyatīti śaṅkitum api śakyate. tathā sati śaṅkaiva na syāt, sarvaṁ mithyā bhaviṣyatīty ādivat*).[22]

Of course, the critics of causality may protest that this criticism is lost upon them. In so far as they behave as practical men of the world, there is no disbelief in the empirical validity of causality. Their doubt of causality is based on metaphysical grounds. Hume remarks: 'My practice, you say, refutes my doubts. But you mistake the purport of my question. As an agent I am satisfied on the point;

but as a philosopher, who has some share of curiosity, I will not say scepticism, I want to learn the foundation of this inference'.[23]

Refering to the above, Prajñākara also replies, well, then, we come to the point. "When the recognised instruments of valid cognition fail to establish any reality corresponding to a widely prevalent idea, it is quite legitimate to hold that the said idea is only a makebelieve or logical fiction (*saṁvṛti*) constructed by intellect, by which we carry on our behaviour in a world of 'as if'. Thus, causal efficiency is a fictive apprehension."

The whole question thus seems to boil down to this. How much credibility should we grant to the criterion of practice or *loka-vyavahāra*? Should we recognise it as the most valid means for determining truth? Or, should we say that it is the source of purely a kind of provisional truth, *saṁvṛti-satya* or *vyavahārika-satya,* called forth by the exigencies of practical life, whereas the ultimate truth, philosophical wisdom or *pāramārthika-satya* is something quite different and higher, truer than this ordinary truth? And thus, causality is true in some sense, but false in another. But, then, we shall be led to one of the fundamental questions of philosophy—the irreconcilable conflict between realism and idealism.

Notes and References

1. *Śvetāśvatara*, i. 1-2.
2. See, for example, *Tattvasaṅgraha* (verses 106ff) and Kamalaśīla's commentary. Also, G. Kaviraj, in Saraswati Bhavan Studies, ii. 95.
3. Śaṅkara on *Śvetāśvatara*, i. 2.
4. Śaṅkarānanda, Dīpikā, *ibid.*
5. *Kalpataru* on *Vedāntasūtra*, ii. 1.33.
6. *Tarkarahasyadīpikā* (Asiatic Society ed.), p. 15.
7. *Ibid.*, p. 13.
8. Outlines of Indian Philosophy, p. 104.
9. *Ibid.*, pp. 103-04.
10. It is an accepted view even in Indian philosophy that in the true sense *sāmagrī* is the cause, since its appearance is followed immediately and invariably by the appearance of the effect. But it is not so in the case of an individual cause, which is called 'cause' in a secondary sense. Thus, in many texts, a distinction is made between *nirupacarita-kāraṇa* and *upacarita-kāraṇa*. (cf. the notion of sufficient condition and necessary condition).
11. *Vaiśeṣika-sūtra*, ix. 2.1.
12. *Animittato bhāvotpattiḥ kaṇṭaka-taikṣṇyādi-darśanāt.*
13. First *stavaka*, verses 4-6 and auto-commentary on them.
14. Potter, *The Encyclopedia of Indian Philosophies*, Vol. ii, p. 54.
15. These five propositions have not been mentioned by Udayana himself in so many words. They are worked out by the commentators. That Udayana had them in mind is, however, beyond doubt, for the fact is corroborated by his way of refutation (in verse i. 5).
16. Sadananda Bhaduri, *Studies in Nyāya-Vaiśeṣika Metaphysics*, pp. 273ff.
17. *Ibid.*
18. *Our Heritage*, Special Number, 150th Anniversary Volume, Govt. Sanskrit College, Calcutta, 1979, *Dharmakirti and His Disciples on the Notion of Causality*, pp. 313-327.
19. Falckenberg, *History of Modern Philosophy* (Calcutta 1962 ed.), pp. 224ff.
20. *Upaskāra* on VS i. 2.1.
21. Bhaduri, *ibid*, p. 279.
22. *Nyāyakusumāñjali*, auto-commentary on iii. 7.
23. Quoted, Bhaduri, *ibid*, p. 280fn.

13

Relation of Causality and Gautama's Concept of God

Nandita Bandyopadhyay

The creator of the world could not come into the history of human thought without creating a problem for his own existence. In the nascent days of theistic speculation the Vedic seer sees the problem in the following shape : If God, the Viśvakarman, created the world where had he stayed before the world was made? Wherefrom did he got the materials for building the world ? [*Ṛgveda* X. 81] The reply is short and apparently simple—God is omnipotent, omniscient and omnipresent. (So the question does not arise.) But the problem did arise, continued to arise and does arise.

The Nyāya philosophy, considered to be the most rational among the theistic systems, inherits the problem, tries to tackle it in its own way, and in the process, has got to modify the meaning of Divine omnipotence by rejecting the sense of absolute independence.[1] It is not then surprising that God enters the *Nyāyadarśana* of Gautama rather from a negative angle as a pointer to the decision that the Supreme efficient cause, quite justifiable, cannot be regarded as absolutely independent in the sense of not depending on anything external to Himself. He, however powerful, cannot simply will the world into existence out of nothing but Himself. The three *sūtras* which directly deal with God in Gautama's work together drive at this conclusion—

(a) *īśvaraḥ kāraṇam, puruṣakarmāphalyadarśanāt* (*NS* 4/1/19)

(b) *na, puruṣakarmābhāve phalāniṣpatteḥ* (4/1/20)

(c) *tatkāritatvād ahetuḥ* (4/1/21)

A confusion has been introduced into the plain meaning of these *sūtras* by Vātsyāyana's introductory remark—"*athāpara aha*". The context is the origin of the world. The preceding view, rejected after examination, seems to refer to the nihilist position that the world has come out of nothing. It means that the cipher is the basic material of the world. But it is difficult to equate this view with that of *Mādhyamika* nihilist according to whom the effect is as much a void as the cause. So it is possible that the view rejected in this context is that of some other atheist, or, may be, some sceptics who think it futile to delve into the origin of the world. The *sūtra*, *īśvaraḥ kāraṇam* etc. comes as a positive contrast to the above view. It is not enough to say that the world cannot come out of nothing. What is required is a positive answer to the positive question—what is then the positive cause of the world ? The reply is attempted in the *sūtra*—"*īśvaraḥ kāraṇam*". But when Vātsyāyana, in his interpretation, introduces the *sūtra* with the remark 'someother says', the question naturally crops up—who is this someother ? Is he the Naiyāyika alone ? It does not seem so from the mode of interpretation offered by Vātsyāyana, Uddyotakara and Vācaspati. To interpret '*aparaḥ*' as '*na paraḥ*', (i.e., 'not alien' and hence the Naiyāyika himself), as has been done by MM Ganganath Jha in his *Khadyota* commentary, seems to be too artificial.[2] The term '*aparaḥ*' seems to refer to the theists in general as a contrast to the atheists whose view has been rejected just before. Vātsyāyana and Uddyotakara on the one hand and Vācaspati on the other approach the three *sūtras* concerned from different angles though they reach the same conclusion. Let us have a look at the plain meaning of the three *sūtras*.

The first *sūtra* which introduces God as the creative cause of the world stands in direct opposition to the immediately preceding examination of the view that the world has come out of nothing. The first *sūtra* is a general statement of the theistic position that the world has a conscious creator. A reason has been attached to bear out the proposition about Divine causality. The reason here is more interesting than the proposition itself, for it brings into prominence a relation between Divine actions and human actions. The exact literal meaning of the *sūtra* is as follows : God is the cause, because human actions are (often) found to be barren. A person doing something to get a result often fails to get it despite his effort. This shows that the attainment of the result of a person's action is dependent on somebody else. If a man were able to achieve and enjoy the result of his action without depending on any assistance from someone else, his action could not have been futile at all. The main purpose of human action is attainment of happiness. But it is not at all rare that a man does something with immaculate precision and preparation with all possible assistance from mundane sources, yet he fails to get the desired result. The action ending in a fiasco only brings misery to the man. Again, sometimes an action is successful, leading to happiness. So happy and unhappy results of human actions point to a Divine Being Whose frown or favour decides the nature of the result of a man's deed. The second *sūtra* (4/1/20) challenges the theistic proposition with a counter-reason. The *sūtra* literally means—No, because the desired result does not come forth without an action on the part of a man. The idea involved in this challenging position has been brought out by Uddyotakara as follows—God is conceived as the Omnipotent Being. Now if it is so, His very omnipotence should have been enough to make a man happy or unhappy without waiting for his actions. Thus human actions would have totally lost their relevance and all men should have been sitting inactive throughout the cycle of creation. That would mean that none should and would have attained salvation because, according to theistic theory, man has to exert himself for salvation. Now all this exertion becomes meaningless, because the Omnipotent God need not wait for any help from any direction. The implication is that Divine omnipotence does away with the very relevance of human action. Moreover, Divine essence being uniform in nature His action too should have been uniform. That means that all His creatures should have been either happy or miserable without their actions having anything to do with their fate.

Now, to meet this atheistic objection, the theist may argue that to bestow the fruit, sweet or bitter, God has to do according to the actions of man. He who does good deeds is rewarded with happiness by Divine grace, and a doer of bad deeds is awarded sufferings by Divine justice. Thus the creation of the world crowded with happy and unhappy people is done by God no doubt, but quite in accordance with the nature of human actions. So omnipotence of God does not mean a whimsical creator, but a supreme judge of human destiny. God has to create the world in order to ensure that creatures may reap the fruits of the actions which were done in their last birth in the last cycle of creation. Thus creation is a display of Divine justice.

This argument does not carry much weight with the atheist for the following reason. By this argument the theists have to admit that God, while generating an effect, is dependent on some other cause which we call the actions of his creatures. A person cannot produce which he himself requires for producing a result. This is approved by our commonsense experience. A potter does not produce the wheel and the rod which are the implements, and earth which is the material cause of the pot. In other words a human creator like a potter has to dpend on the auxiliary causes and the material cause which are external to himself. In that case God has nothing to do with the production of actions which it depends on for conferring the result. This dubious method of escape from the difficulty creates a serious new problem for the theists, for God's omnipotence is now sacrificed to the extent of His dependence on some external causal factors like human deeds. It comes to this that if even God is the cause of the world, He is not the only cause. Had He been all-powerful His own self would have been enough for creation. But He has to depend on something else and so becomes only a cause among causes. Thus He is not that omnipotent cause, and if not omnipotent, He is no God at all. This contention of Pūrvapakṣa is explained by Uddyotakara in the following remarks : "*atheśvaraḥ kāraṇabhedānuvidhanena kāryaṁ nirvartayati, yadapekṣate tanna karotīti prāptam, na hi kulālo daṇḍādi karoti, evaṁ karmasāpekṣaścediśvaro jagadutpattikāraṇaṁ syāt, karmānīśvaro'nīśvaraḥ syāt* " (*NV* p. 456).

The third *sūtra* provides a defence for the first one by clarifying its meaning so as to show that the counter-reason offered by the atheists in the second *sūtra* does not stand. The plain meaning of the third *sūtra* is this that the opponent's reason, '*puruṣakarmābhāve phalāniṣpatteḥ*', is no reason at all *(ahetuḥ)*, because human efforts are also determined by God *(tatkāritatvāt = īśvarakāritatvāt)*. Here God's causality is interpreted in such a way that His dependence on human actions does not detract from Divine power. Vātsyāyana comments that God favours human efforts by helping the desired results to follow. When God withdraws His help man's efforts become fruitless. Uddyotakara explains that to bear fruit an action's influence takes some time to mature *(vipākakāla)* and when God notices this maturity He confers the result on man.[3] Uddyotakara then clearly states that God is only the Supreme efficient cause. He is neither the material cause, nor the auxiliary cause. A creative cause utilises other causes for achieving the result, just as a weaver deftly handles the yarn and the loom for weaving the cloth. Material cause of the world is the atoms (which are as eternal as God) and the auxiliary causes are the human actions. God creates the world by co-ordinating these two types of causes which would have been useless if God would not have handled them for the purpose of creation. So God as the conscious creator is the Supreme cause on which other causes which are unconscious depend for realising their utility. Thus in the final analysis, it is the other causes which are dependent on God for having their causal character. In the field of human creativity it is a matter of common experience that the unconscious material things go to shape an effect only when they are carefully handled by a conscious human agent. The Supreme conscious Being is infinitely more than a man. So what is true in the case of man as regards the relation between a conscious agent and an unconscious material thing is infinitely truer in the case of God. Thus omnipotence of God is not really compromised by His dependence on man's actions, for here dependence only comes to mean that God consciously utilises some unconscious primary elements to yield an effect, which is the world. (According to the Naiyāyikas an action or its influence, i.e. *adṛṣṭa,* is unconscious in itself). The existence of these unconscious elements becomes totally irrelevant without being moved by the Prime Mover.

It is apparent from Uddyotakara's interpretation that the bare general statement of Divine causality such as '*īśvaraḥ kāraṇam*' cannot stand the challenge of the atheists without modification. The statement, '*īśvaraḥ kāraṇam* ', by itself does not make it clear what sort of cause He is—the prime efficient cause or the material cause or the both. Here Uddyotakara leaves no doubt that theism to be rational cannot accept the position that God is both the efficient cause and the material cause. Such an assumption goes against universal human experience. Nowhere in the world we find a conscious creative agent who is at the same time the material of creation. A potter is not himself the material of the pot, nor does he create earth to shape the effect. Even theistic speculations, however high-soaring, have ultimately to conform to basic human experience. Hence we get the dictum—*dṛṣṭānusāriṇī kalpanā* (speculation should be consistent with experience).

The problem of God first raised by the Vedic seer involves a dilemma—If God is omnipotent, omniscient and omnipresent it would mean that before the creation there was nothing else than God, which means that nothing can be co-eternal with God. Hence absolute independence of God demands that He finds the material and implements of creation in Himself. Before the creation there could have been no other cause, whether material or auxiliary, except one God. It is equivalent to saying that God simply wields the world into existence out of nothing but Himself. Such a proposition may satisfy the extreme theism by recognising absolute independence of God, but at the risk of summarily rejecting all evidence of human experience. Thus the dilemma boils down to this : If omnipotence means absolute independence God must have produced the world out of nothing but His will, which goes against the dictum—*dṛṣṭānusāriṇī kalpanā.* If you follow the dictum, Divine omnipotence in the absolute sense has to be sacrificed, even with the grudging recognition that to create the world God had to depend on something else which he had not created.

It goes to the credit of the Naiyāyikas that they are rational enough to accept the second alternative even at the risk of compromising the creator's omnipotence in deference to the demand of human experience. They have clearly seen that the first alternative in its bid to save absolute independence of God would turn Him into an irrational being.

Yet Uddyotakara is keenly conscious that his valiant attempts to make the Prime Mover a rational being are not at all free from difficulties which still remain to be solved. After going to establish the well-known theistic proposition that the unconscious material world presupposes an intelligent creator Uddyotakara again has reverted to the question whether God is quite independent or dependent on something else for creation. His dependence on eternal atoms is recognised without the least hesitation, for the Biblical idea of creation, 'Let there be light and there was light', is revolting to rationalism. But any further dependence such as dependence on human deeds and ensuing *adṛṣṭa (dharma* and *adharma)* seriously compromises the supremacy of Divine causality. If man is to be saddled with moral responsibility he must have a fair amount of independence in his action. If his actions are also willed by God the moral responsibility should, squarely rest on God alone and man should be totally absolved of the responsibility for the so-called virtues and vices. Again, if man is completely independent in his action one can legitimately ask—How a creature of God can go astray under the watchful eyes of an all-seeing God ? How can God allow a man to commit a sin ? Granted that man is independent in his action, yet why should one abuse the independence by doing something bad and why should someone else put independence into right use by doing something good ? Whence does come this difference between good and evil ? If you say that it is purely accidental it is same as to say that something may come out of nothing.

After admitting, without reservation, God's dependence on eternal and uncreated atoms Uddyotakara seems to be at pains to resist any further erosion into independence of God in the process to suggest the compromise in order to explain the relation between God and human deeds. It is not that human deeds and *dharmādharma* or *adṛṣṭa* are totally uncreated by God. The dictum, 'one does not create the instruments of creation' *(yena karoti tasyākartā)* is not absolute *(nāyam ekāntaḥ)*. A person, expert in a good number of crafts, makes a chisel with some other instruments, then makes a rod with that chisel and then makes a pot with the help of that rod. Similarly, God creates material bodies of living beings along with pleasure and pain with the help of *dharma* and *adharma* pursuing the souls from the previous birth for the previous cycle of creation. He also creates *adharma* and *dharma* according to good and bad intentions of beings. Good and bad intentions are again created by means of the memory of pleasure and pain and their instrumental causes experienced by different persons in the previous birth or the previous cycle. Thus the same maker may make both the final product and the instruments of production in turn gradually. Hence the dictum that the maker of something does not make the instruments of making falls through. But what about the first creation of the instruments or the first appearance of human deeds and *dharmādharma* ? Let us admit that actions, *adṛṣṭa* and creation are caught in a chain. But how did God begin the chain ? With what instruments did He create the first instruments of creation? Does the first instrument come out of nothing ? God had to begin His creation at some time. With what instrumental help did He begin? This is a very tough question and Uddyotakara, as the last resort, has to fall back on the eternity of the cycles of creation. Human deeds, *adṛṣṭa* and creation revolve in a cycle which is an endless series having no beginning. In the sense of this revolving series the world is eternal. Hence God's relation with this eternal series is also eternal. So the very question of the first creation and the first instrument of creation does not arise. Let us reserve our comment on this solution for the time being and proceed to the next formidable problem — the purpose and necessity of creation.

Is this creation completely purposeless ? What necessity could have prompted God to the act of creation ? It is a universal human experience that no conscious person except perhaps a sportive child or a lunatic does anything without some purpose. God is the perfect Being. Perfection means fulfilment of everything. So He cannot have any purpose or necessity to fulfil. Simple pleasure cannot be a purpose, for there cannot be any pleasure unattained in the case of Perfect God. For this very reason one should not argue that God creates the world in order to display His infinite power *(vibhūtikhyāpana)*, for it does not detract from His Divinity if there is no such display.

Uddyotakara's reply falls in the expected line that it is the very nature of God to create. He cannot stay without creating. Creativeness is a part of the Divine Essence *(svabhāva)*. So the question 'why' is irrelevant. The earth holds natural objects and beings on her surface. Carrying this burden is a part of her very nature. It is senseless to ask why she does so. Similar is the case with God.

Again the question crops up : If creation is a part of Divine Essence God could not have stood a moment without creation. So there would have been no cessation of creation *(nivṛtti)*. That means that creation would have been a permanent affair, and the world would have been a permanent thing. The gradual creation of the world in a sequence of actions also becomes inexplicable. God would have created the world in a single moment. If the world is not permanent there should have been a complete new world every moment. Yet this does not happen. But why ? Uddyotakara replies that God is not only a creator, but an intelligent creator. So He has to create according to the gradual availability of the instrumental or auxiliary causes like man's action and consequent *dharmādharma*. God has to work in conformity to the sequential appearance of these auxiliary causes. It is to be noted that even in this last leg of reply God's dependence on the auxiliary causes has got to be accepted. Uddyotakara has clearly stated that, while creating the world, God has to rely on and wait for the maturity of *adṛṣṭa (sa khalu pravartamāno dharmādharmayoḥ paripākakālam apekṣate —NV*, p. 463). The appeal to the concept of God's eternal relation to an eternal series of cyclic creations is more a clever device than a convincing argument.

Vācaspati's Interpretation

Vācaspati approaches the *sūtra "iśvaraḥ kāraṇam"* etc. from a different angle. We have already seen how the Vedic seer raised the problem of God. Since God is omnipotent, omniscient and omnipresent the question of His dependence on any external materials and auxiliary causes does not arise, for it would heavily curtail His absolute independence. Apart from that it goes against the very supposition that God created the whole world. The basic constituents of the world are supposed by theists like the Naiyāyikas to be the eternal atoms of matter. Thus God has to depend on something else which is equally eternal as Himself. God cannot create the basis of the world. He can only shape and reshape the world only on the basis of some eternal and hence uncreated elementary constituents. He has no power over the existence of these constituents which do not at all stay on His will or mercy. In this respect God comes nearer to a dependent human creator. It is an absurd theism which recognises God as an absolute creator with the simultaneous recognition that He cannot Himself create the constituents of the world. Along with this, if it is further admitted that God for His creation has to depend on the eternal cyclical series of *karma* and *adṛṣṭa* of the selves, independence of God is further eroded. Uddyotakara's laborious explanation of God's eternal relation with an eternal series of auxiliary causes can only mean an eternal interdependence. But interdependence is also a sort of dependence, for it amounts to admitting that perfect independence of God is impossible.

Hence a consistent theist, true to the proposition that God is all-powerful, cannot but subscribe to the extreme position that God is not only a primary efficient cause, but the only efficient cause and that this efficient cause must also be the sufficient cause without depending on anything other than itself. This can only mean that God creates both the materials and the instruments of creation, which, amounts to the proposition that God creating out of nothing is Himself both the creative and the material cause. This comes to be the meaning of absolute independence. Now Vācaspati thinks that the *sūtra 'īśvaraḥ kāraṇam'* states a proposition about such a causality as in which an absolutely independent creative cause (*nirapekṣanimitta-kāraṇa*), as a logical consequence, leads to the identity of the creative and the material cause. Hence Vācaspati approaches the *sūtra* (4/1/19) as a statement of the extreme theistic position that God is also the material cause of the universe *(īśvaropādānakāraṇatva)*.

With an eye to the various prevalent philosophical traditions of those days Vācaspati shows that God may be the material cause of the world in two different ways — (1) according to the theory of *Brahmapariṇāma* and (2) according to the theory of *Brahmavivarta*. In the former conception *Brahman* or *īśvara* transforms Himself into the phenomenal manifold which is sometimes called the material body of God (e.g. in Rāmānuja's philosophy). Transformation does not mean destruction and hence does not compromise eternity of the primordial principle. God consciously evolves the material world out of Himself along with the individual selves. In this sense matter and individual consciousness are two different modes of Divine expression. In suport of the view that transformation is not annihilation, Vācaspati quotes an well-known observation of Patañjali in the *Paspaśāhnika* of *Mahābhāṣya—"Yasmin tattvaṁ na vihanyate tadapinityam".* (That is also eternal which is not destroyed in its essence, while undergoing transformation.)

The theory of *Brahmavivartavāda* presents a very complicated conception of relation between God and the world. It is the theory of Advaita Vedānta as presented by the school of Vivarta-vādins. *Vivarta* technically means, in contradistinction to *pariṇāma,* an illusory manifestation of something real on which something unreal is superimposed as a matter of false identity covering the nature of reality. A ribbon in darkness is falsely identified to be a snake by a passer-by. Here the ribbon, being the substratum on which the false snake is superimposed, is conceived by the Advaitins as the material cause of the illusory snakes. Since it is the real ribbon which assumes the false serpentine appearance, it must be a cause of the illusory snake. The Advaitins call it a material cause in a peculiar sense. Now, by elevating such a phenomenon of common illusion to the cosmic level the Advaitins conceive the Brahman as the material cause of the world because the world being unreal according to them, the Brahman is supposed to assume the false cosmic appearance.[4] The Brahman is one absolute reality. The world is neither absolutely real, nor absolutely unreal,—not absolutely real for it is considered to be negated by a final awakening of wisdom, nor absolutely unreal for it maintains a protracted stable appearance till the moment of negation. In this sense an object of illusory appearance is beyond definition by absolute existence or absolute non-existence, and hence is beyond both the categories. In Advaita terminology falsity is this indefinability *(anirvacanīyatva)* by the extremes of existence and non-existence *(sadasadvilakṣaṇatva)*. It is only a tentative or relative reality waiting to be negated by the final knowledge of Brahman.

Any rational explanation of this cosmic illusion is impossible to find except the assumption that there is a cosmic principle of illusion *(anādi-avidyā)* operating from eternity. This cosmic *avidyā* is also false and indefinable since the knowledge of the Brahman dispels it for good. The false world is the false transformation of this false *avidyā*. In this sense the world is *avidyāpariṇāma* on the one hand and *Brahmavivarta* on the other. Thus, in the final analysis, the world is the product of two material causes of different types. The one is the substratum Brahman assuming an illusory cosmic appearance and the other is the false cosmic *avidyā* undergoing a false transformation in the shape of the false world. Assuming this fundamental position of the Advaitins, creation itself turns out to be a false process. Yet in deference to the theistic demands pronounced in sacred texts and to the gripping faith nourished by the common people, the Advaitins have got to introduce God and find a place for Him in its philosophical scheme. So it is assumed that the Brahman, falsely conditioned by cosmic *avidyā* assumes the false role of a creator who is called God. Thus the relation between the Brahman and the world is mediated by a so-called creative God who is nothing but the Brahman in the false role a creator. When *avidyā* is finally dispelled by supreme wisdom both God and the world are gone with the same wind. The pure Brahman, the 'single basic reality, is unqualified and unrelated. Hence from the fundamental standpoint, the very question of causality cannot arise in Vivartavāda. It does arise only from the tentative or *vyāvahārika* standpoint and the causality of God is a part of the *vyāvahārika* world which stands to be liquidated in the final count. Vācaspati in *Tātparyaṭīka* has not elaborated the position of the Vivartavādins which he has done thoroughly in his *Bhāmatī* commentary on Śaṅkara's *Brahmasūtrabhāṣya*. In the context of the *Nyāyasūtra* concerned Vācaspati has not touched upon the fundamental position of the Vivartavādins and has kept unsaid the most basic point that, fundamentally speaking, God's causal relation with the world is a part of cosmic unreality.

Remembering this important point concerning *Vivartavāda* let us turn to Vācaspati's criticism of both *Pariṇāmavāda* and *Vivartavāda* from the Naiyāyika standpoint. According to *Brahmapariṇāmavāda* Brahman is the material cause of the universe in the sense that He transforms Himself in the shape of the world. Now Vācaspati goes on to show how the second *Nyāya sūtra* concerned (4/1/20) repudiates *iśvarapariṇāmavāda*. The question that arises in this context is—whether God's transformation is total or partial. A total transformation again would compel the *Pariṇāmavādins* to admit willy-nilly that the Brahman has parts. For the Brahmavādins it would be a proposition too atrocious to be entertained.

Vivartavāda fares no better in this regard. According to the Vivartavādins the world has only an illusory existence. An illusion is a superimposition which occurs when we have only a general but not a specific notion of the substratum. In the shell-silver illusion, for example, a person who is aware of the substratum as a shell cannot take it to be silver at the same time. He entertains the illusion only when he notices in a general way that there is something glittering before him, but does not notice the specific qualities which differentiate a shell from silver. Presence of general knowledge and absence of specific knowledge are jointly responsible for the emergence of an illusory knowledge. Now the Advaitins hold that the Brahman is self-manifest. This self-revelation is termed *svasamvedanapratyakṣa*. Such a self-revelation being the perennial essence of Brahman which suffers no division into parts, then how is it possible for someone to notice only the general character of Brahman and miss its specific character? Brahman being partless, self-revelation brooks no part and as such it should be a total revelation or no revelation at all. Hence there cannot be a cosmic illusion in wihch Brahman is falsely revealed as the world and not correctly as in Itself. In other words *avidyā* cannot partly screen Brahman leaving other part shining.

Thus with the failure of both *Vivartavāda* and *Pariṇāmavāda* the concept of God as the material cause has to be given up and a consistent theist has to fall back on God only as the first efficient cause. So again we come back to the question whether God is *nirapekṣa* or *sāpekṣa* (absolutely independent or dependent to some extent). Futility of human action does not go to establish absolute independence of God, for no result can be achieved without human action. This, according to Vācaspati, is the meaning of the second *sūtra*. The implication is clear. If God could act with complete independence He could have bestowed the result without waiting for the man to act. But man has to act himself. It means that Divine action has to depend on human action. In that case let man be the architect of his own destiny, making Divine action irrelevant and redundant. So one has to choose between the two alternatives. If God is independent in His action man's action becomes irrelevant and if man has to act God's action becomes a dispensable luxury. But the necessity of human action is unquestionable and this makes God's causal action questionable and redundant. This is how Vācaspati looks at the problem.

The third *sūtra*, according to Vācaspati, demolishes three theories about God—(1) *Brahmapariṇāmavāda* (2) *Brahmavivartavāda* and (3) *Nirapekṣeśvara-kāraṇatāvāda*. As a residue, God is retained as the *sāpekṣakāraṇa* of the universe, i.e., as the first efficient cause creating the universe according to human action in the previous cycle of creation. We have already seen in Uddyotakara's explanation how, nevertheless, God's omnipotence can be saved by conceiving that the series of *karman, adṛṣṭa* and *phala* along with the series of cycles is without any beginning. Hence objection against Divine causality embodied in the propositional reasoning 'no human action, no result' can stand only if God is considered as the absolutely independent efficient cause. But the reasoning does not stand *(ahetu)* if the relation between God and man's action is conceived as eternal. The idea is this that eternal interdependence does not detract from Divine independence. From eternity God has been prompting man into action which can produce result with the consent of God. This is the meaning of Vātsyāyana's remark—*'puruṣakāram īsvaro'nugṛhṇāti'*. The very fact that man has to act is ordained by God and this ordinance is operating from eternity.

The later Naiyāyikas down to Gaṅgeśa and his interpreters have added nothing philosophically significant to this basic theoretical position of the elder Naiyāyikas, except trying their best to chisel and polish the syllogistic arguments in favour of Divine causality.[5]

It would not be far-fetched to surmise that Uddyotakara's solution of the relation between God and *karman* by an appeal to eternity has been inspired by the well-known *Brahmasūtra*—*'na karmavibhāgād iti cen nānāditvāt* (*BS*2/1/35).

Again Śaṅkara's observation (on *lokavattu līlākaivalyam, BB* 2/1/33) to the effect that God is creative by nature and one's nature is not subject to questioning, may be prompted by Uddyotakara's Nayāya commentary. Here one should not miss the salient point that Śaṅkara's support for theism in reply to Sāṅkhya atheism is only half-hearted for he is careful to note beforehand that all these talks about God and His relation with human action spring from *vyāvahārika* or tentative consideration, but not from *pāramārthika* or fundamental standpoint (*BS. SBh.* 1/4/23). It is the *Brahmasūtra (vaiṣamyanairghṛṇye na sāpekṣatvāt tathā hi darśayati* (BS 2/1/34), which for the first time in the history of theistic speculation tries to absolve God of moral responsibility for human action and of the charge of partiality and cruelty in the case of his mastery over man's deeds. The *Brahmasūtra* clearly states that God's mastery over man does not mean that He generates the effect of man's action according to Divine whims. But He does it according to the merit or demerit of an action. Without delving into the question whether the author of *Brahmasūtra* himself considers the problems about God and their suggested solutions only from *vyāvahārika* standpoint, whether Śaṅkara is faithful to the spirit of the *Brahmasūtra* in this context, it is indispensable to take into account Śaṅkara's decisive opinion from the fundamental standpoint of Advaita philosophy. Depite all that he has said in favour of theistic faith under the *sūtra 'lokavattu līlākaivalyam* and the *sūtras* immediately following it, Śaṅkara as a *siddhāntin* clearly rejects the solution offered earlier as regards the relation between God and human action. Under the *sūtra 'patyurasāmañjasyāt'* (*BS* 2/2/37) Śaṅkara clearly states that an eternal relation between God and human action and the logically consequent eternity of *saṁsāra* would invite the fallacies of *anyonyāśraya* and *anādi-andhaparamparānyāya,* i.e., the fallacy of mutual dependence and the fallacy of two blind men eternally leading each other by turn.[6] Vācaspati in *Bhāmatī* has clearly and elaborately explained how these two fallacies vitiate the theistic assumption. Vācaspati therein has this revealing remark to his credit — if God had simply decided not to preside over human deeds and destiny the mankind would have been spared all its sufferings. The theistic solution does not solve the problem why and by whom man was prompted to do the evil for the first time. It is moreover difficult to say, between God and man's action, who is the prompter and who the prompted.

The upshot is this that no God can be the first efficient cause and that *Īśvara* or *Brahman* conditioned by *avidyā* is the material cause of the world in the sense of the substratum being the material cause of an illusory world. Thus the Advaitins dissolve the problem of God and creation by dispensing with the world and hence with the creation itself as unreal.

The Saṅkhya philosophy, considered by many to be the oldest philosophical system of India, is avowedly atheist. Its many fine arguments against theism are recorded as Pūrvapakṣa in Śaṅkara's exposition of the *Brahmasūtras*. The *sūtra 'lokavattu līlākaivalyam'* appears as a reply to the Sāṅkhya contention that, if any God has created this world He must have behaved like a lunatic *(unmattavat)*, cruel and partial without any assignable reason. The whole concept of *karman* and *adṛṣṭa* of *jīva* has been introduced by the theists in order to absolve God of the moral responsibility for human sufferings. Kumārila in *Ślokavārttika* repeats the charge brought by the Sāṅkhya against God, when he remarks that it is unbecoming of a benign God to create a world full of sufferings— *'Prāṇināṁ prāyaduḥkhā ca sisṛkṣasya na yujyate* (*SV. Sambandhākṣepaparihāra,* V. 49)

Kumārila further observes that an appeal to *karman* does not solve this moral problem, because an omnipotent God need not wait for human action for His creation and might have quite easily created a perfectly happy world. If *karman* is introduced it is enough for shaping human destiny and God becomes irrelevant. So between God and *karman* you are rationally at liberty to choose the one or the other, but not to decide in favour of the both.

The unmistakable atheistic tradition of Mīmāṁsā is recorded in the *Brahmasūtra 'dharmaṁ jaiminirata eva'* (*BS* 3/2/40). It means that according to Jaimini no God or gods are necessary for producing the result of an action. An action leads to some result by its own nature through its operative influence *(dharma* or *adṛṣṭa)*. But philosophically, the most powerful and significant argument against God comes from Kumārila in the context of the question of the purpose or necessity. Why should God create at all ? We have seen that in reply the theists have finally appealed to the very creative nature of God. But God being creative by nature can only mean that he cannot help creating. Yet God is supposed to be a conscious judge of things. The mark of consciousness is freedom of choice — I may or may not do this, my decision being dependent on sufficient reason and circumstances; So 'God being conscious and independent' would mean that He might have created this world or refrained from creation considering the fact that the product of His action was bound to be a miserable world. But God had no choice. He had to create the world, and that too a world of sufferings, for creation belongs to His very nature which he cannot violate as a matter of choice. If this is so, the most formidable question comes up in the form—what is then the difference between conscious God and unconscious matter? The primordial matter of the Sāṅkhya keeps evolving into the shape of a material world by the natural laws of matter itself. Matter cannot help changing and evolving, just as your God cannot help creating. Matter cannot exercise any choice, neither can God. So the final and almost unanswerable question is posed by Kumārila— *"evameva pravṛttiścet, caitanyenāsya kiṁ bhavet'* (*SV*, ibid, V. 55). If it is the very sportive nature of God to create without any assignable reason what is the usefulness of His being a *conscious Being?* This question is yet to be answered.

Notes and References

1. Vātsyāyana is the first available Naiyāyika to directly assert the existence and character of God. The concept of God has been logically deduced from the *Nyāyasūtras* and, more elaborately, developed by Uddyotakara. A non-existent something can never be the cause of an effect. 'To be a cause' demands its existence before the effect. It is senseless to say that a cause has no existence at all. So it is quite possible to prove the existence of God by means of proving His causeness. — *"Yenaiva nyāyena īśvarasya kāranatvaṃ sidhyati, tenaiva astitvam iti, na hyavidyamanam kāraṇam iti* (*NV*, p. 457).

2. *"na paraḥ aparaḥ svayūthyo naiyāyika iti yāvaditi vārttikābhimatam vyākhyānam"*

   (*Khadyota* on)
   NS 4/1/19

3. Uddyotakara explains : *"Yad yathābhūtam yasya ca yadā vipākakālaḥ tat tathā tadā viniyuṅkte"*.

4. The Advaitins propagate the theory of *abhinnanimittopādānakāraṇatva*. According to them the one and the same Brahman is both the *upādānakāraṇa* (material cause) and the *nimittakāraṇa* of the world. Brahmasūtras like '*prakṛtiśca pratijñādṛṣṭāntānurodhāt* (1/4/23) seek to establish the Brahman as the material cause, while other *sūtras* like *Abhidhyopadeśācca* (1/4/24) show that the Brahman supervises over the worldly creation. A supervising agent is definitely an efficient cause or *nimittakāraṇa*. Emphasis, is, however, laid on *upādānakāraṇatva* which has been strongly challenged by the Nyāya-Vaiśeṣika and Sāṅkhya systems. The intention of the Advaitins is clear from Śaṅkara's comment on the *Brahmasūtra, Patyurasāmañjasyāt* (2/2/37) - *"Tasmād aprakṛtiradhiṣṭhātā kevalam nimittakāraṇam īśvara ityeṣa pakṣo vedāntavihitabrahmaikatvapratipakṣatvād yatnenātra pratiṣidhyate"*.

5. The argument in favour of the existence of God finds a chiselled expression in the following famous syllogism placed by Uddyotakara—*"Pradhānaparamāṇukarmāṇi prāk pravṛtter buddhimatkāraṇādhiṣṭhitāni pravartante acetanatvāt* (on *NS* 4/1/21).

   The newer school, led by Udayana, Vallabha and Gaṅgeśa makes the deduction in a slightly different way *"Kṣityādikaṃ sakartṛkaṃ kāryatvād ghaṭavad iti*" [The world must have a maker, because it is an effect]. Every effect has a maker behind it, for example, pot, an effect has a potter for its maker. Now a maker (*kartṛ*) is he who is endowed with a direct knowledge about the relevant material cause, a desire for doing and a conscious effort. Individuals of inadequate knowledge and power like us are too insignificant to acquire such a great faculty as may suit the creation of this vast universe. So we have no other alternative but to look for an omnipotent and omniscient being who supervises or presides over *(adhiṣṭhātṛ)* the entire creation, and this being is none but God. Viśvanātha, in his *Vṛtti* on the *Nyāyasūtra*, "*Tatkāritatvād ahetuḥ*", reveals an inclination towards this newer line of inference.

6. "*tathā cāyam aparo gaṇḍasyopari sphoṭa itaretarāśrayāhvayaḥ prasajyeta, karmaneśvaraḥ pravartaniya iśvareṇa ca karmeti*".

Bhāmatī on *BS* 2/237

Bibliography and Abbreviations

Brahmasūtraśāṅkarabhāṣya (*BS*) with Bhāmatī, Kalpataru and Parimala, Pandrang Jawaji, 1938.

Nyāyasutras (*NS*) of Gautama with Vatsyāyana's *Bhāṣya* and Viśvanātha's *Vṛtti*, Chowkhamba Sanskrit Series, Varanasi, 1920.

Nyāyadarśana with *Khadyota* of Pt. Ganganath Jha, Chowkhamba Sanskrit Series, Varanasi, 1924.

Nyāyavārttikatātparyaṭīkā of Vacaspati Misra, Chowkhamba Sanskrit Series, Varanasi, 1925.

Nyāyavārttika of Uddyotakara, Chowkhamba Sanskrit Series, Varanasi, 1916.

Ślokavārttika (*SV*) of Kumārila, Tara Publications, Varanasi, 1978.

14

Nyaya Model Knowledge—Base and Relational Representation

Keshab Chandra Dash

Language understanding has become the main topic in theory-oriented research of computational linguistics. This is also gaining its identity in the field of Artificial Intelligence researches. The basic idea of modelling language understanding is to represent the knowledge structure of what holds about the situations, objects, actions and their relations etc. that are referred to by words or described by the sentence or texts. To this effect, AI approach consists in the integration of language information. The term information, in other words, points to the universe of knowables which consists of various concepts, ideas, facts, names and so on. This is an apparent impasse between communcicables and communication, i.e., what one wants to communicate and the way in which it is communicated. This process, in its wider sense, refers to nothing but 'Meaning' which is resolved in the form of content and representation. AI approach aims at the development of methods of qualitative combination of content and representation for simulation on computer.

The relational representation is a kind of internal representation. This is considered from two different points of view. The first is descriptive which deals with static representation of the information embedded in the text. The second one is considered from processing point of view. This deals with the way in which the information is assimilated by the system. In other words, it shows how the information is incorporated with existing knowledge structures and organised in the memory. Thus while designing a representational model of a language, one has to take note of the types of information encoded in a text. At first hand, the levels of representation are delimited, i.e., the relevant units of analysis are distinguished such as:

(1) lexical items, (2) the clause, (3) the sentence and the text as a whole.

Knowledge Base

The area of AI research is well known as expert system or knowledge based system. The expert system points to a computer programme which contains both declarative knowledge and procedural knowledge. The declarative knowledge consists of the facts about objects, events and situations etc. whereas the procedural knowledge takes recourse to the information about action. These two types of expert systems are rule-based and model-based. By rule-based system the procedural knowledge is integrated with the declarative knowledge in the form of production rules. Similarly the model based system is based on a model of the structure and behaviour of the device.

When viewed on above lines the knowledge base is technically known as the component of expert system that contains the systems declarative and procedural knowledge. Further, the knowledge base is divided into three major categories, namely context, parameters and production rules. A context refers to a problem area in the domain of expert system. It provides a convenient way of dividing the larger problem into smaller to meet a specific goal. The parameter is associated with systems conclusion, i.e. the user of the system supplies the values of the parameters in response to questions or problems.

The relationship among values of parameters appear in the form of production rules. In other words, the inference mechanism is encoded in the form of production rules which specify the logical relationship of the values of parameters. The production rule gives ability to the inference engine to infer the values of the facts that appear as conclusions.

Nyaya Model and Representation

On the basis of above discussion we may consider here the Nyāya model of representation from descriptive point of view. Here, we take the lexical representation level. The lexicon has two main function such as: first, it shows its grammatical dependency and secondly, it records some of its semantic properties. From Nyāya point of view a lexicon is judged as a base containing certain knowledge which is expressed in terms of its predicability. In other words, it is a meaningful unit *(śaktam padam)*. In the present context, the base could be rightly termed as a Knowledge Base. The Nyāya System provides certain principles for its representation.

When we talk of computational lexicon it is a fact that the type of information required to be stored in the lexicons of natural language processing systems should be described. The informations are divided into two major categories namely (1) intra-word information and (2) inter-word information. The intra-word information pertains to individual word only. Inter-word information points to the way in which a word is related to other word.

Intra-Word Information

From Nyāya point of view, the structure of a lexicon which provides intra-word information may be presented in the following diagram.

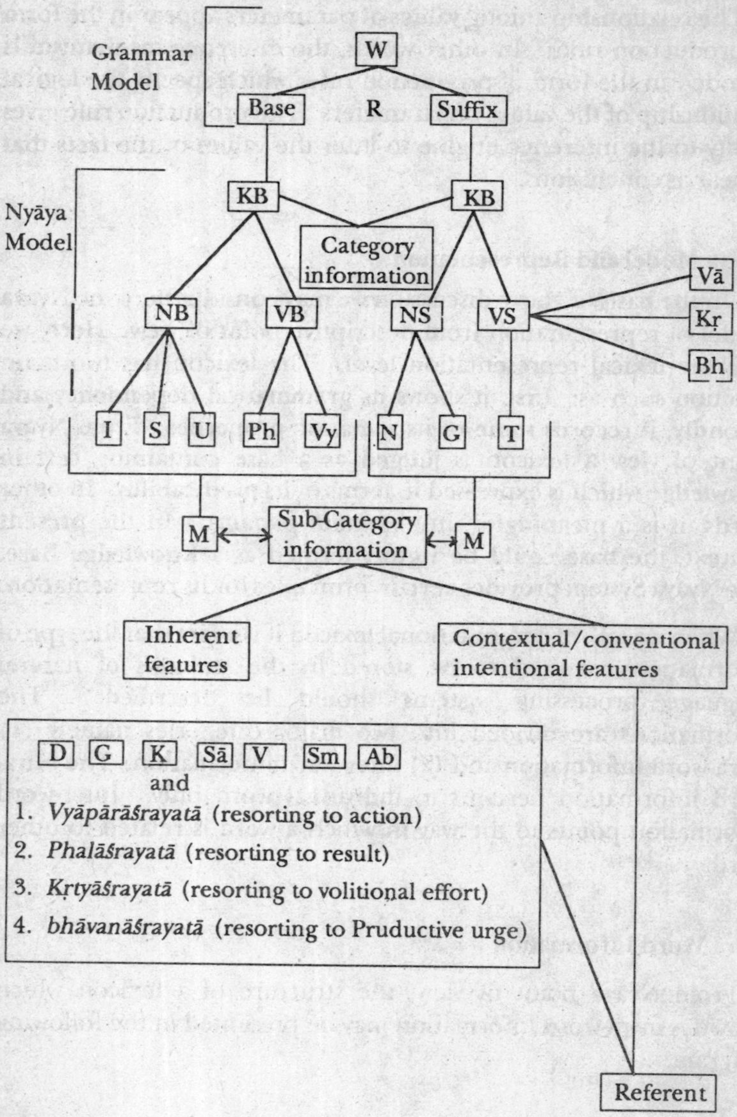
Grammar
Model
W
Base
R
Suffix
Nyāya
Model
KB
KB
Category
information
NB
VB
NS
VS
Vā
Kṛ
Bh
I
S
U
Ph
Vy
N
G
T
M
Sub-Category
information
M
Inherent
features
Contextual/conventional
intentional features
D G K Sā V Sm Ab
and
1. Vyāpārāśrayatā (resorting to action)
2. Phalāśrayatā (resorting to result)
3. Kṛtyāśrayatā (resorting to volitional effort)
4. bhāvanāśrayatā (resorting to Pruductive urge)
Referent

and/or

1. *Vyāpārāśrayatā* (resorting to action)
2. *Phalāśrayatā* (resorting to result)
3. *Kṛtyāśrayatā* (resorting to volitional effort)
4. *Bhāvanāśrāyatā* (resorting to productive urge)

W=Word
R=Relation
Vy=Vyāpāra (action)
KB=Knowledge Base
NB=Nominal Base
VB=Verbal Base

NS = Nominal Suffix
VS = Verbal Suffix
I = Individual
S = Shape
U = Universal

Ph=Phala (result)
N=Number
G=Gender
T=Tence
M=Meaning

Vā = Vyāpārāśrayatā (resorting to action)

Kṛ = Kṛti (volitional effort)

Bh = Bhāvanā (productive urge)

D=Dravya (substance)
G=Guṇa (quality)
K=Karma (action)
Sā =Sāmānya (universal)
V= Viśeṣa (particular)
Sm= Samavāya (inherence)

Ab =Abhāva (absence)
... =Relation
~ ∴ =alternative
Predominant element
↔ =Relational State

This analysis helps in selecting the information by way of specifying the nature of items required for processing.

The general model of processing computational lexicon is considered from the standpoint of parser. For instance, one to one relational pattern is resented in the following manner.

Word →[Morphological analysis]→[Syntactic analysis] → [Semantic analysis]

Similarly, 'one to many relation' between word and its category is presented in the following way.

[ADJ:base: INTIMATE → [ADJ:INTIMATE →
from: positive takes prep:WITH

[Semantic for INTIMATE-ADJ]

[V:base:INTIMATE
tense:Present
Number :Pl]
[V:base: INTIMATE
Intimate for m infinitve]
→ [V:INTIMATE → [Semantics for
complements
that COMP] INTIMATE-V]
[V:base: Intimate
Tense:Present, Per:l
Number : Sg]

A parser ultimately associates each word in full understanding system.

As far as the Indian languages are concerned the morphological and syntactic analysis may be considered from the standpoint of Grammar (Pāṇinian) model.. The semantic analysis which also has its correlation with syntactic analysis may be associated with Nyāya model.

Inter-Word Information

Inter-word information deals with the micro-structural analysis. In other words, it is a relational analysis of the items in a single sentence. The relation which is realised by two items is viewed from both syntactic and semantic standpoint.

An expression is generally found either in Noun-Verb set up or in Non-Noun setup. The N-V and N-N frame-works point to case relationship and non-case relationship respectively. The idea is presented in the following diagram.

1. Noun-Verb frame-work.

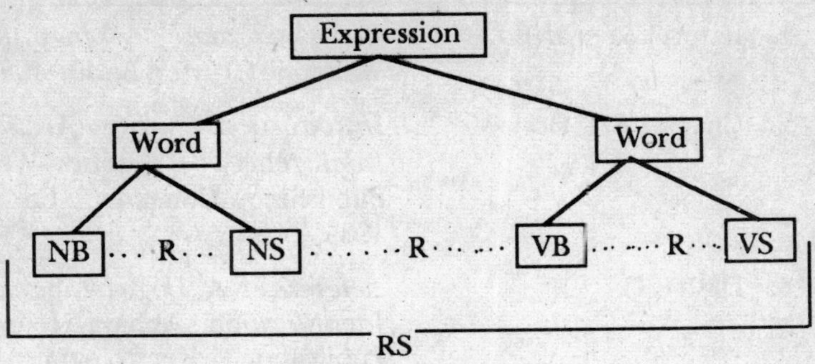

2. Noun-Noun framework

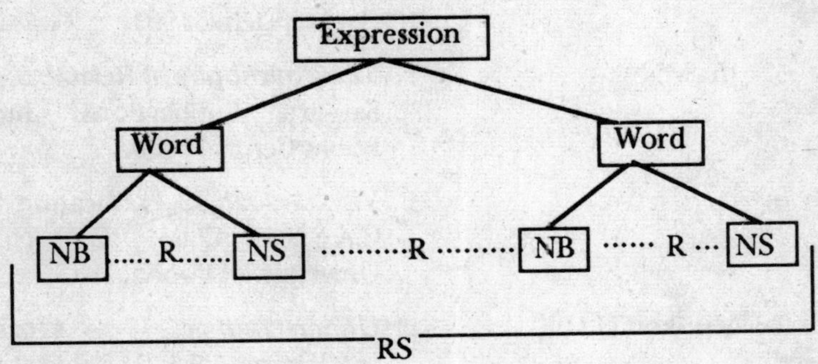

RS = Relational Structure.

Such a mechanism requires contents of the structure as well as extralinguistic and situational features. This has been discussed in detail elsewhere in my book *Relations in Knowledge Representation.*

Moreover, it may be said that the above model can be satisfactorily implemented by considering the nature of relation and the relata as per requirement of the system.

1. Batori I.S., *et al* (Ed.) : *Computational Linguistics,* Walter de Gruyter, Berlin, 1989.
2. Charnik E. & Drew Mc : *Introduction to Artificial Intelligence,* Addison-Wesley Publishing Company, Canada, 1985.
3. Dash K.C. : *Reference: A Logico-Linguistic Identification,* Abhaya House of Publication, Kendrapara, Ctc. 1986.
4. : *Relations in Knowledge Representation,* Sri Satguru Publications, Indian Books Centre, Delhi, 1991.
5. Jha V.N. : *The Philosophy of Relations,* Sri Satguru Publications, Indian Books Centre, 1990.
6. : *Viṣyatāvādaḥ,* Publication of C.A.S.S., Class C, No.16, University of Poona, 1987.
7. Mishkoff H.C. : *Understanding Artificial Intelligence,* B.P.B. Publications, Delhi, 1986.
8. Page E.S. & L.B.Wilson : *Information Representation and Manipulation in a Computer,* Affiliated East-West Press Pvt. Ltd, New Delhi, 1978.
9. Tenskey F.N. : *Principles of Tex Processing* Affiliated East-West Press Pvt. Ltd., New Delhi, 1982.
10. Zorkoczy P. : *Information Technology,* Affiliated East-West Press Pvt. Ltd, New Delhi, 1985.

15

Prābhākara's Concept of Relation

Rajendra Nath Sarma

Relation (*Sambandha*) is one of the most important issues in the systems of Indian philosophy, Rhetorics and in the schools of Grammar. Of all the systems, the Navya-Naiyāyikas deal with the relation to a great extent. The realists like the Naiyāyikas, the Vaiśeṣikas and both the schools of Mīmāṁsā viz., the Bhāṭṭa and Prābhākara admit the real entity of relation. For the Realists it is impossible to acquire a knowledge without the ontological reality of a relation. As a matter of fact, Relation plays a vital role in respect of the process of the production of a knowledge. It is difficult to define a relation, but it can be explained only. A relation supposes at least two things between which it is or it holds. That is to say, there can be no relation unless there are at least two things or objects. Relation, has something to do with the concept of the *pramāṇas* such as *pratyakṣa, anumāna, upamāna, śabda, arthāpatti* and *anupalabdhi.* It has also some functions in respect of understanding *sāmānya* (*jāti*) or generality. Like the Navya-Naiyāyikas, both the Schools of Mīmāṁsā do not admit of relations in various parameters.

The conception of relation is so interesting and all pervasive that on account of its application, the Navya-Naiyāyikas may be regarded as the Relational Logic in the modern sense of the term. In Navya-Nyāya, relations are broadly divided into two types viz, *Vṛttiniyāmaka* (occurrence-exacting) and *Vṛtty aniyāmaka* (non-occurrence-exacting). To the first type, belong three kinds of relations namely, *viśeṣaṇatā* (qualification relation), *saṁyoga* (contact) and *samavāya* (inherence). *Viśeṣaṇatā* may again be either *abhāvīya-viśeṣaṇatā* (relation of absential qualification) or *kālika-viśeṣaṇatā* (relation of temporal qualification).

Saṁyoga is an occurrence-exacting relation. *Saṁyoga* is one of the *guṇas* (quality) which is accepted as a *padārtha*. Like the Naiyāyikas, both, the Bhāṭṭa and Prābhākara Mīmāṁsakas accept *saṁyoga* as a relation. The Prābhākaras have mentioned no definition of *sambandha*. They have also not shown various parameters of *Sambanda* which have been done by the Naiyāyikas. The Prābhākaras accept the relation of *saṁyoga, samavāya* and *saṁyukta-samavāya* (Inherence in the substance contacted). These three types of relation are stated in the context of discussing *sannikarṣa* (conjunction).[1] To be precise, the Bhāṭṭa and the Prābhākaras mean *sambandha* by the word *sannikarṣa*. The Bhāṭṭa Mīmāṁsakas, on the other hand, speak of three types of relation namely, *saṁyoga, saṁyuktatādātmya* (relation of identity in difference of the substance contacted) and *saṁyuktatadatmatādātmya* (Relation of identity in difference of the identified).[2] The Bhāṭṭas do not recognise *samavāya* as a Relation. It has been stated by Nārāyaṇa in his *Mānameyodaya* wherein we find the following verse—*"Rūpādīnāṁ tu saṁyuktadravyatādātmyameva naḥ/ pratītikāraṇaṁ tasmān na sambandhāntarāprekṣā//"* p. 16. Here, the word "*sambandhāntara*" implies *samavāya* and other relations. So, instead of samāvaya, the Bhāṭṭa Mīmāṁsakas accept *tādātmya* (relation of identity in difference).

The Prābhākaras, however, admit *samaya* as a relation but not in the line of the Vaiśeṣikas.[3] The Vaiśeṣikas state that *samavāya* is a permanent or eternal relation between, the two entities of which one inheres in the other. The whole is in its parts, a quality or an action is in a substance or the universal is in the individuals and particularly is in simple eternal substance.[4] Thus, *samavāya* is the eternal relation between any two entities, one of which cannot exit without the other. According to the Vaiśeṣikas, *samavāya* is eternal and one. But the Prābhākaras contend that inherence of the eternal things is eternal and that of the non-eternal things is non-eternal. Thus, according to them, *samavāya* may be both eternal and non-eternal. Here lies the difference between the Vaiśeṣikas and the Prābhākaras regarding the concept of *samavāya*. Kaṇāda has defined *samavāya* as that due to which there arises the knowledge viz, effect exists in the cause.[5] Praśastapāda, however, defines *samavāya* as that relation of the inseparably related and locus-located relationship and which is the cause of such knowledge.[6] Keeping this definition of *samavāya* by Praśastapāda, in mind, Śālikānātha Miśra, a staunch follower of Prabhākara, states that one should understand *samavāya* after having understood the locus-located relationship.[7] The example of *samavāya* of eternal objects is the relation of *ākāśa* and *paramāṇu* and that of the non-eternal objects is the relation of the part and whole. Likewise, the inherence between the community and the individual comes into existence when the individual is produced and perishes as soon as that individual perishes. Moreover, according to the Prābhākaras, *samavāya*, is not produced by action (*samavāyantu saṁyogādbhinnaḥ na karmajaḥ*).

Prābhākaras are, as I think, right in respect of their concept of *samavāya* as a relation which may be both eternal and non-eternal. If two things are not eternal then how can their relation of inherence be eternal? Prabhākara thus, differs from Kumārila in his use of *samavāya* as a means of explaining the relation of the individual to the generality. When a new individual of a class comes into being, what is produced is not the existence of the generality which is eternal, but of the relation of *samavāya* between the individual and the class. *Samavāya* differs from *saṁyoga* in that it does not presuppose the previous existence of the things affected by it and unlike the Nyāya-Vaiśeṣika, Prabhākara does not hold that it is necessarily eternal. This affords an easy answer to the question of the fate of the class character on the destruction of an individual; it does not go away as it has no motion; it does not subsist in the individual which is no longer in being; it does not cease to exist, for it remains in other individual. But inherence between the class and the individual comes to an end. Thus, according to the Prābhākaras, *samavāya* is not necessarily eternal.

We have already stated that Kumārila rejects the concept of *samavāya* as a true category. As he maintains, a relationship can exist only between things which are established as distinct entities and as inherence is supposed to be a relation between things which like the class and the individual are inseparable, it comes to be a contradiction in terms. In fact, the relationship cannot be anything distinct from the things themselves among which it is supposed by the Vaiśeṣikas to subsist.

It may be summed up from the above, that the Prābhākaras never deny *samavāya* but to them, it is necessarily not eternal as conceived by the Vaiśeṣikas.

The Prābhākaras have shown three types of *saṁyoga* viz, *anyatarakarmaja*, *ubhayakarmaja* and *saṁyogaja.*[8] *Anyatarakarmaja* type of *saṁyoga* is that which is caused by the action of either of the two. For instance, the contact of a bird and a post. Here, the contact is caused by the action of the bird.

Again the contact caused by the action of the both, is *ubhayakarmaja saṁyoga* as in the case of two wrestlers.

Saṁyogaja type of *saṁyoga* is one where the contact is caused by the action of a contact. For example, the contact of the body of a man due to the contact of his hand with the tree. It is a case of indirect relation (*paramparā-sambandha*). But a *saṁyoga* is a direct relation (*sākṣāt-sambandha*), because it directly connects two or more substances. Both the Schools of Mīmāṁsā treat *saṁyoga* as the Vaiśeṣikas do.

Another relation is *saṁyukta-samavāya* (inherence in the substance contacted). For example, colour inheres in the jar which is connected through the relation of contact with the eye.

It may be pointed out here that the Prābhākaras' relation of *saṁyoga* is to be understood in a different manner. Śālikānātha Miśra has clearly dealt with this issue in his magnum opus, the *Prakaraṇa-Pañcikā*. He maintains that the relation of *saṁyoga* of the fire and smoke etc. is understood through perception etc. Moreover, from the place and time there arises the knowledge of the object qualified by the relation of *saṁyoga*. So, the knowledge will be like this—these two are contacted and not as this is the contact of these two.[9] Thus, the relation *saṁyoga* comes to be a viśeṣaṇa. *Saṁyoga* is an eternal relation which exists as an accidential quality of two substances related by it. It may be added that relation may be internal and external. While the idealists advocate the theory of internal relation, the realists the external. Bertrand Russell advocates the theory of external relations like our Indian realists. He means by the same that "there are such facts that one object has a certain relation to another. [10] Internal relation is generally accepted by the Idealists. Internal relation is grounded in the nature of terms related, so that the terms would not be what they are apart from the relation.

Sambandha in the *Autpattika-Sūtra*

Prabhākara's view on *sambandha* is also found in his commentary on the *autpattika-sūtra* viz., *autpattikastu śabdasyārthenasambandhaḥtasyajñānamupadeśo 'vyatirekaśca rthe'nupalabdhetatpramāṇaṁbādarāyaṇasyānapekṣatvāt* (MS. 1.1.5).

It is in the *Sabdārthasambandhanityatvādhikaraṇa* wherein it is established that the relation of words and meanings is *autpattika* or natural. Jaimini, by this *Sūtra* states that words, their meanings and the relation between words and their meanings are eternal. Things signified by the words also exist always in some form or other, though individual units of these things have a beginning and an end of their own. As the world has been existing always as it exists today, the words, their meanings and their mutual relation are learnt by the juniors from the senior elderly persons during conversation. Thus, the Prābhākaras maintain that the method of learning the meanings of the words is also eternal.[11]

It may be argued that there can be no relationship between the word and meaning, because none of the several kinds of relations *saṁyoga, samavāya, kārya-kāraṇabhāva* and *viṣayaviṣayībhāva* etc. is possible between the word and the meaning. To this question, the Prābhākaras answer that the relationship between the word and meaning is that of the denoter-denoted or expressed-expresser.[12] The meaning of the word '*autpattika*' is natural, impersonal. The relation comes to be natural because of the letters being natural and the meanings being spontaneous. This is what Rāmāmuja states in his *Tantra-rahasya*. As, Dr. Radhakrishnan sums up, according to the Mīmāṁsakas, "the Vedas are eternal, since the words of which they are composed, are eternal. The relations like between the word and its meaning is natural.[13] Dr. Ganganath Jha also points out that in view of the Mīmāṁsakas, the meaning of the word cannot be comprehended except the hypothesis of its naturality.[14]

The Naiyāyikas, however, do not accept the eternality of *śabda*. According to them, *śabda* is not eternal.[15] So, in their opinion, because of the word being not eternal, its relationship with its meaning is also not eternal. As a matter of fact, word is often found to be destroyed, so that when it comes to be produced (e.g., uttered), again, its relation to its meaning cannot but be artificial, ephemeral and newly made. Moreover, none-ever comprehends the meaning of a word heard for the first time.

But this is not acceptable to the Mīmāṁsakas. As stated by Śabara, the relation between the word and its meaning is also eternal it cannot be regarded as brought about by any (in the shape of God), as there is no proof of existence of such a person.

Words are always taught as accomplished entities having the inherent power of devoting things. If it were impossible for us to comprehend the meaning of words without presuming a creator of this relationship, then alone could there be justification for presuming such a creator. As a matter of fact, however, we find that when senior people are making use of words for their own purposes, the junior who happen to hear those words actually come to understand them; those senior people, too, when they were young, understood the words in the same way, when uttered by their elders. Thus, *vṛddhavyavahāra* comes to serve as the means of understanding the relation of word and meaning as eternal. In the words of Śālikanātha—

> *"autpattikastu sambandhaḥ śabdasyārthena sammataḥ/*
> *vṛddhasaṁvyavahārasya pravāhānāditā yataḥ//* PP, p. 304.

Prabhākara's concept of relation with *abhāva*

While discussing relation in Prābhākara Mīmāṁsā, it will be proper to deal with the concept of *abhāva* (non-existence) according to the system. It is well-known to the readers of Indian Philosophy that while the Nyāya-Vaiśeṣikas admit *abhāva* as a category (*padārtha*), the Bhāṭṭas and the Vedāntins accept the same as an independent *pramāṇa*. But the Prābhākara-

Mīmāṁsakas do not recognise *abhāva* neither as a category nor a *pramāṇa*. *Abhāva* as a *pramāṇa* is introduced by Śabara in his *Bhāṣya* for the first time.[16]

Prabhākara while commenting upon the *Bhāṣya* of Śabara where *abhāva* is established as a *pramāṇa* to prove that absence of a thing refutes the view of Śabara on this point and proved that there is no such category as *abhāva* and so there is no need to accept a separate *pramāṇa* as such.[17] Prābhākaras maintain that *abhāva* is a possible entity and not a distinct mode of reality. *Abhāva* is identical with its locus. It has no reality apart from that of an existing thing. Existence and non-existence are two aspects of the same thing.

Abhāva is constituted by difference. Difference, again, rests upon two terms. *Sambandha* also rests upon two terms. So, *abhāva* is also a relation. The example, 'A is not B' illustrates its truer character. The relational character of *abhāva* is an inference. All relations stand between two terms. *Abhāva* also stands between two terms. Therefore, *Abhāva* is also a relation. Even Western Philosopher Bertrand Russell also holds that negation is a relation since it stands between two terms.

In the view of the Prābhākaras, however, we may conclude that *abhāva* is not at all a relation. The Prābhākaras understood *abhāva* as the *adhikaraṇa-svarūpa*, when we say *ghaṭābhāvavad bhūtalam* (there is an absence of jar on the ground), the absence of jar appears as the qualifier of the ground, qualifierness of which is described by the qualificandness that exists in the qualificand ground. The Naiyāyikas cannot agree with the Prābhākaras who consider *abhāva* as nothing but its locus and do not give independent status of a *Padārtha* to it.

Is relation Viséṣaṇa?

In connection with the treatment of relation, a question arises in one's mind whether relation is a *viśeṣaṇa*. We have already mentioned that *viśeṣaṇatā* (qualification relation) is a relation of the occurence-exacting relation. This is so called because it is considered identical with the *abhāva* which is generally cognised as a qualifier as in the cognition, *ghaṭābhāvavad bhūtalam*. From this it is clear that relation is *viśeṣaṇa*. The Prābhākaras, therefore, regard *saṁyoga* also a *viśeṣaṇa*. In stead of saying that there is the contact between two things, they say "contacted are these two" (*saṁyvktāvimau iti hi pratītiḥ na punar anayoḥ saṁyoga iti*— TR, p. 10).

It may be concluded that unlike the Naiyāyikas, the Prābhākaras accept a few relations as they find it proper to avoid so many relations that may create problem. In any case, Prābhākaras have minimised the number of relations.

Notes

1. *Prābhākarāstu saṁyogaḥ, saṁyuktasamavāyaḥ, samavāya iti tredhā sannikarṣam āhuḥ*, MM, p. 17.

   taṣmāt trividha eva sannikarṣaḥ pratyakṣa-hetuḥ saṁyogaḥ, saṁyukta-samavāyaḥ, samavāyaśceti—PP, p. 134.

2. *Tathāsmākam api tadātmatādātmyaṁ nāma tṛtīyaḥ sammkarṣo'stu, Kā hāniḥ?* MM, pp. 15-16.

3. *Samavāyañca na vayaṁ kāśyapīyā iva nityam upemaḥ,* PP, p. 92.

4. *Ghaṭādīnāṁ kapālādau dravyeṣu guṇakarmaṇoḥ/teṣu jāteśca sambandhaḥ samavāyaḥ prakīrtitaḥ //* BP. K., 11.

5. *Ihedam iti yataḥ kāryakāraṇayoḥ sa samavāyaḥ,* Vs 7.2.26.

6. *Ayutasiddhānām ādhārādheyabhūtānāṁyassambandhaḥ ihetipratyayahetus sa samavaya, PPB under ibid.*

7. *Pratītya hyādhārādheyaṁ sambandhaṁ pratīyāt,* PP, p. 93-94.

8. *Yo hi saṁyogaḥ sākṣāt pratīyate, So'nyatarakarmajaḥ, ubhayakarmaja, saṁyogajo,* PP, p. 141.

9. *Evañca deśakālābhyāṁ saṁyogasambandhasya viśiṣṭasyāvagatiḥ tathāhi saṁyuktāvimaviti hi pratipattiḥ, na punar anayoḥ saṁyoga iti,* PP, p. 204.

10. PE, p. 161.

11. *Kim idam siddhavadupadeśad iti idam nātra kartā śakyate kalpayituṁ vṛddhavyavahārasyānāditvāt. ata autpattikas sambandha iti siddham,* BR under MS 1.1.5, p. 143.

12. *Śabdārthayo stāvatpratyāyyapratyāyakabhāvalakṣaṇas sambandhaḥ, vācya-vācakabhāva iti yāvat. Sa cāpauruṣeyaḥ,* TR, p. 22.

13. IP, p. 389.

14. PIS, p. 150.

15. *Nityaḥ, athānitya iti anityaḥ śabda ity uttaram.* VB under ND, 2.2., 13-39.

16. *Pratyakṣapūrvakatvāccānumānopamānārthāpattināpy akāraṇatvam iti abhāvopi nasti-yataḥ*, SB under MS, 1.1.4.

17. *Abhāvopi pramāṇābhāvaḥ iti kiṁ pramāṇalakṣaṇimdam aum ity ucyate. Kim anena pramīyate uktaṁ nāstīty ayam arthaḥ* —also *na vidmaḥ prasiddheḥ kiṁ bijmiti,* BR, p. 91 under MS. 1.1.5.

References: Original works

1. *Bhāṣāpariccheda* (BP) of Viśvanātha, edited by Pancanan Bhattacharya, Calcutta edition.
2. *Bṛhatī* (BR) of Prabhākara Miśra, Chowkhamba Edition, Varanasi.
3. *Mānameyodaya* (MM) of Nārāyaṇa, Saddarsana Granthamala, Varanasi.
4. *Mīmāṁsā Sūtra* (MS) of Jaimini, Chowkhamba Edition.
5. *Nyāya-Darśana* (ND) of Gotama, Motilal Banarasidass, Delhi.
6. *Prakaraṇa-Pañcikā* (PP) of Śālikanātha, Banaras Hindu University Edition.
7. *Praśastapādabhāṣya* (PPB) of Vātsyāyana, Sanskrit Pustak Bhandar, Calcutta.
8. *Ṛjuvimalā* (RVL) of Śālikānātha, vide, *Bṛhatī*.
9. *Śābarabhāṣya* (SB) of Śabara, vide, *Mīmāṁsā-Sūtra*.
10. *Ślokavārttika* of Kumārila, Chowkhamba Edition, Banaras.
11. *Tantra-rahasya* (TR) of Rāmānuja, Gaekwad Oriental Edition, Baroda.

Modern works

1. Chatterjee, S.C. : *The Problems of Philosophy* (TPP).
2. Keith, A.B. : *Karma-Mīmāṁsā* (KM), Munshiram Manoharlal, Delhi.
3. Jha, G.N. : *Pūrva-Mīmāṁsā in its Sources* (PIS), Chowkhamba Edn.
4. Jha, V.N. : Studies in Language, Logic and Epistemology (SLLE), Pratibha Prakashan, Delhi.
5. Radhakrishnan, S : *Indian Philosophy* (IP), Vol. II.
6. Russell, Bertrand: *Philosophical Essays* (PE), George Allen & Unwin Ltd., London.

16

Function of Relation in Dvaitādvaita Philosophy

N.G. Kamat

Vedānta philosophy has a exceptionally wide range of thoughts. The term vedānta doesn't refer to a single school, but to a group of philosophical systems which believe variously in absolute unity, absolute duality, absolute identity as weli as diversity in different ways. The knowledge of the exact relation between the universal soul and the individual soul occupies a central place in vedāntic thought. That'swhy the vedānta philosophy viz. theistic vedānta satisfies both—the intellectual and the devotee.

The thinkers of theistic school accept three co-eternal principles which are the Brahman—as the cosmic ruler, *Cit*—the subject of experience and *Acit*—the object of experience. Both the *Cit* and *Acit* are the real transformations of the *Brahman*. These two may be different from their cause in forms and functions, but on the other hand they are non-different in essence. So these three realities are different as well as non-different from each other. There comes the mono-dualistic interpretation or *Dvaitādvaita* philosophy to explain this relation.

The doctrine of difference and non-difference or *Dvaitādvaita* is not quite new. Its tradition goes back to the vedic time. The pre-Bādarāyaṇa thinkers like Āśmarathya and Audulomin offered the dualistic-cum-monistic interpretation. Bhāskara, Yādavaprakāśa, Nimbārka and Caitanya are the eminent philosophers of this

Dvaitādvaita philosophy. In the present paper I have concentrated only on Nimbārka's view point.

According to Nimbārka all this verily is the *Brahman*. The *Brahman* is both static and dynamic. In relation to the universe it is active and dynamic, otherwise it is static and serene. The omniscient and omnipotent *Brahman* has transformed himself into the manifest world. His volition is the only reason for the transformation. The Śvetāśvatara declares that he is not supposed to depend on any external implement.[1] All scriptures and Smṛtis show that *Brahman*—the cosmic ruler is alone capable to transform himself. This transformation is without external impelling, real and from within just as milk is turned into the curds.[2]

The Brahman creates both animate and inanimate. The animate or the individual soul is an active agent and enjoyer in all states. Nimbārka has aptly narrated the nature of *Jīvātman* in the third verse of *Vedāntakāmadhenu*.[3] The third ultimate category in Nimbārka philosophy is *Acit* or the material universe. It is also manifested from the *Brahman* only.

The entire expanse of the universe consisting of the corporeal and the incorporeal is different as well as non-different from its source—the *Brahman*. Nimbārka illustrates this concept of *Dvaitādvaita* through the well-known example of the serpent and its coil. The serpent is independent while the coil is dependent. The serpent and coil are substantially same but they do differ in form and function. In the same way the relation of difference and non-difference between the *Brahman* and the universe is equally real and compatible with each other.[4]

Nimbārka elucidates this relation by the theory of the cause and the effect. The effect is implicit in its cause and becomes explicit in the form of the effect. The effect may be different from its cause in attributes, powers, forms and functions. But at the same time it is also non-different from the cause in essence.The relation between the cause and its effect is neither of absolute non-difference nor of absolute difference. The mutual difference and non-difference among these three co-existent realities are as natural as in the causal relation. That'swhy Nimbārka adds an adjective to *Dvaitādvaita* as natural or *svābhāvika*—*Dvaitādvaita* philosophy.

The *Brahman* is both the material and the efficient cause. He creates the mutable and the immutable at the time of creation. At the same time he rewinds also the universe as a spider creates and rewinds its[4] web.[5] According to his will he becomes the creator as well as the object of the creation. It is well established on the ground of the scripture and *Smṛti* texts. Hence in the scriptures the *Brahman* the unmanifest controller is said to be the source. Then he alone is the material cause. Because the word *Yoni* i.e. source occurring in the Muṇḍaka, denotes itself the material cause. The creation of the universe is nothing but the mere modification.

Modification is of two kinds. One is *svarūpa-pariṇāma* as accepted in *Sāṁkhya* philosophy. The second type of transformation is *śaktī-vikṣepa-lakṣaṇa-parīṇāma* . Nimbārka admits the second, terming it as *Brahmaśaktikāraṇavāda* and explains it through the offen-quoted example of the transformation of milk into curds. There is no external impelling factor which prompts for the creation. The *Brahman* creates the universe for mere sport without any external motive.[6]

An objection may be raised that *Brahman* who has no external factor is not the creator of the world. Because in daily life it is always found that external implements like stick, wheel and potter are employed to create the pot. Nimbārka replies that there is no need of such things. *Brahman* creates himself through modification. His powers are infinite.[7] He modifies himself into the form of the world through his very nature. He does not require any external accessories for creation.

Here one may take the example of clay and dish or gold and bracelet to prove the causal relation as well as the relation of difference and non-difference between the cause and the creation. The dish and clay both are different in name and shape but there is also non-difference so far as the clay is concerned. So the relation between the cause and the effect is that of difference and non-difference. There is no such rule that a material cause and its effect must be absolutely similar. Because the causal relation itself proves the difference as well as non-difference. The cause itself assumes the shape and the attributes of the effect as milk changes into curds naturally.

There is another objection that if the *Brahman* is the material cause then he will himself become an enjoyer of pleasure and pain in the form of the individual soul. There will be no distinction between the enjoyer and the controller. Nimbārka refutes kthis objection by giving the example of the sun and its ray.[8] Though the individual soul is a part of the *Brahman*, the *Brahman* is not affected by the deeds of the individual soul. Just as the sun is devoid of the merits and demerits of its rays. Similarly the Brahman is also aloof from pleasure and pain.

The individual soul is neither absolutely different nor totally non-different from *Brahman*. Because there is a causal and part-whole relationship between them. His existence and activities are under the control of the *Brahman*, which may be named as whole. So the creatorship of the world is not possible to any part other than the Supreme Reality.[9]

So to sum up, the function of the relation in *Dvaitādvaita* philosophy centres around the theory of causation. Nimbārka accepts *Brahmakāraṇavāda* and explains the universe along with individual soul as a self-transformation of the *Brahman*. Naturally, he admits three ultimate principles. As a result of causal relation between unity and plurality, both are real and different as well as non-different from one another. It is the peculiarity of *Dvaitādvaita* philosophy.

Notes and References

1. न तस्य कार्यं करणं च विद्यते न तत्समश्चाभ्यधिकश्च दृश्यते।
परास्य शक्तिर्विविधैव श्रूयते स्वाभाविकी ज्ञानबलक्रिया च।।
Śvetāśvatara, VI. 8.

2. यतः क्षीरवत्कार्येण ब्रह्म परिणमते। नशे 1.23;
कृत्स्न जगत्सृष्टयादिव्यापारहिं ब्रह्मैव। 'स कारणं
कारणाधिपाधिपः Śvetāśvatar VI. 9)'
सर्वस्य वशी सर्वस्य ईशानः (Bṛhadāraṇyaka IV. 4.22')
'मयाध्यक्षेण प्रकृतिः सूयते सचराचरम् (Gitā IX, 10)' इति।। IV.4. 20.

3. ज्ञानस्वरूपं च हरेरधीनं शरीरसंयोगवियोग योग्यम्।
अणुं हि जीवं प्रतिदेहभिन्नं ज्ञातृत्ववन्तं यमनंतमाहु;।।
vedāntakāmadhenu 3

4. मूर्तामूर्तस्याप्रतिषेध्यत्वं दृढयति - मूर्तामूर्तादिक विश्वं
स्वकारणे भिन्नाभिन्नसंबंधेन स्यातुमर्हति
भेदाभेदव्यपदेशादहिकुंडलवत्।। III. 2.27.

5. ब्रह्मैव निमित्तमुपादानं च। 'तदात्मानं स्वयमकुरूत'।
(Taittiriya II. 7) इत्यात्मकृतेः।... सर्वज्ञ सर्वशक्ति ब्रह्म स्वशक्तिविक्षेपेण जगदाकारं स्वात्मानं परिणमय्य अव्याकृतेन स्वरूपेण शक्तिमता कृतिमता परिणतमेव भवति।। I 4. 26. 'यथोर्णनाभिः सृजते गृह्णते च ... तथाक्षरात्संभवतीह विश्वम्।।' Muṇḍaka I. 1.7.

6. 'यद्भूतयोनिं परिपश्यन्ति धीरा' (Muṇḍaka I. 1.6.)
कर्तारमीशं पुरूषं ब्रह्मयोनिम् (Muṇḍaka III. 1.3.) इति ... योनिशब्देन ब्रह्म गीयते अतो ब्रह्मैवोपादानम्।। I. 4.27.

7. सा देवता सर्वशक्त्युपेता (Śvetāśvatara VI. 8) सर्वकर्तुं समर्था भवति।। नन. 1. 29; अस्याऽचिन्त्यविचित्रसंस्थान - संपन्नस्य असंख्येयनामरूपादि विशेषाश्रयस्याचिन्त्यरूपस्य विश्वस्य सृष्टिस्थितिलयः यस्मात् सर्वज्ञानान्तगुणाश्रयाब्रह्मेशकालादिनियन्तुः भगवतो भवन्ति।। I. 1.2.

8. ब्रह्मणो जगदुपादानत्वे जीवरूपेण ब्रह्मण एव सुखदुःख - भोक्तृत्वापत्तेर्वेदप्रसिद्धो भोक्तृनियन्तृविभागो न स्यादितिचेत्। अविभागेऽपि समुद्रतरङ्गयोरिव तयोर्विभागःस्यात्। II. 1.13.

जीवस्य परमपुरूषांशत्वे अंशी सुखदुःखं नानुभवति यथा प्रकाशादिः स्वांशंगतगुणदोषवर्जितो भवति।। II. 3.45.

9. अंशांशिभावाज्जीवपरमात्मनोर्भेदाभेदौ दर्शयति। परमात्मनो जीवोंऽशः 'ज्ञाज्ञौ द्वावजावीशानीशौ'' (śvetāsvatar I. 9) इत्यादिभेदव्यपदेशात् 'तत्त्वमसि (chāndogya VI. 8.6.) इत्याद्यभेदव्यदेशात्।। II. 3. 42;

अप्राकृतस्य आनन्दमयस्य सर्वशक्ते; पुरूषोत्तमस्य तु न कुतः। कामात् संकल्पादेव... सोऽकामयत बहुस्याम् (Taittiriya II. 6) इत्यादिश्रुतेः।। I. 1.19.

17

Form and Function of Relation in Viśiṣṭādvaita Philosophy

P. Srirama Murti

Different Philosophies enumerated the categories they accepted in consistent with their world views. Both in their ontologies and epistemologies they accept certain relations that are necessary to explain the various activities of the world. But relation itself is not accepted as a category often for fear of the fallacy of reductio ad absurdum i.e. *anavasthā*. Relations exist between substances, between substances and qualities, actions etc. Generally *saṁyoga*, conjunction is accepted as relation between two concrete substances and it is recognised as a quality by itself. But the relation between a substance and its qualities is said to be a different relation called *Samavāya*—inherence. It is also recognised as a substance some times. The relation of *abhāva* and the substratum where the *abhāva*, absence of a thing is spoken of is considered to be the relation of *Viśeṣaṇa - Viśeṣya-bhāva*—qualified and quality. The Viśiṣṭādvaita Philosophy has got its own views in this regard.

According to the Viśiṣṭādvaita Philosophy there are two distinct classes of categories *prameyas*, namely *Dravya* and *Adravya*—substances and non-substances. The *Dravyas* are of six kinds—(1) *Prakṛti,* nature (2) *Kāla,* time (3) *Bhogavibhūti* and *Nityavibhūti*, the divine manifestation of *Prakṛti* here and in the highest region of creation (4) *Dharmabhūta jñāna*, the attributive knowledge (5) *Jīva*, the individual soul and (6) *Īśvara*, the Universal soul or God. The *Adravyas*—non-substances are ten; *Sattva, Rajas* and *Tamas*, the three qualities of *Prakṛti, Śabda, Sparśa, Rūpa, Rasa, Gandha*—the qualities of the five *bhūtas; Saṁyoga*, conjunction, the relation and *Śakti*, potency, the causation in all causal substances. *Prakṛti* is the same as that in the Sāṅkhya philosophy with a difference. In Viśiṣṭādvaita Philosophy the will of *Īśvara* is responsible for the revelation and manifestation of its charms. It is also eternal and all pervasive and it serves the interests of *Īśvara* as an instrument in the cosmic functions.

Saṁyoga—conjunction as a *Sambandha*, relation is defined as the cause for the knowledge that the things are in conjunction and it is two-fold—*Kārya* and *akārya*—what is caused and what is not caused. The first variety is again of two kinds—one caused by the motivation of both the things coming into contact and the second what is caused by the motivation of one of the two coming into contact.

The example for the first is the contact between two goats fighting and the example for the second is the contact between the man and the post. The conjunction which is not caused is that between two all pervading objects like *Kāla* (time) and *Īśvara* (God). It is sometimes objected that two all pervading (*Vibhudravyas*) things cannot have contact between them. The following is the answer of the Viśiṣṭādvaitins. The Śruti passage.

अन्तर्बहिश्च यत्सर्वं व्याप्य नारायण स्थितः

Nārāyaṇa, the supreme Lord, remains pervading all from inside and outside. This authority of the Veda is cited in approval of their contention.

Viśiṣṭādvaitins accept three Pramāṇas namely *Pratyakṣa, Anumāna* and *Āgama*. They hold that all perception is attributive only (*Saviśeṣa*). In fact all knowledge is considered only attributive *Saviśeṣaviṣaya*. Both determinate and indeterminate perceptions are proved to be *saviśeṣa* attributive. The distinction of what is called indeterminate knowledge *Nirvikalpakajñāna* is in that the recurrence (*Anuvṛtti*) of the quality is not known since it is perceived for the first time. It may be noticed here that *jāti* is not accepted as a separate category but as a configuration—*samsthāna*. Each body is a distinct configuration.

When it comes to sense relation i.e., *Sannikarṣa*—conjunction alone is accepted. All others are classified under *Samyuktāśrayaṇa* dependence on what is in contact. Even *Samavāya* relation between *Avayavin* and *Avayavi* is explained as *Samyuktāśrayaṇa*—

अत्र वृद्धा विदामासुः संयोगं सन्निकर्षणम्।

संयुक्ताश्रयणञ्चेति यथासंभवमूह्यताम्।।

vide *Tattvaratnākara* of Paraśarabhaṭṭāraka. It is said that one and the same object is a part with reference to a particular position and the unitary perception makes it a whole—which is only an aggregate of the parts. Further the relation *Samavāya*—inherence should exist in a substance by some relation which could be only *samavāya*. If this is accepted there is the logical fallacy of infinite regress—*anavasthā*. The relation between sound *Śabda* and ear which is *Akāśa* only is said to be *Samyuktāśrayaṇa,* for sound is found in ether which is in conjunction with the ear. Thus *Samavāya* is not accepted as a separate relation by the Viśiṣṭādvaitins.

Abhāva, non-existence is not accepted as a separate category by the Viśiṣṭādvaitins. It is grasped by *Svarūpasambandha* itself. So the relation of *Viśeṣaṇa-Viśeṣyabhāva* postulated by Naiyāyikas for the perception of *Abhāva* is not accepted.

The Viśiṣṭādvaita Philosophy has integrated the *Pāncarātra* tradition with the Vedic tradition of thought. It has accepted three real objects namely *cit, acit* and Brahman the sentient entities, *Jīvas;* the inaminate world *prakṛti* and the God—Brahman. They together, however, form a single whole for the first two do not exist without the third and they exist for Him and they are pervaded and controlled by Him. It is the *cit-acit-viśiṣṭa*-Brahman that is the reality. Before creation it was undifferentiated and after creation they are differentiated. In support of this criterion they stand by the *śrutipramāṇa*—Emphasizing on the validity of Ghṭakaśrutis—the Vedic passages speaking of the relation, and immanence of God in respect of the individual souls and nature.

It is held in the Viśiṣṭādvaita Philosophy that, the individual souls and the nature form the body *śarīra* of the universal soul and the relation is called *śarīra-sarīri-bhāva*—body-soul-relation. What is a *śarīra*? In *Nyāyasūstra* 1-1-11 it is explained as the support of the effort *ceṣṭa* and sense (*indriya*) and enjoyment (*Bhoga*) चेष्टेन्द्रियार्थाश्रयः शरीरम्. But according to Rāmānuja it is more. Śarīra—a body is liable to be held or controlled in its entirety for the purpose of the spirit and is thus merely a means to its end.

चेतनस्य यद्द्रव्यं सर्वात्मना स्वार्थे नियन्तुं धारयितुं

शक्यं तञ्चेष्टैकस्वरूपञ्च तत्तस्य शरीरम् - AHIP, P. 293

This idea is also expressed in defining it as *śeṣa-śeśi-bhāva*—the relation of end and means. The concept has originated in Mīmāṁsā. According to Jaimini शेषः परार्थत्वात् 3-1-3-2 in the context of *yoga*—substance or *kriyā* useful for the accomplishment of the sacrifice in *śeṣa*—it is explained by Śabara as—

तस्मात्पारार्थ्यमेवैकं युध्यते शेषलक्षणम्।

परोद्देशप्रवृत्तिश्च पारार्थ्यमभिधीयते।।

It is in essence its being motivated to accomplish the interests of the other. In brief Maṇḍana puts it as यो यदर्थः स तच्छेषः one that is for the other is the means of the other.

Rāmānuja adopts this in the following words—

अयमेव हि शेषशेषिभावः परगतातिशयाधानेच्छया

उपादेयत्वमेव यस्य स्वरूपं स शेषः परः शेषी -

Vedārthasaṁgraha.

What is accepted for bringing about greatness to the other and what exists only for that is *śeṣa*—the other is *śeṣī*. Since the inanimate nature and animate beings are there only to serve the interests of the God, the inanimate world and animate beings are *śeṣa*—means and he, the God, is *śeṣin*. This is established by the *śruti* passages like—सर्वस्य वशी, सर्वस्येशानः

Further *Śeṣa-śeṣibhāva* also implies the relation of superiority-inferiority. The relation between the superior *Jyāyān* and the inferior *kanīyān* is that the latter exists for the sake of the former and it is dependent on the former. Such relation is *śeṣa-sesita.* The superiority of God to individual souls and nature is due to greatness of the qualities God and also due to His prior existence, being the prime cause of all.

कालतो गुणतश्चैव प्रकर्षो यत्र तिष्ठति।

शब्दस्तं मुख्यया वृत्त्या ज्यायानित्यभिधीयते।।

Ahimbudhnyasambita A H I F, III, p. 53

This superiority of God is accepted by a man who is wise and enlightened and he adores Him.

The external material objects exists for the sake of the souls—as materials of enjoyment and also constituting the bodies thereof—and both the external material objects and the individual souls exit for the sake of God—*Īśvara*—as the final and śeṣin and are controlled and supported by him.

Generally those qualities that are invariably found with a substance are accepted as *Prakāras* of that substance. But in such cases no possessive suffixes are added. But when a substance is spoken of as the possessed, suffixes are added. To this objection Rāmānuja says—such a distinction should not be made—when there is invariable coexistence in the case of the two substances. There can be *Prakāra-Prakaribhāva*—the mode and modified relation, in that case also.

धातिर्वा द्रव्यंवा गुणोवा न तत्रादरः कश्चन द्रव्यविशेषंप्रति विशेषणतयैव यस्य सद्भावः तस्य तदपृथक्सिद्धेः तत्प्रकारतया तत्सामानाधिकरण्येन प्रतिपादनं युक्तम्-

Vedārthasamgraha, p. 191, Tel. Edn.

When a particular thing—generality or substance or a quality—is found as a quality of another substance and it exists invariably with it—it is proper to speak of it as a mode of it for they are always found coexistent.

Now the inanimate nature and individual souls being the body of the universal soul—God are found to be ever coexistent with him and they exist for His sake and therefore they are rightly spoken of as the modes Prakāras, of the God—*Īśvara*. This relation is *Prakāra-Prakāribhāva.* The relation between the three eternal objects is *Viśeṣaṇaviśeṣyabhāva.* It is in fact this relation that has given the system its name Viśiṣṭādvaita.

18

Form and Function of Relations in Vīraśaiva Philosophy

M. Sivakumara Swamy

The philosophy of Vīraśaivism designated as *Śakti-viṣiṭādvaita, Śivādvaita, Dvaitādvaita* or *Viśeṣādvaita*, showed its vitality as a system of *Vedānta* for the first time in the *Siddhānta-śikhāmaṇi* of Śivayogi-Śivācārya (10th Cent. A.D.). It developed as a full-fledged system in the hands of Śrīpatipaṇḍitārādhya (1070 A.D.) who gave that form to it by writing a *Bhāṣya* on the *Vedāntasūtras* of Bādarāyaṇa. Śrīpatipaṇḍitārādhya made use of the *Vīraśaiva* material available in the *Upaniṣads, Śaivāgamas, Śaivapurāṇas* and the *Siddhānta-śikhāmaṇi* and built it up as a system of *Vedānta* on par with other systems of *Vedānta*. Later works like *Kriyāsāra* of Nīlakaṇṭhaśivācārya, *Śivānubhavasūtra* of Moggeya Māyideva (1400-1500 A.D.), *Vīraśaivānandacandrikā* of Maritoṇṭadārya (1650 A.D.) and *Śivādvaitamañjarī* of Svaprabhānanda-Śivācārya (1650 A.D.) have strengthened the system with scholarly discussions and arguments in a bid to defend its doctrines against the criticism by rival systems.

Like the other systems of Vedānta, this system also discusses about the philosophical concepts of *Brahman, Jīva, Jagat* and their mutual relation. In common with its sister systems of the *Śaiva* fold, it has a theory of causation consisting in the evolution of thirty-six principles. It has emphasised in particular the special feature of '*Śaktiviśiṣṭatva*' in the case of *Paraśivabrahman, Jīva* and *Jagat* and has established an inseparable '*tādātmya*'—relation among them. Similarly it has put forward a relation of the nature of 'difference' (*bheda*) and 'non-difference' (*abheda*) between *Śiva* and *Śakti, Śiva* and *Jīva* as well as *Śiva* and *Jagat*. These philosophical concepts are presented in brief to facilitate the highlighting of the form and function of relation in their context.

Paraśivabrahman

Paraśivabrahman is the substratum of all and the cause of all. He is glorified as *Brahman* in the *Upaniṣads*:

Brahmeti vyapadeśasya viṣayam yam pracakṣate;
Vedāntino jaganmūlaṁ tannamāmi Paraṁ Śivam. [1]

He is of the nature of '*sat*', '*cit*' and '*ānanda*'. He with his *Śakti* is the material and efficient cause of the world. This is in conformity with the *Muṇḍaka* statement—'*Yathorṇanābhiḥ sṛjate gṛhṇate ca*'.[2] The *Taittirīyaśruti 'Yato va imāni bhūtāni jātāni* '[3] shows that He is the efficient cause of the world and the other part of the *Śruti* '*Yatprayantyabhisaṁviśanti*'[4] shows that He is also the material cause of the world:

Jagadupādāna - Parameśvaraśaktestu tadekadeśavṛttitvam.
Tasmādabhinnanimittopādānakāraṇatvam na tvekakāraṇatvam.[5]

He has the five fold activity as creation, maintenance and dissolution of the world and binding and liberating individual souls— '*Sṛṣṭisthitisaṁhārāvirbhāvatirodhānāni pañcakṛtyāni*'.[6]

Śaktiviśiṣṭatva

At all times He is '*Śaktiviśiṣṭa*', inseparably associated with *Śakti* who makes Him realise '*asmi*', '*prakāśe*' and '*nandāmi*', i.e., His *Saccidānanda*— nature. This is the nature which she shares with Him. As described by the *Nāsadīyasūkta*, He who is called 'That One' (*Tad Ekam*) was breathing in a windless state with His own power (*Svadhā - Śakti*) then, when nothing else had come into existence:

Na mṛtyurāsīd amṛtaṁ na tarhi
na rātrya Aahna āsīt praketaḥ;
Ānīdavātam svadhayā tadekam
tasmāddhānyanna paraṁ kiñcanāsa. [7]

The *Śvetāśvataropaniṣad* corroborates it:

Yadā tamastanna divā na rātriḥ
na sat na cāsat Śiva eva kevalaḥ
Tadakṣaraṁ tatsaviturvareṇyam
Prajñā ca tasmātprasṛtā purāṇī. [8]
Parāsya Śaktir vividhaiva śrūyate
svābhāvikī jñānabalakriyā ca.[9]

There was no sign of day or night. There was That One alone, i.e., there was Siva alone. There was in Him that *Śakti*, the ancient *Prajña.* That is called *Vimarśaśakti* assuming many forms as *Jñānaśakti, Icchāśakti* and *Kriyāśakti.* It is innate and natural to *Śiva*:

Yathā candre sthirā jyotsnā viśvavastuprakāśinī;
Tathā Śaktirvimarśākhyā prakāśe Brahmaṇi sthirā.[10]

Just as moonlight revealing all objects is eternal in the moon so in *Śakti* called *Vimarśā* eternal in the effulgence in the form of *Brahman*. Thus it is clear that *Śiva* is eternally *Śaktiviśiṣṭa.*

Concept of Jīva

Following the Śruti-statement that all creatures are one quarter of God—"*Pādo'sya viśvā bhūtāni*",[11] the *Vīraśaiva* philosophers regard the *Jīva* as a part of *Śiva*:

Anādyavidyāsaṁbandhāttadaṁśo jīvanāmakaḥ;
Devatiryaṅmanuṣyādijātibhede vyavasthitaḥ.[12]

The *Jīva* is His part itself separated from Him due to its association with beginningless nescience. The *Jīvas* are many in accordance with the differences in species as gods, animals and human beings. Śrīpatipaṇḍitārādhya says that the individual soul is a part of *Śiva* just as a ray of light is a part of a luminous thing:

Prakāśavajjīvaḥ paramātmano'ṁśaḥ. [13]

This is an echo of the Upaniṣadic statement:

Yathā sudīptātpāvakāt visphuliṅgāḥ
sahasraśaḥ prabhavante sarūpāḥ;
Tathākṣarādvividhāḥ somya bhāvāḥ
prajāyante tatra caivāpi yanti. [14]

Just as thousands of similar-looking sparks emerge from the well-lit fire, so the various objects emerge from the Immutable One and finally merge into it again. These *Jīvas* are real, many, eternal and atomic. *Śiva* resides in the hearts of all as their impeller (*preraka*) to make them active and experience the joys and sorrows. This view is in accordance with the *Śruti* 'Tatsṛṣṭvā tadevānuprāviśat':[15]

Māyī Maheśvarasteṣām prerako hṛdi saṁsthitaḥ;
Candrakānte yathā toyaṁ sūryakānte yathānalaḥ
Bīje yathāṅkuraḥ siddhastathātmani Śivaḥ sthitaḥ. [16]

Maheśvara endowed with Māyāśakti resides in the hearts of all as their impeller. Just as water is naturally found in the moon-stone, fire in the sun-stone and sprout in the seed, so is *Śiva* in the soul.

Nature of the World

In speaking about *Jīvas* one aspect of the world known as *Acarajagat* or *Bhoktṛprapañca* has been covered. The other aspect is the *Acarajagat* or *Bhojyaprapañca*. *Paraśivabrahman* being the material cause of both, the world as a whole cannot be a false appearance. It is not different from Him. It is nothing but the unfoldment of His *Śakti*. This is the true view of the *Upaniṣads*.

Relation/Relations Involved

Coming to the relation/relations involved after a brief account of related concepts, it may be noted that there is a '*tādātmya*' relation basically between the respective pairs of concepts as *Śiva* and *Śakti*, *Śiva* and *Jīva* and *Śiva* and *Jagat* and at the same time there is the relation of 'difference-cum-non-difference' between them.

Firstly, as regards *Śiva* and *Śakti*, a relation has to be thought of because they are conceptually distinguished as 'one possessing power' (*Śaktimān*) and 'the power' (*Śakti*). Here comes the idea of '*Śaktiśaktimatorabhedaḥ*'[17]; *Śakti* is non-different from *Śiva* as the former is the qualification and the latter the qualified (*viśeṣaṇa* and *viśiṣṭa*) and as both cannot remain separately from each other.

Further their relation is said to be innate, inseparable and natural. Yet the difference as Śakti and Śaktimān cannot be ruled out. Thus there can be neither absolute difference (*bheda*) nor absolute non-difference (*abheda*), but a 'difference-cum-non-difference' should be accepted between *Śiva* and *Śakti*. Here the relation between *Śiva* and *Śakti* which is basically a natural, innate and inseparable one comes to be looked upon as one of difference-cum-non-difference. This relation has to be accepted for the purpose of explaining the conceptual duality and functional non-duality between *Śiva* and *Śakti* in the five-fold action of creation, maintenance, dissolution, bondage and liberation of the world of beings and matter. The world is as real as its cause, the *Śiva-Śakti*-synthesis.

Śiva and *Jīvas* are '*Śaktiviśiṣṭa-s*'. *Śiva* is endowed with *Sūkṣma-cidacidātmaka-śakti,* i.e., omniscience and omnipotence and *Jīvas* have *Sthūla-cidacidā-tmaka-śakti,* i.e., limited knowledge and limited power of action. The *Śruti* about two beautiful birds (*dvā suparṇā*) expresses difference between *Śiva* and *Jīva*. The *Śrutis* about non-difference between *Śiva* and *Jīva* (*Tattvamasi*, etc.) express non-difference between the '*aṁsin*' and '*aṁśas*'. Hence a relation of the nature of difference-cum-non-difference should be accepted between them. The *Jīvas* are parts of *Śiva* and they are nothing but His parts:

Jīva-Brahmaṇor bhedābheda evāṅgīkartavyaḥ

Jīvā Brahmaṇa aṁśā eva, na tvitare .[18]

There is no contradiction between difference and non-difference as far as the *Jīva* and *Śiva* are concerned. *Śruti* admits both difference and non-difference between *Śiva* and *Jīva*. Śrīpatipaṇḍitārādhya asserts this on the ground that *Śrutis* should be taken as the authority:

Na ca bhedābhedayor virodha iti vācyam.

Vayaṁ śrutiprāmāṇavādinaḥ .[19]

He asserts that this view is supported by scripture, reason and experience.

As regards scripture, it may noted that a *Śruti* says "*Pado'sya viśvā bhūtāni*".[20] Hence the *Jīvas* are parts of *Śiva*. The *Bhagavadgītā* says "*Mamaivāṁśo jīvaloke jīvabhūtaḥ sanātanaḥ* '.[21] The *Jīva* is a part of *Śiva*, as a ray of light is a part of a luminous thing, as a white Cow is apart of the genus of Cow. A part is a qualification of a qualified object; a qualification is a part of a qualified object. Though the former is a part of the latter, there is difference in their nature. A ray of light is different from the luminous thing. Similarly the *Jīva* is different from *Śiva*. Yet it is non-different from *Śiva*, because it cannot exist separately from Him. The *Jīva* as a qualification always exists as dependent upon *Śiva* Who is the principal. The *Śrutis* expressing non-difference show that *Śiva* is the Inner Controller of the *Jīva*:

> *Viśeṣaṇaviśeṣyayoraṁśāsitve'pi svabhāvavailakṣaṇyaṁ dṛśyate. Evaṁ Jīva-parayorviśeṣaṇaviśeṣyakṛtaṁ svabhāvavailakṣaṇyam āśritya bhedanirdeśāḥ pravartante. Abhedanirdeśastu pṛthaksiddhyanarha-viśeṣaṇānāṁ viśeṣyaparyantatvamāśritya mukhyatvenopapadyate.* [22]

The analogy of the fire and sparks figuring in the *Muṇḍakaśruti* '*Sudīptātpāvakāt*, etc.' is also utilized for establishing the same view.

Similarly the relation between *Śiva* and *Jagat* is also of the nature of 'difference-cum-non-difference'. The *Jagat* is an expression of His power; it is thus non-different from Him. It is different from Him because it is transcended by Him.

Thus, in conclusion, it can be said that the *Vīraśaiva* philosophers have postulated a relation of *Bhedābheda* between *Śiva* and *Śakti*, *Śiva* and *Jīva* and *Śiva* and *Jagat* with a view to adhering to the spirit of the *Śrutis* and achieving harmony between *Bhedaśrutis* and *Abhedaśrutis*. Śrīpatipaṇḍitārādhya makes the following observation on the stand of the *Vīraśaivas*:

Dvaitādvaitamate śuddhe viśeṣādvaitasaṁjñake;
Vīraśaivaikasiddhānte sarvaśrutisamanvayaḥ. [23]

Another necessity is as a result of the path of spiritual development they have chosen. The path is called *Ṣaṭsthalamārga* consisting of *Bhakta, Māheśvara, Prasādin, Prāṇaliṅgin, Śaraṇa* and *Aikya*. The first three stages are practically *Dvaita*-oriented, as they lay emphasis on the duality of the worshipper (*Pūjaka*) and the worshipped (*Pūjya*) in the worship of the *Iṣṭaliṅga*. During the third stage an awareness of the internal *Liṅgas, Prāṇaliṅga* and *Bhāvaliṅga* becomes more tangible. The fourth stage onwards there is the *Advaita*-oriented development and the worshipper while worshipping the *Iṣṭaliṅga* establishes a *yoga* with the internal Prāṇaliṅga and practises its worship with the abstractions of his pure thoughts and feelings. The *Jīva* becomes instilled with *Śivabhāva* and in the *Śaraṇasthala* there is the experience of 'Sakhya', the joy of communion. Finally the *Aikya*-stage is marked by the experience of *Samarasaikya*.

Jale jalamiva nyastam agnāvagnirivārpitaḥ
pare Brahmaṇi līnātmā vibhāgena na dṛśyate .[24]

This is the stage of Jīvanmukti.

Notes and References

1. Śivayogi-Śivācārya: *Siddhāntaśikhāmaṇi*, Pañcācārya Electric Press, Mysore, 1972 (Kannaḍa script), 1.2.
2. *Muṇḍakopaniṣad*, 1. 1.7.
3. *Taittirīyopaniṣad*, 3.1.1.
4. *Taittirīyopaniṣad*, 3.1.1.
5. Śripati-paṇḍitārādhya: *Śrīkarabhāṣya*, I. 1.2.
6. Ibid., I. 1.4.
7. Ṛgveda, X. 129.2.
8. *Śvetāśvataropaniṣad*, 4.18.
9. Ibid., 6.8.
10. *Siddhāntaśikhāmaṇi*, 20. 32.
11. *Ṛgveda*, X. 90.3; *Chāndogyopaniṣad*, 3.12.6. (*Pādo'sya sarvā bhūtāni*).
12. *Siddhāntaśikhāmaṇi*, 5.34.
13. *Śrīkarabhāṣya*, II. 3.43.
14. *Muṇḍakopaniṣad*, 2.1.1.
15. *Taittirīyopaniṣad*, 2.6.2.
16. *Siddhāntaśikhāmaṇi*, 5.34-35.
17. *Śrīkarabhāṣya*, II. 1. 14.
18. Ibid., 2.3.40.
19. Ibid., 2.3.40.
20. *Ṛgveda*; X. 90.3; *Chāndogyopaniṣad*, 3.12.6 (*sarvā* for *viśvā*)
21. *Bhagavadgītā*, 15.7.
22. *Śrīkarabhāṣya*, II. 3.43.
23. Ibid., Introductory Stanza.
24. *Siddhāntaśikhāmaṇi*, 19.42.